Teaching Climate Change

Teaching Climate Change

Fostering Understanding, Resilience,
and a Commitment to Justice

Mark Windschitl

HARVARD EDUCATION PRESS
CAMBRIDGE, MA

Paperback ISBN 978-1-68253-834-0

Library of Congress Cataloging-in-Publication Data is on file.

Published by Harvard Education Press,
an imprint of the Harvard Education Publishing Group
Harvard Education Press
8 Story Street
Cambridge, MA 02138

Cover Design: Wilcox Design
Cover Image: South_agency/E+ via Getty Images

The typefaces in this book are Adobe Garamond Pro and Avenir Next.

Contents

*This book is dedicated to young people
throughout the global community who will
help regenerate the Earth through storytelling,
bearing witness, teaching their elders, and
disrupting the social norms of modernity.
We will need all your talents.*

*And to my father, who passed away
during the time I was writing this book.
His acts of kindness and love sustained
generations of our family.*

CHAPTER 1

The Leap

OUR CHILDREN ARE ALREADY aware that the Earth is being transformed. They know this less because of what they hear in classrooms and more because they spend much of their lives online where there is no escaping stories about explosive wildfires, torrential floods, and species vanishing along with their habitats. These accumulating spectacles are signs that the world they will inherit is becoming unfamiliar, even dangerous. This shadow curriculum, however, also connects them to images of young people in places like Nairobi, Paris, and Seoul who are marching in the streets to rally for hope, for radical changes in how we live with the more-than-human parts of our environment, and for the urgency of *now*. They are right, because the unthinkable is rushing toward us with increasing speed.

It would be comforting if the steady diet of ominous warnings could be dismissed as alarmism, but the cold truth is this: humans have precipitated unnatural changes in the environment that now threaten the sustainability of life on our planet. This started two hundred years ago when we learned to exploit fossil fuels for the energy stored in their chemical bonds. We extracted from the earth the remains of ancient plants and animals, reconstituted by time into tar sands, anthracite, oil shales, boghead coal, and other organic deposits. We refined these, transported them, and burned them in our engines and furnaces. Today the cost of cheap energy is that we are throwing about

33 billion tons of carbon dioxide into the atmosphere every year, and this is warming our planet at an unprecedented pace, disrupting our climate dynamics, and imperiling our ecosystems.[1]

For the first time in history, one species has become the dominant geophysical force on Earth, altering the most basic processes of the air and oceans that all life depends on. We have crossed over into the time of the *Anthropocene*, a new epoch marked by existential threats to the environment and uncertainty that will likely last for millennia. To avoid the worst effects of climate change, we will have to limit increases in atmospheric temperatures to 1.5 °C (2.7 °F) above preindustrial levels. In practical terms, this means a complete decarbonization of the world's energy and transport systems, industrial production, and land use by 2050. This sounds like the distant future, but reaching this target will require a more immediate downward wrench in global emissions by 2030. For the country that has contributed more greenhouse gases to the atmosphere than any other—the United States—this means a 40 to 50 percent cut within a few years.[2] The window for action at this scale is closing fast, and as of 2023, the world is still moving in the wrong direction, *adding* record amounts of these gases to the thin layer of air circulating above us.

Surprisingly, the barriers to energy transformation are not insurmountable; the solutions are known and technically within our grasp. It is the extent to which we can influence human behavior that will determine our fate, and this is where public education can be a force for social change. Most students realize that the Earth's systems are conspicuously unstable and know who is responsible. In a national study of 2,293 adults and 629 teenagers, 78 percent of the older respondents indicated that climate change was happening and that humans were causing it (see figure 1.1).[3] Sounds like impressive public awareness of the crisis, but the teens made an even bolder statement, as 85 percent agreed that change is happening and that we are driving it. Teens and young adults ages eighteen to twenty-nine were also about 10 percentage points more likely than adults ages thirty and older to say climate change will cause a great deal of harm to people in their generation and to future generations. In another survey of over 1,200 thirteen- to eighteen-year-olds, 80 percent of teens believed climate change was happening, and most of these respondents believed that humans were at least partially responsible.[4] This combination of awareness and concern leaves an open door for us as educators to start conversations about the environment in our classrooms, knowing that on average, the large majority of students will be a receptive audience.

Schools can provide spaces for students to explore climate phenomena they are passionate about, but we can do better. As professional educators we can help them appreciate diverse points of view on climate issues; take critical non-Western perspectives on our relationship with the natural world; be open to changing their minds in response to well-grounded arguments by classmates; become interested in situations, problems, and places they were previously unaware of; and envision their lives in multiple possible futures. These outcomes are not fostered by scrolling through daily news feeds or social media posts; they require sustained intellectual work in the company of others. Ideally, teachers can be powerful and positive socializing influences for students, helping combine the energy they bring to the classroom with unflinching questions about how and why the world is changing. To do this

Figure 1.1 Adults and teens who believe in human-caused climate change

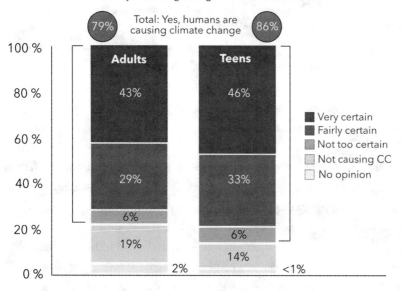

Do you think that human activity is or is not causing changes to the world's climate, including an increase in average temperature? If yes: How certain are you that human activity is causing changes to the world's climate?

Source: Kaiser Family Foundation/Washington Post Climate Change Survey, 2019, https://www .washingtonpost.com/context/washington-post-kaiser-family-foundation-climate-change-survey -july-9-aug-5-2019/601ed8ff-a7c6-4839-b57e-3f5eaa8ed09f/.

work, we must school ourselves on the varied psychological reactions young learners have to environmental threats, and students' nascent worldviews that shape how receptive they are to messages about risks or proposed solutions. Without considering the issues above and what students bring to the table, we risk failing them in ways that will matter profoundly to their generation.

This book is not just about teaching climate fundamentals. It will also help you prepare students to reconceptualize environmental and social conditions beyond their communities so they can become part of larger movements that work toward increasing resilience for all humans and for the natural world. This is not the only book you'll ever need; rather, it is a springboard for deepening your own learning about key climate change ideas, helping you identify resources that support transformative experiences for you and your students, and mobilizing other educators to create coherent trajectories of learning from elementary through high school. Reimagining our roles and responsibilities in the world is the basis on which change depends. We can take this leap together.

TO TEACH CLIMATE REALITIES, WE MUST PREPARE OURSELVES DIFFERENTLY

Confronting Intimidating Content

Climate change cannot be effectively taught or learned if we treat it like other science topics. It isn't a neatly compartmentalized body of knowledge but a planetary puzzle that implicates every part of the natural world. *Climate* used to refer to characteristic weather patterns in a region, but scientists now view climate as a set of integrated global-scale processes, linking the Earth's atmosphere, oceans, land, and life. *Climate change* refers to the full range of cascading effects, as atmospheric levels of greenhouse gases (GHGs) rise and different parts of the Earth's systems respond to higher temperatures. Outdated conceptions of climate change may lead some to think that it's only about what's happening above our heads, when in fact it is also about ocean circulation, ecosystems, crops, carbon sinks, urban heat islands, and ultimately the influence of emissions by *Homo sapiens* on everything we should care about.

This means that the subject matter is expansive and mind-bogglingly interwoven. Seeking out the most important ideas for teaching climate change is like entering a vast and unfamiliar museum. There is no information desk and no sign that says "Start Here." You wander into exhibits showcasing the Atmosphere, the Oceans, the Amazon, the Greenhouse Effect, Hurricanes, Human Consumption, and Renewable Energy. Occasionally you pause to watch videos of ice shelves collapsing or offshore wind turbines being towed into place. You pass through the Gallery of Models, which features data visualizations depicting possible futures—animated maps show how little-known diseases could spread in a warming world, what will happen to the quality of the air we breathe, and how the cost of renewables could plummet in response to material innovations and government policies. With every space you venture into, the growing sprawl of ideas makes it harder to imagine how all this could be contained, much less organized, in a coherent curriculum. You wonder, *How can I sort through all this to locate the most generative ideas for my students? What are the connections, the unifying themes? How much of this do I have to know?* You feel overwhelmed.

In a dark way, climate change represents an opportunity for students to dive more deeply into the complexities of Earth's systems because they have to understand not only how these behave in their natural state, but how they are now responding as familiar causal mechanisms are being thrown out of whack and perturbing other connected systems. Students are no longer studying just "the oceans" or "the Arctic" or "habitats," but how their dynamics are becoming permanently disrupted, and what that means for life on Earth.

Dealing with Myths and Knowledge Traps

Climate change is unlike other topics in the science curriculum because it is mired in mythologies about the crisis itself and humans' capacity to deal with it. In his book *Uninhabitable Earth*, David Wallace-Wells describes the "comforting delusions" people cling to:

> That global warming is an arctic saga unfolding remotely. That it is strictly a matter of sea level and coastlines, not an enveloping crisis sparing no place and leaving no life undeformed; that it is a crisis of the "natural" world, not the human one; that those two are distinct, and that we live today somehow outside or beyond or at the very least defended against nature, not inescapably within and literally overwhelmed by it; that wealth can be a shield against the ravages of warming; that the burning of fossil fuels is the price for continued economic growth, that growth and the technology it produces will allow us to engineer our way out of environmental disaster.[5]

None of these assumptions are true of course, except the part about the wealthy being less impacted than poor communities—but even that will only be for the short term. Most people see climate change as a problem remote in space (not here) and time (not yet). They compartmentalize it as an environmental issue or a scientific dilemma, but much less so as a "people problem."[6]

Knowledge traps are different from delusional thinking. These keep us from recognizing the complexity and scope of climate change. For example, many people assume that *either* humans are causing climate change *or* it is a result of natural processes, viewing these as mutually exclusive.[7] Scientists point out however, that natural processes and human influences have worked together to destabilize our climate.

Teachers also have to compete with retrograde messaging about climate change from fossil fuel groups and conservative think tanks. For decades, these folks have been manufacturing doubt about anthropogenic changes to the atmosphere, disputing whether climate change is happening at all, what is causing it, and if it is worth being concerned about. Their primary strategy has been to downplay any suggestions of scientific consensus about these matters. Denialist groups have urged educators to "teach both sides of the climate change debate" when there is no serious debate. While it is hard to gauge the effect of a campaign of falsehoods that continues today, we know that adults believe that only around 67 percent of scientists agree humans are causing climate change, with middle school and high school students estimating about 70 percent agreement.[8] The number is, in fact, closer to 97 percent.

One example of counter-messaging these denialist narratives was developed by Ed Maibach, a climate communication scientist.[9] The box below

Scientists agree.
It's real.
It's us.
It's bad.
But there's hope.

Source: @MaibachEd, June 25, 2018, https://twitter
.com/maibached/sttus/1011267883664662529

presents his spare but elegant statements that encapsulate the realities of our environmental crisis. Every assertion is backed by science and focuses our attention on what is important to know. If we explore with students the "why" behind each of these lines with real-life cases, it can help them tie together essential parts of the climate change story and recognize our collective obligations to act.

There is yet another knowledge trap: the more students learn, the more they can feel besieged by the rhetoric of threat and doom. This can slide into apathy, as their fears become tinged with guilt.[10] You can tell, even in this introductory chapter, that one of the primary tensions of climate change teaching is communicating the raw urgency of the crisis even as we offer talk of solutions and hope. So what are the alternatives to a curriculum of anguish or pushback? Studies of both public communication and science classrooms have documented positive responses to pedagogies that directly connect preservation of the environment to human concerns and well-being.[11] Teachers who've managed this successfully have portrayed nature as the web of life that puts humans in kinship with animals, plants, the air, land, water, and sun. Every member of the web is alive in different ways and we can thrive only in mutual interdependence with them. Students have also responded positively when they're helped to understand what is at the root of climate disruptions and how we might mitigate warming, rather than dwell on its most dire impacts.

In terms of solutions, there is an astonishing array of innovations being tested now to decarbonize our lives, including reforms for how we use land, decrease food waste, and produce energy. These are referred to as *drawdown strategies*. *Drawdown* is a milestone in reversing climate change, marking the future point in time when carbon dioxide in the atmosphere peaks and then drops, reversing the climb of global temperatures. Students are amazed at the potential remedies that move us closer to drawdown, and one of the pleasures of diving into these together is finding out that the most consequential changes we can make are not what gets attention in the media. Surprisingly, the redesign of air-conditioning and food refrigeration takes the top spots. The unsexy process of reducing methane leaks from oil fields is also higher on the list than installing those majestic wind turbines across the landscape. Drawdown strategies, whatever form they take, can infuse hope into your curriculum.

Confronting Issues of Climate Injustice

The first lesson of climate justice is that destabilizing change is happening in every corner of the world. The kinds of tidal surges that regularly flood New Orleans and permanently inundate an additional 65 square kilometers of Louisiana every decade are also swamping the Sundarbans—a mangrove forest of about 10,000 square kilometers in the delta opening out to the Bay of Bengal.[12] In California, wildfires are so massive and intense that they create their own weather systems and have incinerated more than 6,000 square miles a year, but conflagrations like these now char landscapes in Australia, Greece, and Canada. Dryland ecosystems that encompass 46 percent of the terrestrial landmass on Earth are devolving into deserts in places as diverse as China, West Africa, and Peru.[13]

The message here is not that the effects of climate change are inescapable, but that the pain will not be shared equally. One study suggests that rising sea levels in India could permanently submerge some of the country's most fertile lands and precipitate the migration of up to 50 million people in that country, with another 75 million being displaced in neighboring Bangladesh. A one-meter rise in sea level could drive more than 10 percent of the population of Vietnam from their homes.[14] The scope of these humanitarian catastrophes is hard to comprehend. Half a billion people in Southeast Asia are at risk of becoming climate refugees, and the burden of these impacts will be borne largely by the region's poorest people, disproportionately by women.

The global mismatch between greenhouse gas emissions and the burden of climate consequences is enormously inequitable; twenty of the thirty-six highest-emitting countries are among the least vulnerable to the negative impacts of future climate change.[15] Conversely, eleven of the seventeen countries with low or moderate rates of GHG emissions are the most likely to experience serious negative impacts. Many countries, including the United States, are free riders that benefit from fossil fuel consumption while causing others to bear climate burdens. It is a sign of our privilege in an affluent society that so many of us can remain indifferent to human suffering and unmoved to action.

In American classrooms, it is possible that students learn about climate-related impacts in all their technical detail without any acknowledgment of how these phenomena affect millions of women, children, and men whose well-being are at risk because of the consumption habits of others in faraway places. These impacted communities are largely in the Global South—regions of Latin America, much of Africa, South Asia, and Oceania—but can include populations and places outside these areas that have been politically or culturally marginalized. These peoples have endured prolonged histories of colonization and empire-building by wealthier nations that expropriated resources like minerals, plants, and raw materials to enrich the North, often leaving chaos and environmental ruin in their wake. Ongoing colonization and its cultural violence also applies to Indigenous communities spread across the Americas, Australia, China, and Scandinavia. They and their lands are now subject to climate-induced vulnerabilities—to use a sanitized phrase—yet many of their families have carbon footprints that are small fractions of those living in more affluent parts of the world.

For our part as science teachers, we are slowly improving how we address the mechanisms and fallout of climate change; however, we rarely contextualize our lessons with the history of how we got to this point, not only through historical oppression but also in terms of more contemporary corporate gaslighting and political foot-dragging. For climate change education to mean something beyond addressing standards with students, we must confront the inequitable social conditions that have produced the problem in the first place: namely, colonialism and its intimate relationship with a model of economic development that prioritizes resource extraction and unfettered growth over sustainable limits. This is where climate justice should be integrated—a concept that brings together interests in the quality of life for present and future generations, equity in resource allocation, sustaining Indigenous cultures, and living within ecological limits. Grassroots climate justice movements have identified several guiding principles that can become part of a school curriculum:[16]

- Slowing carbon dioxide emissions and the exploitation of fossil fuels
- Ensuring just transitions to renewable energy
- Protecting vulnerable communities and including their participation in decision-making
- Having the courage to act in the face of uncertainty
- Ensuring intergenerational justice
- Demanding US leadership on global efforts to combat climate change

Teaching for climate justice will be intimidating for many of us—we never encountered this as students, nor were we trained for it. Still, communities at risk should have their stories told and studied, not hidden because we are uncomfortable sharing them with students or because our inaction threatens their very existence.

TEACHERS AND TIPPING POINTS

The sheer scale of the climate crisis can make us question the impact we are likely to have, but let's think what might happen if educators acted together. In the United States, our schools serve about 57 million children, each of whom spends approximately 180 days under the care and guidance of teachers. Each year, students should have the opportunity to expand their climate-relevant knowledge and develop more informed visions of a desirable future. It is not realistic, however, for one heroic teacher in each school to take all this on. Rather, a successful model should include teams of educators and administrators, from early elementary through high school, planning coherent trajectories of student experiences with climate change ideas that, over time, build increasingly sophisticated and socially conscious understandings.

We should think of education as playing a central role in cultural transformations, not just by influencing one child at a time, but also by developing "just enough" social influence among the many to re-cast climate narratives in our communities and helping students understand how they can take action in the world. I refer to changes in how youth see their relationship with the natural world and how they could embrace a less consumptive life, resist the messaging from powerful organizations seeking to preserve the status quo, and demand more responsive public institutions. If you are working in the K–12 system or in community education, your team can have an enduring and positive effect on learners. We should not opt out of this in the name of protecting curricular turf or imagining "this too shall pass." These are not solutions, and climate change is not going away.

It is no longer an exaggeration to point out that the children sitting in front of you belong to the last generation capable of reversing the climate crisis. The pace of change, then, is critical. In any system, change can happen slowly but steadily, it can be sporadic or stall out entirely. Then there is the *tipping point* model. There are different definitions depending on the system you are referring to; however, nearly all share the same criteria. Here's the technical version: a tipping point is the threshold at which small shifts accumulating over time suddenly trigger rapid nonlinear change that is accelerated by positive feedback mechanisms and leads to a qualitatively different and often irreversible state of the system.[17] In plain language, this means that when the limits of a system has been pushed, little by little, there can come a time when a single event or just a nudge sets off a wave of rapid, self-reinforcing, and unpredictable changes that can permanently alter how the system works.

There are scary tipping points. For example, permafrost across the Arctic is beginning to thaw and release methane into the atmosphere—a greenhouse gas that is about thirty times more potent than CO_2 over a one-hundred-year period. If this further accelerates atmospheric warming, then even more methane will vent, fueling a new and unwelcome cycle in the climate crisis.[18] There are other kinds of tipping points, however, that lead not to environmental catastrophe, but to social transformations built on principles of sustainability and justice. Education has played a major role in shifting norms of participation in civil rights movements, gender equity in the workplace, and health-related issues such as air quality.[19] More consumerist examples include installations of rooftop solar panels and buying electric vehicles, which have both been shown to be contagious, spreading fastest in communities where they are most visible.

Importantly, the power of groups does not come from their authority or access to resources but from their commitment to a cause. There is anecdotal evidence that student-led climate strikes around the world, driven by organizations like the Extinction Rebellion (XR) in Europe as well as the Sunrise Movement in the United States, seem to have sparked a wave of pro-environmental action in politics and broader social consciousness about sustainability.[20]

When major shifts in public sentiment gain momentum, they are usually the result of intensive social mobilization. Naomi Klein, author of *This Changes Everything*, describes how education might bring us to a tipping point.

> Activism becomes something that is not performed by a small tribe within a culture, whether a vanguard of radicals or a sub-category of slick professionals, but sometimes an entirely normal activity throughout society—it's rent payers associations, women's auxiliaries, neighborhood assemblies, sports

teams, youth leagues, trade unions. During extraordinary historical moments—both world wars, the aftermath of the Great Depression, the peak
of the civil rights area—the usual categories dividing "activists" and "regular
people" became meaningless because the project of changing society was so
deeply woven into the project of life. Activists were quite simply, everyone.[21]

Education is not mentioned here, but aren't public schools the places
where every child can have something to say about the common good, not
to mention their own futures? Worldwide, people's educational backgrounds
are the single strongest predictors of climate change awareness.[22] Adolescents
who hear others discussing the topic of climate change—including science
teachers, parents, friends, and their favorite news sources—are more engaged,
have more accurate risk perceptions, and are more concerned. They view the
issue as more personally relevant, and have higher expectations that their generation can adapt to climate change.[23] In a survey of US teens ages thirteen
to seventeen, about one-quarter report that they *already engage politically* on
the issue of climate change by participating in protests or school walkouts, or
contacting government officials.[24] Students of color stand out as more likely
than others to join in political action around climate change. Hispanic teens
(41 percent) and Black teens (37 percent) are more likely than White teens (24
percent) to believe people need to act within the next year or two in order to
prevent the worst effects of climate change.

Committees from the US National Academy of Sciences assert that increasing the quantity and quality of climate coverage in primary and secondary education is key. This is a start, but it is playing by the old rules, still inside
the box. Case in point: a nationally representative sample of 1,500 middle
school and high school science teachers found that virtually all students hear
about climate science at some time during their secondary education, but according to the survey methodology, simply having it mentioned in the classroom would suffice as coming into contact with the topic.[25] The authors were
clear about the problem:

> The patchwork of exposure does not appear to be in any way cumulative. Some
> students are likely to encounter little more than a discussion of climate change
> consequences, such as rising sea levels. Others will learn about greenhouse
> gases, but without the scientific foundations that explain the greenhouse ef-
> fect. Overall, the evidence suggests that few will encounter sophisticated and
> reinforcing instruction in multiple classes taught by different teachers.

When climate ideas do make an appearance, they are often folded in with more traditional content as ancillary topics rather than being taught as core material. Even in courses where climate change is addressed, the time devoted is rarely more than a week each year; some studies indicate the median time spent is one to two hours.[26]

Teachers at the forefront of designing climate curricula agree that coordinated and cumulative learning experiences for students are needed. Ideally, topics should be taught beginning at least by middle elementary and continue through high school. Currently, students are probably encountering some important climate-related phenomena repeatedly and others not at all. This ultimately brings up a broader question of policy making around the science curriculum. Whether it occurs at the level of a science department, an individual school, or better, at the level of school districts or states, a well-structured yet flexible K–12 trajectory gives students the best chance to engage deeply and critically with climate phenomena and sustainability.

WE NEED TO PULL ALL THE LEVERS

Some of the most critical work we need to do is developing new narratives that reframe our collective efforts around sustainability and justice. Naomi Klein proposes a radical tack that must become core to the educational mission. The task is to articulate "an alternative worldview to rival the one at the heart of the ecological crisis—embedded in interdependence rather than hyper-individualism, reciprocity rather than dominance, and cooperation rather than hierarchy."[27] If this sounds idealistic, it's because I am talking about a social movement. What mobilizes people about climate change is being grounded in an ethos of caring for the planet as it cares for us. This presents a counterweight to moral compromises like appeasing skeptics in the community or delaying action on climate for political expedience.[28] The truth must be framed effectively to be widely embraced, and teachers, as public intellectuals, have the clearest pathway to educate the next generation about climate stewardship and resilience.

Teachers can immerse students in conversations they may not have access to outside the classroom and, along the way, cultivate new knowledge, social norms, ways of using language, and understanding how to exercise agency for change. No one intervention will work by itself—not policy, technological breakthrough, or educational transformation. We will have to *pull all these levers* at once, and this is why our role is so crucial.

CHAPTER SUMMARIES

Climate change is an unfolding story that implicates every branch of the science we teach; academic content is becoming inseparable from humanity's relationship with the natural world and our response to a crisis that may impact the Earth for generations. The following chapters address key parts of this story that inform and inspire, fostering climate consciousness that students will carry into adulthood. Some chapters address the latest science in approachable terms. Others will help you design opportunities for all students to engage in sensemaking and disciplinary activity around climate change. Several chapters put you in less familiar territory with modeling the future, dealing with denial in the classroom, or supporting activism by students. These ideas form the larger context in which you can design transformative experiences for students. This is preferable to wading into a sea of online lesson plans, hoping to find a few that work magic for you. We can all do better with support from these chapters and from colleagues who are reading and perhaps changing along with us.

Chapter 2: A Vision for Climate Change Teaching. Young learners become more invested in science when they are challenged to explain real-life phenomena that are relevant to them. They can seek out connections between drought and recent wildfires, imagine creative ways to store solar energy for later use in a neighborhood power grid, or engineer defenses against toxic algae blooms in a nearby lake ecosystem. Because effective phenomena are real-world puzzles, there are most often multiple causes for what is happening, and several possible versions of scientifically credible explanations or solutions. This is why well-curated events are essential if you envision your classroom as a knowledge-building community. Such communities work together to understand complex phenomena, revising and improving evidence-based explanations over time. They build on students' everyday knowledge and experiences as assets to do collective sensemaking work. Events or processes that work really well are just challenging enough to require deep dives into several key science ideas, sustaining students' intellectual curiosity for weeks. Phenomena are more compelling to young learners if people become part of the storyline, in part because so much of climate change is manifested in social injustices to vulnerable populations. In this chapter I share examples of events and processes related to a variety of climate change topics, provide details about why some work better than others with students, how you might modify existing phenomena to be more relevant to your students, and how to maintain an equitable classroom in which students learn how to learn.

Chapter 3: A Primer on Core Climate Change Ideas. This chapter explores five science domains that encompass what is important to know about the mechanisms of climate change and downstream consequences: (1) the greenhouse effect, (2) the carbon cycle, (3) the oceans and cryosphere, (4) impacts on biodiversity and ecosystems, and (5) weather extremes. These sections won't be encyclopedic; there is already enough information available out there for more in-depth reading. Rather, I will provide specialized content that you need for teaching. Each domain is broken down into more granular but fundamental concepts that, when understood by students, empowers them to explain a wide range of phenomena in the world. I will describe how students typically think about content in these areas, including common alternative conceptions and knowledge gaps. The chapter shows how events and processes related to these domains are affecting human communities around the world. It also offers guidance on how to identify illustrative case studies and locate other trustworthy resources with more information.

Chapter 4: Solutions: Helping Students Envision Sustainability and Resilience. You'll hear a lot about drawdown in this book; this is the inflection point when levels of greenhouse gases in the atmosphere stop climbing and start to decline. This chapter explores the technologies, changes in life habits, and policies that can accelerate movement toward drawdown. The range of possible engineering solutions to climate change is eye-opening for students who may be familiar only with wind turbines and solar panels. There are plenty of surprises about building designs, food production, the development of high-tech materials, reforms in land use, and other innovations that have bigger payoffs for stabilizing the climate than do electric vehicles. The diversity of potential solutions utilizes concepts from all school science subjects—biology, earth science, physics, and chemistry.

Chapter 5: Dealing with Disinformation and Skepticism. Climate change is contested terrain. Adults hold different worldviews about the environment that influence their receptivity to ideas about sustainability. Children also come to us with combinations of concern and apathy toward the climate, some of which results from being socialized every day to believe skeptical narratives about the climate spread by the fossil fuel industry or others who feel it their right to exploit the environment in ways they choose. These influences are powerful and can impact how students learn from us. We also know that confrontational "take-it-from-me" pedagogies may trigger pushback from students and cause even pro-environmental learners to feel cynical about the future. There are, however, approaches that do not make students defensive but rather allow them to focus on inquiry into a changing world and solutions as a core part of the curriculum. I'll share recommendations for working productively with students in classrooms where there can be widely diverging beliefs about how humans should relate to the natural world.

Chapter 6: It Matters How You Frame the Story. Framing is the use of rhetorical strategies to influence how an audience adopts perspectives about an idea or event. It's a communication strategy in which the messenger (a teacher in our case) selects case studies, language, and imagery to expand how others can interpret climate stories and, in the process, stimulate new insights. For example, I show how some teachers elevate the idea that all humans are intimately connected to the environment. The frame used is that of Indigenous relations with the land, sky, water, and all living beings. I also advocate that teachers make visible the consequences for human communities as essential for students to understand the science in meaningful ways. I describe the importance of helping students develop explanations for events that not only require deep knowledge of the science, but also reflect social justice orientations.

Chapter 7: How Do We Know That Happened? Reconstructing the Past to Understand the Present. Scientists are recording the state of our Earth's systems in real time using technologies like submersible drones in the watery parts of the world or satellites in orbit around the planet, as well as humble instruments like field notebooks. But these are today's modes of data capture— what about the past few centuries or millennia? How do we know that the 420+ parts per million of carbon dioxide in the air today is an increase over tens of thousands of years ago? And if so, is it simply a roller-coaster of natural variation that has little to do with human influence? This chapter acquaints you with the diverse sources of paleo-data that scientists use to estimate what the Earth was like long ago. Among these are the chemical contents of stalagmites from caves, types of pollen or samples of ancient air trapped in glaciers, and micro-fossils in sea floor sediments. The chapter will also help teachers decide how to address questions of evidence with students: What counts as credible data? How do we know what we know? Are there alternative explanations? These conversations help learners develop identities as capable knowers of the natural world.

Chapter 8: Our Possible Future(s): Data Visualizations and Climate Models as Sensemaking Tools. Here we'll make the jump from the past into the present. I refer to the present as the last few decades in which science has accumulated an almost uncountable number of physical and biological observations of different Earth systems. This vast repository, in its raw form, is too complex for us to wrap our heads around. This is where data visualizations become an indispensable tool for scientists and everyday folk to comprehend how features of the environment co-vary with one another—for example, how the numbers of a particular bird species vary by altitude on a mountainside over the past 100 years, or how the power generated by offshore wind turbines changes seasonally. It's hardly possible for students to grasp what is happening with the climate or solutions unless they are given the opportunity to study these representations, ask questions, pause, and perhaps reorganize their thinking about the workings of the world. In the second part of this chapter, I turn to the future. To glimpse what might be happening in the next few decades, we must rely again on visualizations, specifically climate models. Models and how they project the future always have uncertainty built into them. This uncertainty is important to understand, in part because it is a core feature of all science and because skeptics have cited it as evidence that scientists can't agree about anything. All the more reason that students should develop fluency with data that goes into and comes out of climate models.

Chapter 9: Helping Students Show What They Know: Building Models and Explanations. Here is where students do the modeling. Research in classrooms confirms deeper student learning when they model phenomena like ecosystem disruptions, extreme weather events, or the greenhouse effect. Developing and using models serves as a sensemaking process that allows students to predict and explain phenomenon, and makes their thinking visible as well as shareable in the classroom. There are many types of models that we should be using to teach climate change—graphs, equations, computer simulations, physical replicas, charts, and so on. However, conceptual models are unique in that they require students to create their own representations for describing what is happening and explaining why. Modeling means more than just representing ideas; it's a process of changing your thinking over time about complex events in the natural world. This is a focus of work in all knowledge-building communities.

Chapter 10: Activism and Self-Care for the Long Haul. Young people on every continent are entering into public debates that provoke dissent from prevailing norms of consumption, fossil energy use, and the unjust use of power in decision-making. These are climate activists who mobilize others to change individual behaviors for the sake of sustainability and equity, and they pressure economic and political actors toward the same ends. Their aims interweave issues of social injustice with environmental challenges such as pollution and biodiversity loss. This chapter describes what educators can do to inspire collective action and demand climate justice at the political and social levels. It provides a picture of how children can become part of a movement that changes how we think and see ourselves in the world. An important but overlooked feature of activism is the need for self-care, because we are in this for the long haul. Tips on preserving your life balance and energies are included.

CHAPTER 2

A Vision for Climate Change Teaching

THIS IS AN INVITATION to deeply meaningful work. It is rooted in a vision of what we want for our children and how to work toward those goals. A vision for teaching must be something we can wrap our minds around, especially so when it involves the complexity of climate change; only then can it be translated into action. We can see such a vision play out in a seventh-grade classroom in western Washington where students were exploring how an Iñupiat community just below the Arctic Circle was dealing with the decline of sea ice and the consequences for their tiny island village. One young girl in the community observed, "Even winter is retreating from our island. The seal hunters can't venture out there on foot or on snowmobile. It's too dangerous."[1] Over the course of this unit, students dove into data to find out why climate change is heating up the Arctic four times faster than the rest of the world, how sea ice plays a role in local ecosystems as well as Indigenous cultures, and how its disappearance could be linked to greenhouse gas emissions a half a world away.

The teacher wanted her students to explain what was happening to their world and why. She wanted them to understand the basis for claims about past climate conditions as well as projections for different possible futures. Learners were asked to frame problems related to climate change, deliberate how these problems could be addressed, and weigh the risks of inaction.

The teacher made clear to her students that climate change is not just a science problem but also an adaptive challenge for all of humanity that requires new ways of seeing and being in the world.[2] In some situations, for example, problems are narrowly framed as individual behaviors like overconsumption, energy-intensive transportation habits, and waste—this is the default perspective for most Americans.[3] In these cases, it seems self-evident for educators to raise students' awareness of their own contributions to these problems and to shift toward more sustainable life choices. Not all problems, however, are about individuals' carbon footprints. In other situations, they are rooted in environmental racism, corporate greenwashing, or runaway models of capitalist expansion. In these cases, the role of educators is to help students use their deepening science knowledge to recognize exploitation and imagine equitable solutions. We have to acknowledge to students that two levels of explanation—scientific and justice-oriented—are necessary to move society toward sustainability and compassionate governance.

YOUR CLASSROOM AS A KNOWLEDGE-BUILDING COMMUNITY

When students take up the long-term challenge of developing causal explanations for complex environmental phenomena or designing climate solutions, their learning is deeper and more durable than when merely exposed to repeated rounds of new information and activity each day. Developing explanations, though, is no magic bullet. Success in these classrooms is the result of more diverse opportunities for intellectual work along the way. For example, classroom studies consistently show that students benefit from sensemaking conversations with peers, chances to model what they think is happening in the environment, invitations to connect the science to their own lives, freedom to determine what information they still need, and time to reflect on their progress.[4] This fosters students' epistemic agency (taking action to find out what we know and how we know it) as they shape the work of the classroom community.[5] I'll say more on these opportunities in a moment.

These activities provide intellectual momentum for one another if you set up your classroom as a knowledge-building community. Within this structure, children's ideas are routinely made visible, and many different student contributions become part of the curriculum, including everyday experiences that they feel are related to the topic, their partial understandings, wisdom from their family members or friends, and concepts developed from previous instruction. This kind of knowledge creation is not aimed at "landing on right answers" (there aren't any for authentic problems) but more serious work like identifying or reframing problems in new ways, providing supportive or disconfirming findings for claims, and offering novel perspectives on socioscientific issues.[6] Some of this work is done through individual reasoning, but much of the thinking is done as a collective with peers, where conjectures are coaxed out onto the social plane of the classroom and many voices work together to disambiguate, connect, and make meaning of ideas. The end game for students is to iteratively refine explanations and justice-oriented solutions that have value in the real world.

To get a knowledge-building project underway, anchoring events play a crucial role. The phrase "anchoring event" refers to any complex phenomenon or potential climate solution for which students can develop models and explanations over the course of a unit. These events can take place in a short time frame like a catastrophic flood, or they can be longer processes like the transition of the Amazon from a biodiverse rainforest ecosystem to a less diverse grassland ecosystem. Some anchoring events are challenges like selecting the most feasible and effective way to store energy generated by renewable sources like wind or solar. A good anchoring event is made even more effective when it is accompanied by a compelling essential question. An essential question cannot be answered with a yes/no response, but rather it requires critical thinking. For a unit on oceans and the atmosphere, an essential question could be "Where on the Earth has the climate changed most in the last twenty years and why?" A unit on the carbon cycle could be guided by the question "What might be the benefits and who might be harmed by geo-engineering projects as strategies to mitigate climate change—like pumping reflective aerosols into the atmosphere or dumping fertilizers for plankton into our oceans?"

All good anchoring events motivate students to construct explanations for what is going on and why. These are not just a couple of sentences with key vocabulary worked in. They are *elaborate* and *evidence-based* accounts that require learners to *draw on a wide range of science and social concepts* and to engage in *multiple investigations* in order to assemble a causal narrative or storyline for the target phenomenon. What makes these "why" explanations challenging is that they always involve things and actions that are not directly observable. This is why the teachers featured in this chapter prompt students explicitly to write about or model "what you cannot see as well as what you can." The unobservable things and actions that underpin a causal explanation may not be directly evident to our senses or even to instruments. These, for example, can work at a micro scale (the absorption and re-radiation of infrared waves by greenhouse gases); they can happen quickly (the creation of carbon dioxide during combustion in car engines); they take a long time (past warming of global temperatures over millennia); or they are abstract (albedo or the sequestration of carbon by plants). Using these theoretical goings-on to explain what we can see and hear in the world is some of the most demanding intellectual work students can engage with.

Is this effort worth the time? Let's put it this way—the more students make sense of new ideas, the more they will see new connections. This allows their knowledge to evolve into a kind of organic network of varied concepts with roots and branches; it can even self-organize and extend itself horizontally to help students make meaning of new topics.[7] We should provide opportunities, then, for learners to expand, revise, restructure, and reprioritize their ideas.[8]

These strategies succeed where "lessons in boxes" fail. In too many classrooms, a topic is announced—something like the carbon cycle or ocean acidification—and then with minimal context or input from students, instruction takes off. In the teacher's mind, every new idea is properly sequenced and connected. In the mind of the student, however, every day is something new but unmoored to previous lessons or anything they are genuinely concerned about. Too often, recitations of canonical science concepts are accompanied by vocabulary or procedural labs that students are obliged to take notes on for the purposes testing later. When science is dished out in discrete chunks like this, students don't have opportunities to do systems thinking, which would allow them to reason how individual components act together to generate complex events and processes in the world. The knowledge-in-pieces approach also causes students to struggle with potentially generative ideas like cycles and feedback loops. Without these tools, they lean on oversimplified causal chains to express how natural systems behave.[9] Students who don't perceive any coherent narrative in the curriculum or authentic puzzles to solve are justified in asking: How does this idea matter in the world? Why should we care?

EXAMPLES OF KNOWLEDGE-BUILDING CLASSROOMS IN ACTION

What does it look like when teaching is both coherent and responsive to students' ideas? I'll give an overview of three classrooms in which knowledge-building practices are the norm. As you get a sense of the activity in these classrooms, you'll likely pick up on a family resemblance among them that goes beyond using an anchoring event. These similarities matter and will be highlighted later.

Third Graders Study Biodiversity and Effects of Deforestation on Ecosystems

Carolyn's students were eager to find out what unusual creatures live in a rainforest and how plants and animals there interact. The lights in the classroom were dimmed, and they settled in as a video panned from the dark forest floor with a swarm of passing army ants, upward into the light-dappled understory where emerald tree boas and jaguars languished in the branches, then still higher into the canopy where macaws, sloths, and monkeys fed on abundant fruits and leaves. Although the video focused on the diversity of this ecosystem, the closing took an unexpected turn. It showed towering trees suddenly shuddering as if shaken by an invisible hand, then crashing to the forest floor. Among these fallen giants, heavy machinery became visible, roaring and spewing diesel fumes into the air. Students watched in silence. When the room lights came back on, Carolyn knew that the clear-cutting scene would be what many students remembered but she planned to help them later understand why this was happening and what might be done to preserve the rain forests. As with all knowledge-building classrooms, Carolyn attended to what students already seemed to know or be puzzled by and then adjusted the curriculum. She ended the class by asking them to share how they thought different species interacted with one another and then to draw a conceptual model of those links.

What followed was a series of activities introducing concepts that students could stitch together for themselves as the unit progressed, in order to comprehend the impacts of deforestation (see unit trajectory in appendix A). Carolyn's essential question was: "How do we know that losing some of the tropical rain forest is damaging to ecosystems and people?" The lessons included different ways that scientists study trees and how a typical climate helps trees to thrive as well as play key roles for other organisms in the ecosystem. All this set up investigations about how trees take up and store carbon dioxide, how tree rings provide clues to past climate conditions, and how effects ripple when these tropical rain forests are cut down. Students explored how Indigenous peoples who had taken care of these forests were now being displaced, and what actions students could take to interrupt the loss of community and destruction of ecosystems like the rain forests. Along the way, they were engaging in scientific practices nearly every day, including explanation, modeling, data interpretation, and gathering necessary information to understand what was happening. They got used to asking for more data to fill in their knowledge gaps. At other times they would announce, "We need to talk more about . . . " just so they could air out new ideas together. Carolyn periodically asked how their thinking was changing and what questions they felt would help them make progress. She prompted them with the same three questions in one form or another, every few days: "What do we know now and why do we think it's true?" "What resources or information do we still need in order to improve our understanding of what is happening here?" "Why does this matter for people and communities?"

Seventh Graders Connect Arctic Warming with Greenhouse Gas Emissions a World Away

Jessica based one of her climate change units on the book *My Wounded Island*, the story mentioned earlier in this chapter about an Alaskan village on Sarichef Island where climate change is literally at the doorstep. Students began by reading how the central character, a young girl named Imarvaluk, felt that there was a monster consuming the surrounding sea ice and now threatened to devour her village. The essential question for the unit is "What is happening around her island, and far away, that puts this village at risk?" The winter expanses of solid ice are critical to family hunting excursions there, and in warmer seasons, large patches of broken-up ice buffer the island's coastlines from the wave impact of stormy seas. Jessica had her students talk about questions this story raised for them. They wrote these on sticky notes, which gradually filled a whiteboard on the side of the room. A quick survey told her that students already knew this was the result of climate change but felt unsteady about the details. For example, many of their notes expressed the same two partial understandings that children around the world hold—that "pollution" is somehow responsible, but students are not sure what kind or how it does its damage. They also knew that the greenhouse effect was part of this story; however, the most common final phrase on the notes was ". . . but I don't know exactly how that works." To see as much of their initial thinking as possible, she asked them to sketch what they believed was happening on a model template that had the island pictured on the left and "the rest of the world" on the right.

Over the next five weeks, these students sorted through ideas that helped them build explanations about both sides of that template—what is happening in Alaska and how it is connected to choices people continue to make a world away from this little island. They explored weather versus climate; how the Iñupiat people have developed a deep knowledge of natural cycles of weather and living systems that they see themselves part of; the influence of human behaviors on the carbon cycle, on the greenhouse effect—the anthropogenically amplified version of it—and on ecosystem disruptions in polar regions brought about by planetary warming. In one activity, students compared the carbon footprint of the average American with others around the world, prompting them to ask what makes their own lives so carbon intensive. Another activity had students making sense of data about increasing carbon dioxide levels in our atmosphere over the past fifty years and why the northern polar regions are now warming faster than anywhere else on Earth. Figure 2.1 shows the storyline of lessons for Jessica's unit, with early elicitation of students' ideas and their initial models, then a few days later a chance to revise those models, and at the end, final models and written explanations. All three teachers I discuss here follow the same broad pattern, including the seven opportunities labeled below the figure as "threaded throughout the unit."

As in Carolyn's classroom, students had opportunities to figure out how all these ideas might fill knowledge gaps or support a hypothesis they favored. Jessica's version of this asks some combination of the following: (1) How are ideas from different days connected? (2) What does [this new idea] mean to you? and (3) What do you need to learn more about? At one point, Jessica shared an aerial photo of Sarichef in which students could see that individual

Figure 2.1 Trajectory of *My Wounded Island* seventh-grade unit with selected lessons

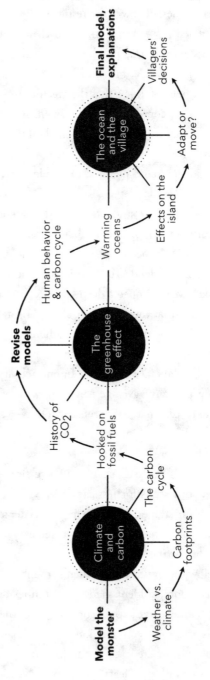

Opportunities threaded throughout unit: 1) Epistemic conversations, 2) modeling, 3) revising ideas, 4) making meaning of data, 5) metacognitive reflection, 6) students' ideas becoming part of curriculum, 7) conversations about who is doing harm and who is being impacted?

homes were perilously close to the sea. The island itself seemed defenseless against the massive swells of dark water. For some students, this was no longer an abstract problem; a quick online search confirmed to them that this was not a fictional case. Students' final models showed cars with billowing exhaust coming from their tailpipes and zoom-ins of carbon dioxide trapping heat in the atmosphere. Part of the template also asks students to propose solutions for Sarichef. Some wrote that "citizens can build a big [sea] wall" and "they could put solar panels on their roofs." This reminds us that students' understanding can become scientifically sophisticated in many ways yet overestimate humans' capacity to deal with problems of this scale.

High School Students Want to Know: What Is Stressing Out the Pikas?

Molly teaches in a conservative rural community east of the Cascade Mountain Range. She feels that she has an obligation to address climate impacts and gets surprisingly little pushback from students because, in her words, "they're seeing it, we have a longer wildfire season, the smoke season lasts forever, we have heatwaves like never before, and drought." Molly decided to teach an interdisciplinary unit centering on a small mammal—the pika—that her students knew was becoming scarcer in the foothills outside town. Although the pika was the main actor in the unit, the curriculum focused not on biology but on physical and geological science. Pikas depend on the local snowpack in the winter to provide insulation against freezing temperatures (they don't hibernate) and its runoff in the summer that cools the surrounding environment just enough for them to avoid heat exhaustion. But this ecosystem is changing. Students noticed that with a small rise in overnight low temperatures, winter precipitation now falls more often as rain than snow.

Molly wanted to connect with students' lives, so she started the unit by talking about stress on living organisms and then asked students what stressed them out. They were not reluctant to share: tests, sports, needing to fit in, friendships, fear of failure, family, talking about the future, and the list goes on. Molly had students consider what stresses could accumulate for pikas, and what the result might be. Students then transitioned to creating an initial model of the pika and their environment, which indicated to Molly that they were already bringing sophisticated ideas into this unit. Among these were that pikas experienced problems when they sought a survivable habitat that included new kinds of competition for food and tried to fit into a new ecosystem they have a role in disrupting.

Over the course of this unit, the students explored topics like the greenhouse effect, the role of freezing and thawing cycles that create the fractured stone fields pikas prefer for cover, and the conservation of energy as water vapor becomes snow and melts again (see unit trajectory in appendix A). As in Carolyn's and Jessica's units, the students recognized each lesson as a clue that helped solve a challenging puzzle. All lessons finished with similar questions: "What did we observe?" "What caused these trends?" "How does this help us understand the pika's situation?" Molly pressed them to integrate these ideas with what they already knew, in order to make claims and argue for their emerging explanations. In their final models, some students drew the hydrosphere, atmosphere, geosphere, and the biosphere and then wrote or drew how these systems interacted in predictable ways. Other students built trophic pyramids to explain the changing role of the pikas in an environment that was becoming inhospitable and dangerous.

Lessons Learned About Anchoring Events

All three teachers grounded their units in compelling phenomena, which helped them sequence their lessons and set the stage for student engagement. Over the last few years, hundreds of teachers have circulated valuable feedback on how to choose anchoring events. Here is what they recommend (more detail is available in the book *Ambitious Science Teaching*[10]):

Anchoring events should relate to students' interests and experiences. This increases their motivation to learn, but also allows them to capitalize on their background knowledge as they develop explanations. Relevant contexts for study would connect to some aspect of students' lives (i.e., relating to their home, culture, school, peer network, or out-of-school experiences). Other contexts can involve their local community, physical surroundings, or the history of a region where they live.[11]

Explanations for anchoring events should require students to integrate a number of important science ideas together. In one high school biology classroom, students were asked to figure out how to restore California's kelp beds that, over the last fifteen years, had diminished by 90 percent through various human impacts. This unit, however, was not just about these enormous ribbons of brown algae; students drew on ideas such as the sequestration of carbon by both plants and kelp, the support kelp beds give to entire ecosystems, and the sources of near-shore pollution that stress kelp and other organisms. Each of these science ideas became more meaningful when students figured out how it was linked with others in this unit. They also applied what they learned to other "blue carbon" ecosystems around the world, which include mangrove forests, seagrass meadows, coral reefs, and coastal watersheds.

Anchoring events are more puzzling and complicated to explain if they are about events or systems that don't behave as expected, about something that stops happening, or about problems that aren't where you would expect them to be. In other words, don't study systems behaving normally—they are too simple and no longer how the world works. On the North Carolina coast, for example, vast stands of red maples, sweetgum, and bald cypress are turning into ghost forests of withered branches and ashen stumps because of saltwater creeping in below ground. Why is this happening *now* and how is it affecting the ecosystem? An anchoring event can also focus on problems that are overlooked when climate solutions get discussed. For example, the technology behind wind turbines is fascinating, but the bottleneck preventing more widespread use is how to store the energy they generate. Some companies are using the wind energy to pull a train filled with concrete up an incline (referred to as the "rubble express"). Then, when the wind dies down and energy has to be withdrawn from the system, the train begins a controlled descent, releasing its stored energy through regenerative braking, just like some hybrid cars. There is a whole menagerie of massive, quirky batteries being tested now—they are worth studying for their engineering and their dramatic transformations of energy from one form to another.

Anchoring events should allow students to construct different types of explanations and models. We want students to know that there are many ways to show what they know, and that viable explanations for an event can take different but equally credible forms. Teachers have to announce this early in the school year when students first start modeling and writing explanations because learners often feel they have to have right answers or converge on models should show the same events in the same ways.

When you start seeking out anchoring events, you'll reach the limit of your own subject-matter understanding. It is important to work with your colleagues, asking them how they understand the science and current climate events. There are abundant content resources online for every dimension of climate science, but the sheer volume of these can be intimidating. Use this book to identify phenomena with potential, as well as to pass over flashy but trivial climate stories in the media. Even when you make good choices, you'll never get rid of the feeling that there is always one more thing to read.

Developing a unit that works for a knowledge-building community has to be done in the summer or be the focus of a long-term collaboration with teaching peers during the school year. Developing one good unit (don't shoot for perfection) is genuine progress. A clunky or so-so anchoring event will engage your students far better than none at all. Adapting existing high-quality units is another option—sometimes all they need is a well-chosen anchoring event to motivate students and tie lessons together.

DESIGNING LESSONS FOR SENSEMAKING AND AGENCY

The arc of a unit begins with students sharing what they know and wonder about at the start, then revising their thinking over the course of several lessons, and finally working with peers to culminate their thinking with evidence-based explanations, models, or other authentic performances. But as you can tell by the vignettes of the three classrooms, teachers must provide specific opportunities for students to grow. For example, students experience deeper learning when they have regular interactions to process new ideas with peers.[12] Especially powerful are epistemic discussions, also known as "How do we know?" conversations in which students deliberate whether certain claims about the environment or human influence are consistent with science and they debate the applicability of different kinds of evidence for explanations of events.[13] Epistemic conversations also can focus on the accuracy of predictive climate models or how Indigenous ways of knowing and traditional Western science can be used together to help vulnerable communities adapt to climate risks.

Effective climate instruction incorporates firsthand data (student-generated) or secondhand data (generated by others) into discussions about causes and effects, trends over time, cycles, or feedback loops. Data can support talk about how scientific knowledge is constructed, and students need to understand how evidence supports or challenges assertions about climate change. This includes how to counter claims that are skeptical of anthropogenic warming.[14]

The scientific practice of modeling motivates students' understanding of a wide range of phenomena associated with climate change.[15] Modeling makes student thinking visible and can prompt them to revise their thinking over time—a key norm in a knowledge-building community. Modeling also supports systems thinking. Systems are things that have parts and relationships that allow the whole to behave in ways that individual components cannot. Systems can interact with one another (e.g., ecosystems with atmospheric systems). They can also comprise smaller subsystems (e.g., transportation systems as part of carbon-intensive food systems). In climate change teaching, there are diverse examples of systems such as food webs, a solar farm's connections to an electrical grid, or a set of Indigenous agricultural practices designed for a particular landscape. Students who model come to realize that systems can have inputs, internal processes, and outputs, and that lots of human actions can perturb natural systems in unexpected ways.

Students learn to regulate their own learning by engaging in metacognitive work. This simply means periodically questioning one's own state of knowing and developing a repertoire of ways to improve it. Teachers prompt students to consider: What knowledge gaps do I still have? What resources might I need to make progress on my models or explanations? What is the best way to show what I know? The teachers I've worked with use these questions in exit tickets and do a quick review of trending responses. When students get support for monitoring their current levels of understanding, they are more likely to take steps to improve their learning, including moves to identify relevant tools, knowledge they need, peer input, and other resources. Put another way, part of successful teaching is to help students *operate more independently of you* as the year progresses.

As climate change educators, we have the added task of inspiring action. Both in-school and out-of-school programs have found ways to instill a sense of self-efficacy and to motivate young people to act by translating global problems to a scale that they can grasp. Students have examined the origins of climate impacts in their region of the country or in their own backyards, and then proposed public communication or engineering strategies that they could design and help implement.[16] Other programs focused on how climate disruptions have impacted vulnerable human populations and what socially just solutions would look like. Some of these curricula help students see the connections individual behaviors have with carbon emissions or mitigation efforts.[17] But this brings up a tension. Foregrounding personal behaviors like cutting food waste at home or ditching carbon-intensive fast fashion may distract students from engaging in the necessary community-level activity and broader forms of activism. At this time, mobilization for environmental resilience has to happen at the level of neighborhoods, cities, or governments, and mostly through targeted political action. Opportunities for empowered work like community action projects or protests can be transformational for students. These can help them and their families feel a sense of direction and much needed self-efficacy to create changes that matter.[18]

All these recommendations are part of a larger vision for learning and climate consciousness. But we should also be prepared to address traumatic experiences, especially among students who are directly exposed to climate change threats and families who have the fewest resources to protect themselves against harm. This includes those who will lose their homes and their livelihoods. We must build students' own capacities for dealing with strong emotions and supporting others in building theirs. As climate scientist Susanne Moser writes:

> The task is not to dramatize suffering or turn victims into exhibits, but—quite the opposite—to validate the emotional responses to change, explain how they are normal responses to extraordinary circumstances, and then to give space to people to support their processing of them, individually and together with others. Communicators of transformative change and those going through it (who may be one and the same) will need to create or seek out calm spaces and times for rejuvenation and healing.[19]

The final chapter in this book will deal with these issues of eco-anxiety. You may find it surprising that many of the self-care measures described in the literature identify activism as one way to build a sense of agency and hope about the future.

COORDINATING A SEQUENCE OF CLIMATE CHANGE EXPLORATIONS ACROSS COURSES

Students benefit from subject-matter coherence across different time scales. *Within a lesson* they learn to connect ideas if we thoughtfully sequence talk opportunities and material activity. Similarly, the steady focus on improving explanations and models *over a unit* helps students consolidate a wider range of concepts. We should extend this logic to *an entire year's curriculum* and even to students' *experiences over several years*. By coordinating what gets taught about climate change and when, committed educators in a school can have a multiplier effect on student learning. Imagine teaching a high school unit about the role of the oceans in climate sustainability if students have already investigated ocean currents, warming, and acidification in previous grades. You would not have to start from scratch, spending precious time reintroducing basic ideas, but rather you could launch instruction from students' prior experiences and build toward richer, more advanced ideas. I've visited many classrooms at the start of the school year where students jumped right into scientific arguments with peers, using savvy interpretations of complex data or demonstrating all kinds of modeling techniques to show what they knew. When I ask the teacher how this is possible, the answer is always the same—"They had Mr. or Ms. 'so-and-so' last year; that's where they got this head start." I should expect this by now, but I am still amazed at what a vertically connected and cumulative curriculum can do for students.

You can start a coherence project by building trust with teachers at other grade levels around the issue of climate change instruction, perhaps reading a couple of articles or a book together and suggesting you collaboratively create a road map of key topics at different grades. Just the reading and the mapping can take the better part of a year. Then, before you get into the weeds about who should teach what, brainstorm long-term climate change goals for your learners. This is a place where you could invite former students, teachers from other subject areas, and community members to participate in the conversation. What do we want our children to know, value, and be able to do? What capacities (like critical thinking, compassion, sense of agency, or an orientation toward justice) do we want students to develop across years? Just this beginning step has been useful for teacher groups; many educators we know have reported epiphanies about what peers and students value. You will want to revisit this conversation as you learn more about what colleagues are currently teaching and what their students experience at each grade level.

Another conversation focuses on what counts as a climate change topic. Would a generic ecosystem unit fit the profile? Probably not, or only if it is modified to explicitly address climate, mitigation, human impacts, and so on. Nor would a unit on the chemistry of plastics be appropriate unless the teacher asks students to link them to fossil fuels and perhaps the greenhouse gases they emit when they are incinerated (only 9 percent are recycled in the United States).[20] Even a unit on the greenhouse effect might not count because of the way it is taught, as unrelated to human emissions or failing to mention its cascading effects on other systems. Without shaming any colleagues, map out what is being taught now and add enough description so others know if the current curriculum links to climate change are explicit or implicit, direct or indirect. Working backward from what your team (including students, other faculty, community members) has listed as its values, think of other student experiences you'd want to design into a multiyear curriculum. As part of this, identify the science standards that you could address, but bear in mind that some standards speak directly to climate change, others to human impacts on the environment, still others to designing adaptations, and some focus on more generic science ideas that could easily be woven into a climate change unit. Don't dismiss a standard just because the word "climate" is not in it. That being said, if you feel there are important climate-related ideas or opportunities for a certain grade level, and yet there are no standards related to that particular science, you have to decide what is truly in the best interests of your students. My inclination would be to teach it.

Collaborating teachers that I work with have helped identify different categories of standards that all link to climate change, but in different ways. Table 2.1 describes these categories. When we select from the *Next Generation Science Standards*, we mean disciplinary core ideas and performance expectations.

Placing standards in these categories is a judgment call. What really matters is that these can get you thinking about standards that you may not have thought were connected to climate change or resilience. This will help you design lessons, courses, and multiyear trajectories that help your students build coherent climate-related ideas over time.

Table 2.1 Categories of standards applicable to climate change

Category of standard	Criteria for this category of standard
Direct references to climate	Refers to climate system or weather dynamics
Direct references to climate change	Mentions that climate changes, either naturally or through anthropogenic forcing
Direct or indirect (negative) human impacts on climate	Encompasses direct anthropogenic influences on climate or that exacerbate existing climate change risks
How humans will be affected by climate change	Describes present or future climate-related risks for humans or for the more-than-human world
Engineering for mitigation or adaptation of climate risks	Engineering standards that directly reference challenges with lowering or adapting to specific climate risks
Foundational geophysical knowledge, potentially applicable to climate change	Expresses a fundamental idea from the domains of chemistry, physics, or earth sciences more broadly that students could use to understand or incorporate into an explanation for a variety of climate change phenomena
Foundational biological knowledge	Expresses a fundamental idea from the domain of biology that students could use to understand or incorporate into an explanation for a variety of climate change phenomena
Downstream biological effects	Describes a scientific principle that could be used to understand or explain biological systems phenomena that are part of a cascade of climate change effects
Foundational engineering applications	Engineering standards that refer to broad principles which could be used to study, mitigate, or adapt to climate change risks; these may or may not explicitly mention climate change

There are no long-term planning sequences that work for all teacher teams. I do suggest, however, that you ask some version of these questions early on:

- How might we include phenomena that could be understood most deeply if situated in a local context?
- Where might there be opportunities for involvement with the community?

- In what parts of a yearlong or multiyear trajectory should we address climate anxiety?
- How can we discuss Indigenous worldviews that present generative views of the living world and humans' roles in relation to the land, air, and water?
- When should we address both the scientific and social dimensions of climate change solutions?
- How should we engage students in activism around climate change and environmental justice?
- How do we build on these experiences in a coordinated way over time?

Using these questions as a guide, you can prevent unintentional gaps, mixed messages, and redundancies in what students are asked to grapple with; each unit or course then offers footholds for the next. I cannot overemphasize the value of building trust among colleagues and giving this process a couple of years to unfold without undue pressure.

CHAPTER 3

A Primer on Core Climate Change Ideas

IF WE WANT TO BUILD specialized knowledge for teaching something as complex as climate change, it helps to create conceptual categories. The following sections—think of them as mini-chapters—offer a starting place for this; they are based on five broad science domains that are climate-relevant and show up in the standards: the greenhouse effect, the carbon cycle, oceans and the cryosphere, impacts on ecosystems and biodiversity, and extreme weather. This is not an official framework, but it can be used to consolidate what you already know about climate change and extend that knowledge. You will likely reorganize ideas within these categories as you read, find generative connections between the categories, or recreate them to serve your pedagogical needs.

Each of the categories is home to complex large-scale systems which are difficult for students to visualize. Classroom research consistently demonstrates how students benefit from systems thinking, which is, in turn, critical for comprehending climate change processes and solutions. While this is true, I argue here that we are overlooking an even more important cross-cutting science concept—that of stability and change. In our altered world, *in*stability and change now characterize most natural systems. Although systems thinking provides a shared language about interrelationships among parts and the whole, or inputs and outputs, the inclusion of stability and change allows students to explain dynamic equilibrium (e.g., of healthy ecosystems), feedback loops, (e.g., sea ice disappearing as open water absorbs more light), the irreversibility of system changes (e.g., slowing of ocean circulation), and tipping points (e.g., conditions leading to the collapse of Antarctic ice shelves). We cannot be confident that our students will think in terms of systems unless they understand these concepts and their role in the growing disequilibrium of normally stable processes.

For the five categories, I'll describe how students typically think about content in these areas (if the research is clear), including common initial conceptions and knowledge gaps. I will also share how events and processes related to these topics ultimately affect human communities around the world. After reading, you should be able to set up productive conversations with colleagues about the science, sequence experiences for learners, identify what new ideas to include and which to reject, and perhaps become better informed citizens.

Think of these sections as launching platforms that orient you to big ideas in each category. More importantly, they provide guidance on how to *seek out additional resources* to continue more purposeful and directed learning on your own. Many government-sponsored agencies and intergovernmental organizations now have extensive consumer-friendly information resources for understanding every science idea related to climate change. These include the National Oceanic and Atmospheric Administration (NOAA), the World Meteorological Organization (WMO), the World Health Organization (WHO), the National Aeronautics and Space Administration (NASA), the US Environmental Protection Agency (EPA), the US Global Change Research Program (USGCRP), the United Nations Environment Programme (UNEP), the US Geological Survey (USGS), the National Center for Atmospheric Research (NCAR), the National Academy of Science (NAS), the Intergovernmental Panel on Climate Change (IPCC), and Project Drawdown.

What's helpful about these sites is that they curate and organize the world's most well-vetted science information. They also include data on human risks and case studies of how different kinds of data are collected. They make clear the uncertainties in the climate record and what that means for different communities.

SECTION 3.1

The Greenhouse Effect

Where It All Starts

The greenhouse effect begins the climate change story and drives nearly every other process we associate with planetary warming. At its core, the greenhouse effect explains the interactions of energy from the sun with gases in our atmosphere and the Earth's different surfaces.[1] The sun generates the full spectrum of radiant energy that travels in waves through space; however, much of what reaches the Earth's atmosphere does not penetrate it, especially shorter-wavelength ultraviolet, x-rays, and radio waves. What does make it to the Earth's surface is radiation that we can see as visible light, ranging from violet (shorter wavelengths) to red (longer wavelengths). As this energy passes through our atmosphere, some is reflected back into space by clouds and small particles and some is absorbed by substances such as water vapor, soot, and ozone. About 29 percent of the energy is reflected back into space by the atmosphere, the land surface, and the sea surface.[2] The percentage of solar radiation reflected back into space is called the *albedo*. Albedo is affected by clouds, snow cover, the extent of ice sheets, sea ice, glaciers, and oxygen and nitrogen in the atmosphere. In general, lighter-colored substances (clouds, ice, and snow) reflect more radiation.

The Earth ends up absorbing the remaining 71 percent of energy, mostly visible light, which heats the land, ocean surface, and atmosphere. How does this happen? Both the surfaces and the atmosphere re-radiate this energy in a different form called *infrared radiation* (IR). This IR is commonly referred to as heat or thermal energy because the IR emitted by any object (including our own bodies) depends on its temperature—this is what night-vision goggles detect. The higher an object's temperature, the more infrared energy it emits. This is half the story. The IR emitted by Earth's surfaces moves outward in waves like ripples in a pond. Some of this re-radiated IR then travels into the

39

atmosphere, where much of it is absorbed by water vapor and long-lived green-house gases such as carbon dioxide.[3]

Why do greenhouse gases absorb IR when other gases don't? A CO_2 molecule has a carbon atom bonded to two oxygen atoms. Because of the shape, the bonds can bend back and forth like springs, and they happen to wobble at the same frequency that the IR waves hit them (the phenomenon of resonance).[4] This is similar to a sound wave that has a unique frequency, and if it matches the frequency of a nearby glass, it will cause it to vibrate or even shatter. When the bonds rebound, the carbon dioxide molecules then re-radiate this IR in random directions rather than just downward to Earth. Without the presence of CO_2, some of the infrared would have been lost to space, but instead, this greenhouse gas ends up redirecting IR toward the Earth's surface, warming it. The IR that radiates back toward Earth heats both the surface and the lower atmosphere, adding to the IR they already absorbed directly from sunlight. In fact, if averaged across the whole planet, the surface receives as much radiation from the atmosphere as it does from the sun.[5] It's surreal that warming on a planetary scale can be traced back to the nanoscopic vibrations of greenhouse gas molecules.

Figure 3.1.1 shows a seventh grader's model of the greenhouse effect that accurately represents many key processes. Point A on the model shows the kinetic energy of "particles" from the sun; at B the student depicts how, as radiation hits the surface, it can be re-emitted as IR, which causes molecules to move faster; C indicates that CO_2 is "reflective" and can send some IR back to Earth; D shows that molecules like O_2 allow IR to pass through into space; at E it appears that both the atmosphere and the Earth's surface heat up as a result of re-emitted IR. As with most student models, some adjustments could be made; for example, there are actually no molecules accompanying incoming solar radiation, and technically, CO_2 absorbs and re-emits rather than reflects IR energy. Nonetheless, this student has clearly made sense of a complex and invisible set of processes.

The *natural* greenhouse effect moderates life on Earth. The surface temperature of any planet is determined by two factors: the net amount of incoming solar energy it receives, and the heat-trapping properties of any greenhouse gases in its atmosphere. Increasing the concentration of greenhouse gases, whether artificially or naturally, shifts the balance between incoming solar

Figure 3.1.1 Seventh-grader's model of the greenhouse effect

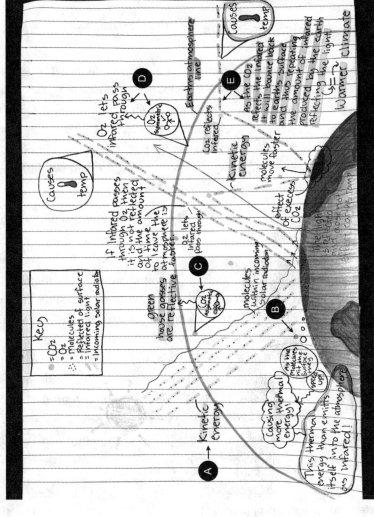

energy and outgoing heat energy, making the planet warmer. Without green-house gases, Earth would be like Mars, a frigid –18 °C (0 °F).[6] In contrast, the atmosphere of Venus is a massive reservoir of carbon dioxide—retaining 154,000 times as much as the Earth. Our planet under these conditions would be like a furnace at about 400 °C (750 °F).

WHAT OTHER GASES ARE RESPONSIBLE FOR WARMING?

We often hear the phrase *greenhouse gases* (GHGs), indicating that there are others in addition to carbon dioxide. Some are even more effective at trapping and re-radiating energy than CO_2, because of their molecular structures.[7] On the other hand, common gases like nitrogen molecules (N_2) and oxygen molecules (O_2), which make up more than 90 percent of Earth's atmosphere, have much simpler structures and do not absorb IR. I'll start by adding more context about carbon dioxide, then describe other major GHGs.

Carbon dioxide. Carbon dioxide is released through natural processes such as respiration and volcanic eruptions and through human activities such as deforestation, land use changes, and burning fossil fuels. Beginning around 1950, human production and consumption of goods increased dramatically, leading to even greater fossil fuel exploitation. Because of this, scientists call the period from 1950 to the present the Great Acceleration.[8] We've since added an enormous amount of carbon dioxide to the thin shell of our atmosphere, as of 2023, dumping 2.2 *trillion* tons of it into the air. About 45 percent of that remains circulating above our heads today. After a pulse of CO_2 is emitted into the atmosphere, a small portion of it cycles out quickly; however, 40 percent will remain over the next 100 years and 20 percent will remain for 1,000 years. About 10 percent will take 10,000 years to turn over. This literally means that the heat-trapping emissions we release today are determining the climate that our children and grandchildren will inherit.

Water vapor. Some people are surprised to hear that water vapor is the most abundant heat-trapping gas. So why aren't we worried about it? The reason is that it has a short life cycle in the atmosphere—ten days on average—before it becomes rain or snow and falls to Earth, so it can't accumulate the same way carbon dioxide does. But water vapor is part of a vicious cycle in which, as more CO_2 is emitted into the atmosphere and the Earth's temperature rises, more water then evaporates into the Earth's atmosphere, which in turn increases the temperature of the planet. The warmer atmosphere can then hold more water vapor than before, further amplifying the cycle (an example of positive feedback).

Methane. This greenhouse gas is generated by human activity. This includes the decomposition of wastes in landfills, wood burning, agriculture, ruminant digestion (by bacteria in the guts of cattle, sheep, and goats), and manure management associated with domestic livestock. On a molecule-for-molecule basis, methane is about twenty-five times more active a greenhouse gas than carbon dioxide, but also one that is much less abundant in the atmosphere. Methane is the main natural gas that we use for power generation, heating, and cooking. Natural gas leaks (called "fugitive emissions") at production and processing facilities and through distribution pipes are a major source of methane emissions. It takes about a decade for methane (CH_4) emissions to cycle out of the atmosphere.

CFCs and HFCs. Humans create coolants to refrigerate food and air-condition living spaces. Chlorofluorocarbons and hydrofluorocarbons are artificially produced for these purposes. HFCs and CFCs are a few thousand to 10,000 times more potent than carbon dioxide, but thankfully they are being phased out and replaced with alternatives like ammonia that are safer for the environment.

CAN WE BLAME THE SUN FOR SOME OF THIS?

Some climate change skeptics suspect that differences in the sun's output of energy is causing the Earth to warm now. This seems like fair game since the sun is the source of energy that drives our climate system. Indeed, studies show that solar energy variability has played a role in past climate fluctuations.[9] For example, a decrease in solar activity coupled with an increase in volcanic activity (spewing millions of tons of aerosols into the atmosphere) is thought to have helped trigger the Little Ice Age between approximately 1650 and 1850, and the cooling of Greenland from 1410 to the 1720s. However, the amount of solar energy that we receive has always followed the sun's natural eleven-year cycle of minor ups and downs with no net increase in insolation since the 1950s. Over that same period, global temperature has risen markedly. It is therefore extremely unlikely that the sun has caused global warming trends during the past half-century. It's us.

HOW STUDENTS AND TEACHERS THINK ABOUT THE GREENHOUSE EFFECT

Many children and adults assume that all kinds of unnatural pollutants are to blame for warming.[10] But because people usually think of carbon dioxide as a natural component of the life cycle and necessary for plants, they resist the idea that it is driving climate change. Reasoning from the unnatural pollutants theory, people mistakenly assume that the problem must be toxic gases that "eat holes" in the ozone layer which, their logic tells them, allows more heat from the sun to pass through our atmosphere and warm the planet.

Most elementary students recognize the importance of the greenhouse effect.[11] However, they also believe that incoming UV rays create an ozone hole that warms up the planet and melts polar ice. Many middle school and high school students consider the depletion of the ozone layer a cause of increased temperatures in the Earth's atmosphere; they confuse different types of radiation such as solar and terrestrial radiation, longwave and shortwave, ultraviolet and infrared. About half of middle school students consider acid rain and gases produced by rotting waste as contributors to global warming.

A national survey of 1,500 science teachers highlights the critical work we must take on in addressing causal mechanisms for planetary warming.[12] Most respondents considered it essential to discuss CO_2 as an important heat-trapping gas. However, the underlying story—that the atmosphere and surfaces on Earth absorb and transform incoming radiation into IR, which is then reabsorbed and re-radiated by CO_2—was considered a priority by only about a quarter of respondents, and by very few biology or middle school science teachers. One in five educators even declined to rate the priority of this topic. Just as problematically, some surveyed teachers viewed factors that were not significantly related to climate change as high-priority topics. Specifically, they cited pesticides, depletion of ozone, and aerosol spray cans as important to address for a unit on greenhouse gases. Although these are each important contributors to environmental pollution, none are directly relevant to a unit on greenhouse gases or global warming.

Taken together, studies like these indicate that we should be preparing ourselves to explore with students the chain of causality from the sun's energy streaming into our atmosphere to the re-emission of infrared energy by greenhouse gas molecules. It should also be made clear to young learners that things can be bad for the environment but not play a major role in warming the climate.

Carbon Cycling

Where It Stays and Where It's Going

Carbon is always on the move. It circulates around the planet, taking on different forms and playing different roles in our Earth systems, often in ways that are not apparent to us. Students need to understand how and why carbon moves, in particular the processes that transfer it among different "sinks." A carbon sink is any reservoir, natural or otherwise, that accumulates carbon-containing compounds for an indefinite period. Sinks are important because they help keep carbon dioxide out of the atmosphere (which is a sink itself). The distinctions between a reservoir and a sink are of little practical consequence for K–12 teaching, and I'll use the terms interchangeably in this book. By far the largest sink of carbon (excluding rock) is the deep waters of our oceans, which are thought to contain about 25 percent of the CO_2 emitted by human activities and fifty times more carbon than our atmosphere.[1] Other sinks include sediments at the bottom of the oceans, soils, permafrost, vegetation—primarily in the Amazon, the northern boreal forests, and vast kelp beds—and our atmosphere. If the prime takeaway from section 3.1 was "stop burning fossil fuels," the big lesson from this one is "don't abuse the sinks."

Transfers of carbon between these reservoirs are referred to as "fluxes." Some fluxes are sensitive to climate. When global temperatures increase, for example, a positive feedback loop can occur as carbon accelerates its transition from sinks like the oceans back into the atmosphere.[2] This increasing amount of carbon dioxide in the atmosphere then leads to further climate warming via the greenhouse effect, intensifying the carbon flux from the oceans into the atmosphere. These are known as "carbon cycle–climate feedbacks," and this is how global warming can spin out of control when self-reinforcing loops kick in.

FAST AND SLOW CARBON CYCLES

K–12 textbook images of carbon cycles can be oversimplified and often obscure how carbon circulates. They seldom include how long greenhouse gases stay in the atmosphere; they underplay the effects of other GHGs like methane and disregard how sinks work. Some representations don't explain the time it takes for carbon to move and often omit anthropogenic influences within the cycle. Even the term "cycle" can be misinterpreted as carbon moving in a circle, with atoms in a particular reservoir all moving in unison to another one, packing their bags and decamping together. The fact is that carbon atoms in the atmosphere may be captured by plants, dissolve into the ocean, or be removed through the process of rock weathering, processes that vary in time and consequences.[3]

On a global scale, carbon moves around in a *fast* cycle through rapid exchanges among the oceans, the terrestrial (land) biosphere, and the atmosphere. Simultaneously, carbon also moves around in a *slow* cycle, traveling between geological reservoirs such as deep soils, the deeper ocean, and rocks. These redistributions of CO_2 among geological (nonliving) reservoirs can take hundreds of thousands of years or longer.

Figure 3.2.1 shows the major fluxes in the fast carbon cycle and the main reservoirs of the carbon cycle as a whole (both the fast and slow carbon cycles).[4] Reservoirs are indicated by parentheses noting the gigatons of carbon (GtC) they hold. Arrows indicate fluxes of carbon between reservoirs; flow rates are in gigatons of carbon per year (GtC/y). Where there is a "+," the following number indicates the contribution from human activities, primarily through burning fossil fuels, cement production, and land use changes.

The Fast Carbon Cycle

The fast cycle can be observed in a human lifespan because it involves living systems. Exchanges of carbon between the atmosphere and the terrestrial biosphere occur through photosynthesis and cellular respiration. Carbon is removed by plants from the atmosphere through photosynthesis, which helps them form biomass (aquatic plants and phytoplankton and go through this process with CO_2 dissolved in the oceans). Carbon dioxide is returned to the

Figure 3.2.1 Fast and slow carbon cycles

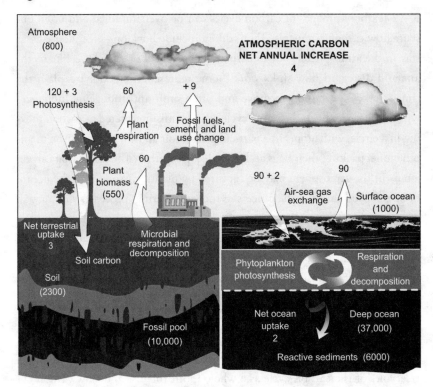

Source: Carbon Cycling and Biosequestration: Report from the March 2008 Workshop, DOE/
SC-108 (Washington, DC: Us Department of Energy Office of Science, 2008), https://genomic
science.energy.gov/carboncycle/report/.

atmosphere through plant respiration and microbial decomposition of organic
matter on the ground and in the soil. Fire and other disturbances such as in-
sect outbreaks and timber harvesting can be thought of as an accelerated respiration processes, adding to the amount of carbon entering our atmosphere.[5]

Four processes move carbon from plants and return it to the atmosphere,
but all involve the same chemical reactions of combining biomass (containing
sugars from photosynthesis) with oxygen. The first three processes are respiration and the last is combustion:

- Plants go through the process of respiration, breaking down their sugars
  to release energy they need to grow and reproduce.

- Animals (including people) eat plants and break down the sugars to get energy.
- Living organisms die and decompose (are digested by microbes).
- Fire consumes biomass.

In all instances, oxygen combines with sugars to release water, carbon dioxide, and energy. The carbon dioxide that's released as a by-product in these respiration or combustion reactions usually ends up in the atmosphere. The fast carbon cycle is so tightly tied to plant life that satellites can track the growing season by monitoring how CO_2 fluctuates in the atmosphere. During the Northern Hemisphere's winter, when fewer land plants are growing, atmospheric carbon dioxide concentrations climb. During the spring, when plants begin photosynthesizing again, concentrations plummet. This is the Earth "breathing."

The Slow Carbon Cycle

The only fast part of the slow cycle is the exchange of CO_2 between the air and the surface of the oceans. At this interface, carbon dioxide gas both dissolves into and ventilates out of the oceans in a steady trade-off with the atmosphere. About 1 million tons of carbon dioxide cross from the air to the sea *each hour.*[6] Once in the ocean, some carbon dioxide reacts with water molecules to release hydrogen ions, making the ocean more acidic. This is one of the few ways that emissions in the atmosphere directly disrupt an Earth system without being involved in the greenhouse effect.

Before the industrial age, the oceans vented carbon dioxide into the atmosphere in balance with what it received, mostly from the process of rock weathering. The weathering process begins with rain, which is usually slightly acidic after absorbing CO_2 from the atmosphere on its journey to the ground. The acidic rain reacts with the rocks and soils it lands on, gradually breaking them down into minute grains and forming a compound called bicarbonate. Eventually, this bicarbonate washes into the oceans, where its carbon is stored in dissolved form for hundreds of thousands of years or locked up for even longer in the sea floor. However, since CO_2 concentrations in the atmosphere have increased, the ocean now takes more carbon from the atmosphere than it releases.[7] Over millennia, the oceans will absorb up to 85 percent of the extra carbon humans put into the atmosphere, but the upper layers are already "getting full" and the bottleneck is becoming the transfer of carbon from surface waters to the deep ocean. As with other processes in the slow carbon cycle, this takes an extraordinary amount of time, about 500 to 1,000 years.[8]

The slow cycle maintains a balance that prevents all of Earth's carbon from entering the atmosphere (as is the case on Venus) or from being locked up entirely in rocks. This process acts like a thermostat, keeping Earth's temperature relatively stable.[9] For example, if the planet were to warm significantly, this would accelerate the chemical weathering of rocks, taking more CO_2 out of the atmosphere, which would then cool the climate back toward its original equilibrium.[10] Conversely, if the planet were to cool, weathering would slow, allowing CO_2 to accumulate in the atmosphere, thus warming it. This process is dynamic, meaning that for shorter time periods—tens to hundreds of thousands of years—the temperature of Earth can vary before balance is regained. This is part of the reason the Earth swings between ice ages and warmer interglacial periods on these time scales.

INTERACTIONS BETWEEN CLIMATE CHANGE AND THE CARBON CYCLE

Left undisturbed, the fast and slow carbon cycles maintain a relatively steady distribution of carbon among the atmosphere, land, plants, and oceans. But when anything jacks up or depletes the amount of carbon in one reservoir, the effect ripples through the others. Today, we are perturbing the carbon cycle. We do this not only by burning fossil fuels but also by misusing land. When we cut down forests, for example, we remove part of a sink—a dense growth of plants that had stored carbon in wood, leaves, and roots. By removing a forest, we not only destroy habitats, but also eliminate plants that would normally pull carbon out of the atmosphere as they grow. As of 2023, deforestation accounted for about 14 percent of all human-caused carbon dioxide emissions.[11]

This is not the end of the human disruption story. When we simply dig up and expose soil, this releases carbon from decayed plant matter into the atmosphere. Humans are currently emitting just under a billion tons of carbon into the atmosphere per year through land abuses, and this is why land reform is a critical lever for reversing climate change. Global warming can also "bake" the soil, accelerating the rate at which carbon seeps out of the ground. This is of particular concern in northern regions, where frozen soil—permafrost—is thawing. Permafrost contains rich deposits of carbon from plant matter that had accumulated for thousands of years because the cold slowed its decay. When these soils warm, the organic matter finally breaks down and carbon— in the form of methane and carbon dioxide—escapes into the atmosphere. Current research estimates that permafrost in the Northern Hemisphere holds a massive 1,600 billion tons of organic carbon. If just 10 percent of this permafrost were to thaw, it could release enough GHGs to raise Earth's surface temperatures an additional 0.7 °C (1.3 °F) by 2100.

What about fossil fuels? Even without humans extracting coal, oil, and natural gas, the carbon in these reservoirs would still leak slowly (over millions of years) into the atmosphere through volcanic activity as part of the slow carbon cycle. Our extraction of these fuels, however, accelerates this process. By doing so, we move the carbon from a relatively immobile pool (fossil fuel reserves) to a relatively mobile pool (the atmosphere), or put more simply, we shift these enormous carbon reservoirs from the slow cycle to the fast cycle.[12] As a result, concentrations of CO_2 and CH_4 in the air have increased dramatically. Atmospheric CO_2 has increased from a preindustrial abundance of 280 parts per million (ppm) of dry air to more than 420+ ppm in recent years— the highest concentration in 2 million years.[13] Methane has increased from a preindustrial abundance of about 700 ppb (parts per billion) of dry air to the current 1,900 ppb. These concentrations are at their highest point in at least 650,000 years.[14]

WHAT HELPS STUDENTS UNDERSTAND HOW CARBON MOVES?

You will likely teach only a subset of the ideas in this section, but for students to understand even the most elemental conceptions of the carbon cycle, they'll need more than a lesson or two. Students will benefit from extended opportunities to make sense, through dialogue and examinations of data, about why carbon now moves through the atmosphere, land, oceans, and living organisms differently than it did in the past.

Students can also create, evaluate, and revise their own carbon cycle models, using them as sensemaking tools along the way. In a science class, this could help them grasp how biological processes are part of a global carbon system and understand the relationships between carbon cycling and climate change.[15] When students merely examine carbon cycle models in textbooks or passively listen to teachers' renditions of these complex processes, it short-changes their understanding of the underlying mechanisms. In one study, high school students were asked what might happen in the carbon cycle if fossil fuel emissions stopped immediately. They relied on a "good versus bad" rule of thumb, not paying attention to quantitative pools or fluxes at all, but simply connecting well-intentioned actions with positive outcomes. One student predicted a steep drop in atmospheric CO_2 and reasoned: "If it's cut down and [we] maintain a low-level use, the air will clean up and it will be good for animals and humans."[16]

Secondary students also tend to compartmentalize carbon movement between plants and animals yet are still sketchy about the roles carbon plays in photosynthesis and cellular respiration.[17] They confuse the varied types of transfers and transformations of carbon within fast and slow cycles and are unsure of the sources of CO_2 for either anthropogenic or natural outputs. These struggles, unsurprisingly, lead to misunderstandings of how the carbon cycle is related to global climate change.[18]

When you teach about the carbon cycles, it's good to help students understand how it works rather than just describing its details and vocabulary. Each arrow in figure 3.2.1 represents a transformation of carbon from one form to another and/or its transfer from a source to a sink. Each of these processes is influenced by other factors in the diagram, and the more students understand these interconnections, the more they will be able to comprehend the scale of the problems we face as well as what decarbonizing solutions are feasible. Consider inviting students to show how the carbon cycle is related to the greenhouse effect, ocean acidification, drawdown, deforestation, photosynthesis, or the energy held in carbon molecular bonds. They'll generate their own insightful ideas about climate change that may not show up in any textbook. A deep understanding of the carbon cycles would indeed help students explain a lot about the changing world they are living in.

No Place Is Too Remote

Our Oceans and Cryosphere

There are two immense stores of water on the planet that students may not recognize as part of the climate system. The first are the oceans, covering two-thirds of the Earth's surface. The second are vast tracts of ice and snow in the polar regions, along with glaciers at high altitudes. Both illustrate how climate change places its imprint on some of the most remote places in the world. We'll start with the oceans because they are being impacted by climate shifts in ways that end up destabilizing weather patterns across continents.

WHAT IS CHANGING WITH OUR OCEANS?

The oceans support all life on Earth in ways that are not always apparent. They provide much of the oxygen we breathe and absorb enormous amounts of carbon dioxide. The oceans influence the water cycle, which, in turn, supports habitats and even the migration patterns of terrestrial species. They do this by distributing heat around the world in currents (underwater rivers) that, until recently, ensured stable conditions for ecosystems everywhere to flourish. It is not an exaggeration to say that the oceans regulate the climate system, and our students need to know how.

Sadly, we are degrading the oceans' vitality in three ways: through warming, acidification, and deoxygenation. Warming is the most well-documented impact. Surface temperatures have risen on average 1.5 °F (0.7 °C) since 1900, and unsurprisingly, more than 90 percent of this extra heat can be traced back to the greenhouse effect, making oceans both the largest heat sink and the largest carbon reservoir on the planet.[1] This warming impacts sea levels, disrupts ocean circulation, and endangers marine ecosystems. The specifics remind us that everything is connected: changes in ocean and atmospheric temperatures have altered ocean currents, which then influence the abundance of plankton communities that form the base of ocean food webs. When we think of photosynthesis on Earth, what comes to mind is the Amazon or Canada's boreal forests, but scientists estimate that 50–80 percent of the oxygen on Earth comes from plankton drifting in the oceans' upper layers.[2]

Marine circulation provides heat energy for the Gulf Stream, which is an ocean current that transfers warm water from the Gulf of Mexico northward into the Atlantic Ocean. It extends all the way up the coast of the United States to Canada, then arcs its way eastward to bring much needed moisture to Europe. The Gulf Stream is just the surface part of a much bigger oceanic flow called the Atlantic Meridional Overturning Circulation, or AMOC. As with all things related to climate change, this story doesn't end with what's normal. The AMOC is at its weakest in more than a millennium, and a warming climate is the probable cause.[3] Scientists now predict that the AMOC could slow down more dramatically by the end of this century *regardless* of future greenhouse gas emission scenarios. If a collapse of this circulation were to occur, it would likely cause abrupt shifts in regional weather patterns and the water cycle, such as a weakening of the African and Asian monsoons, strengthening of Southern Hemisphere monsoons, and drying out of Europe.[4] It could also raise sea levels across the northeast coast of North America and disrupt the flow of vital nutrients that phytoplankton need to grow in the North Atlantic. This is a future that, by climate scientists' estimation, is only modestly likely, but if it were to become reality, it would disrupt climate patterns and devastate ecosystems, sparing few regions of the world.

In addition to warming, excess carbon dioxide in the atmosphere has a direct effect on the chemistry of the ocean. The oceans absorb CO_2 through a chemical exchange at its surface. When CO_2 dissolves in seawater, algae and plants use some of it as fuel for photosynthesis, potentially benefiting many of these species at the base of the marine food chain. But water and carbon dioxide can combine to form carbonic acid, souring the water. The carbonic acid then reacts with carbonate ions in the water to form bicarbonate. The problem is that animals like coral and oysters need those same carbonate ions to create their shells. With fewer carbonate ions available, the animals need to expend more energy to build their shells, which end up being thinner and more fragile. There's a double whammy here in that more acidic water can also dissolve the carbonate shells of marine organisms, making them pitted and weak.

The third effect of atmospheric CO_2 is that as the oceans warm, oxygen concentrations in their surface waters decline. Warmer water holds less dissolved gases, and that includes oxygen. Oxygen, like CO_2, dissolves into the ocean at its surface, but because oceans are warming near the surface and warm water becomes more buoyant, it no longer mixes easily with the less oxygenated and cooler water below it.[5] This reduces the vertical transfer of oxygen below the surface, which negatively impacts ecosystems, especially their processes of photosynthesis and respiration. We see this in the increasing number of coastal and estuary "dead zones."

All three of these effects—warming, acidification, and deoxygenation—interact with one another and with other stressors like pollutants in the ocean environment. For example, down the length of the Mississippi River, nitrogen fertilizer runs off the land and infiltrates the Gulf of Mexico. This mixes with human sewage to become a part of a biochemical stew that triggers massive algal blooms. The algae eventually decay en masse, creating large zones with very low oxygen and low pH.[6] Marine pollution (any human-generated waste that natural systems cannot assimilate) compounds the impacts of climate change. The dreck we dump into our waters becomes deadly to all aquatic life. In the oceans, fish ingest microplastics shed from larger objects like bags or toys, which then make their way up the food chain, transferring toxic chemicals along the way.

Unhealthy oceans will have profound economic, social, and health consequences. This is a survival issue for people in poorer countries who depend on the sea as an essential source of food. The impact is already being felt in coastal areas around the world, where rural fishing communities are unable to sustain themselves, due in part to breakdowns in ocean food chains. If this weren't problematic enough, diminished access to food and loss of livelihoods will lead to political crises and climate migration, especially in the Global South.

Here's another reason why action to restore ocean health is critical. A quarter of CO_2 emissions that human activity generates each year is absorbed by the oceans. If emissions increase, the ocean and land carbon sinks are projected to take up progressively larger amounts of CO2 in *absolute* terms; however, they will become less effective at this in a few decades, in part because the ocean is becoming saturated.[7] That means the *proportion* of emissions that can be taken up by the land and oceans will decrease over time. This will result in even higher proportions of emitted greenhouse gases damaging our atmosphere.

SEA LEVEL RISE AND RISKS ON OUR COASTS

Although the open ocean is a deep mystery to many, lots of us have first-hand knowledge of coastal areas. Our coasts are home to diverse ecosystems such as beaches, intertidal zones, reefs, salt marshes, estuaries, and deltas that all support a range of important services, including fisheries and storm protection. Coastal wetlands, for example, are a first line of natural defense against erosion, flooding, and storm surges. They also serve as natural sinks for greenhouse gases; the uptake is referred to as "blue carbon" and is stored by seagrasses, coral reefs, kelp, and mangrove forests. Per hectare, marine ecosystems can hold up to five times more carbon than a terrestrial forest, but when these deteriorate, carbon is released back into the environment.

Coastlines are now more vulnerable than ever because sea levels are projected to rise, on average, ten to twelve inches in the next thirty years, which matches the rise measured over the last hundred years (1920–present).[8] If you live near a coast, then you know that risks from sea level rise are already being compounded by high tides and storm surge flooding, saltwater intrusion into coastal aquifers, and elevated groundwater tables.[9] By 2050, moderate (typically damaging) flooding is expected to increase *tenfold*, and can be further intensified by the local conditions listed above.

The sheer scale of rising sea levels makes it difficult to imagine how human communities can adapt. The rate of sea level rise in South Florida has tripled in recent years, exacerbating tidal flooding. To cope, one couple in Liberty City is replacing the old seawall around their home, adding several vertical feet to hold back the waters.[10] "That's the price you pay to live here," the homeowner said. She added that she's not a "global warming scaredy-cat" and has no plans to leave. She also questions the scientific consensus about the connection between human activity and climate change. "We've had ice ages and all sorts of other things—droughts, famines. We really have very little control over that, I can't predict what's going to happen in 100 years. I'm not going to be here in 100 years." This rugged individualism and a breezy dismissal of known science will be a poor bulwark against the gathering forces of the Atlantic Ocean. The homeowners' tiny backyard seawall and the larger one now being raised around Miami will provide only the temporary illusion of safe refuge.

THE CRYOSPHERE

The global cryosphere—the frozen regions of the Earth—holds almost three-quarters of the planet's fresh water. It also shrank by about 33,000 square miles, an area the size of Lake Superior, *per year*, between 1979 and 2016.[11] Scientists have documented disappearing ice sheets, dwindling snow cover, and loss of Arctic sea ice. "The cryosphere is one of the most sensitive climate indicators and the first one to demonstrate a changing world," said author Xiaoqing Peng, a physical geographer at Lanzhou University in China. "Its change in size represents a major global shift, rather than a regional or local issue."[12] Stunning new research indicates the Arctic is now warming at least four times as fast as the rest of the world.[13]

Those of us teaching science need to recognize that land ice and sea ice play very different roles in the climate change narrative. Land ice refers to glaciers and ice sheets, while sea ice floats in the ocean. Land ice covers much of Antarctica and Greenland. Combined, these two regions hold over 99 percent of the Earth's fresh water in frozen form. Greenland's ice sheet, however, is disappearing rapidly, and NASA reports that added water from Antarctica's melting ice sheet now makes up 20 to 25 percent of current sea level rise.[14] In the Arctic (which has no land beneath it), sea ice is also melting.

Though the Antarctic continent stays frozen for much of the year, rising temperatures in the Pacific have changed how air circulates around the South Pole, which in turn affects ocean currents. Unusually warm, deep ocean water is now welling up toward Antarctic coastlines, lapping at the frozen underbelly of ice sheets that jut out over the ocean, weakening them from below. These ice sheets often hold back immense glaciers (mostly on land) from moving slowly into the sea. Thwaites Glacier in western Antarctica is the widest on Earth, spanning about eighty miles and extending to a depth of about 2,600 to 3,900 feet. Warming ocean water is not just melting Thwaites from below; it's also loosening the glacier's grip on the submerged seamount, making it even more unstable.[15] As the glacier loses its hold, it then becomes more prone to surface fractures that could spread until the ice shelf that keeps it back from the ocean disintegrates. The breakup of this ice shelf won't immediately increase sea levels because it already floats on top of the water (as when melting ice cubes in a glass of water do not raise the level of the liquid). But without the ice shelf acting as a restraining force, the land-based parts of the Thwaites Glacier will start to move more quickly toward the sea. If the entire glacier succumbs to this fate, it will raise global sea levels by several feet. Island nations and coastal communities would be inundated. Already 80 percent of the 1,190 Maldives islands are just a meter above sea level, making accelerated sea level rise an existential threat for the nation's 540,000 citizens.

Climate scientists are virtually certain that mountain and polar glaciers are committed to continue melting for decades or centuries. Continued ice loss over the twenty-first century is a foregone conclusion for the Greenland ice sheet and likely for the Antarctic ice sheet.[16] But the cryosphere is the setting for yet another potential tipping point—the thawing of permafrost in northern latitudes, which releases into the atmosphere its stores of carbon from partially decomposed plant and animal remains. This permafrost is a carbon-rich deposit made up of dead organic matter that began to accumulate hundreds of thousands of years ago. Estimates indicate that just within the uppermost ten feet of this geological layer, the soil holds ten to twenty pounds of carbon per square foot of surface area.[17] If this begins to melt and decompose, it is more likely to release the carbon as methane than carbon dioxide. Although the total mass of methane that would be released is one-third of the mass of CO_2, it has eighty-five times the greenhouse heat-trapping effect that CO_2 does over a twenty-year period. This, unfortunately, would be a "game over" scenario for our efforts to heal the Earth. Figure 3.3.1 shows how all the climate-relevant indicators being recorded in our oceans and cryosphere are headed in the wrong direction.

HOW DO STUDENTS UNDERSTAND THE OCEANS AND CRYOSPHERE?

Students' knowledge of how climate change impacts our oceans is often fragmented, rarely in the form of clear cause-effect relationships, and not always reflective of oceans as systems. Even secondary students see climate change as something that could be addressed by improving the water quality of the oceans through reducing litter and getting rid of pesticides.[18] Some lump environmental issues together in ways that are not transparent, believing ocean

Figure 3.3.1 Components of the ocean and cryosphere and how climate change affects them

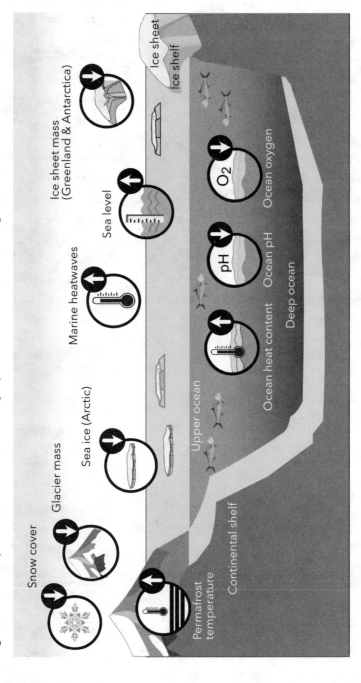

Source: Adapted from Nerilie Abram, Jean-Pierre Gattuso, Anjal Prakash et al., *Special Report on the Ocean and Cryosphere in a Changing Climate,* chapter 1, IPCC 2019, https://www.ipcc.ch/site/assets/uploads/sites/3/2019/11/05_SROCC_Ch01_FINAL.pdf.

and air pollution to be at the root of global warming. High schoolers also have mixed understandings of how the polar regions are implicated in climate change. In one study, students focused on the essential question: Why might the Arctic be warming faster than the rest of the world?[19] They were asked to offer initial theories for this phenomenon, and although about a third of responses were related to actual causes—the decline of sea ice leading to the increased absorption of energy from the sun, and the altered ways in which warm air now circulates from the equator to the Arctic—the majority of beliefs were not directly connected to this phenomenon. These included volcano eruptions in Iceland, pollution, plate tectonics, and deforestation. Even the dynamics of glaciers are not well understood. Most believe they are static land features and form by the sudden freezing of huge amounts of water, rather than snow accumulating and being compressed into ice over centuries.[20]

Given these challenges for students, educators might find it helpful to explicitly teach about our oceans and atmosphere as systems that interact with one another in newly disruptive ways as a result of climate change. Lessons on the multiple causes of sea level rise could also help learners connect the oceans with changes, both present and future, in the cryosphere.

Ecosystems and Why We Care About Biodiversity

When we act as responsible stewards of the more-than-human world, ecosystems reciprocate by providing us with clean air and water, pollination, medicines, nutrient cycling, buffers against floods, and even carbon storage.[1] We depend not just on other living things, but on intact healthy ecosystems in ways we might not even realize.

Ecosystems have to be able to move energy, nutrients, and organic matter through an environment. This is what makes them healthy. They accomplish this through (1) primary production, which is the process by which plants use sunlight to convert inorganic matter into new biological tissue, (2) nutrient cycling, in which essential nutrients are captured and released, and (3) decomposition, which is how organic waste such as dead plant and animal tissues is broken down and recycled.[2] More and more, human activity interferes with these core functions, which then tests the *resilience* of ecosystems, meaning their ability to cope with disturbances and respond or reorganize in ways that maintain their essential functions as well as their biodiversity.[3] Some ecosystems, however, are already reaching their adaptation limits; these include some warm-water coral reefs, coastal wetlands, rainforests, and polar and mountain habitats.[4]

If we want students to understand how climate change is affecting living systems and to design solutions for ecological resilience, three ideas are key—the role biodiversity plays in ensuring healthy ecosystems, the limited ways that organisms can respond to accelerated changes in the environment, and how additional stresses that humans are placing on living systems make them more vulnerable. Each idea sheds a different kind of light on ecological relationships and problem-solving possibilities.

WHY BIODIVERSITY MATTERS

Biodiversity is the inherited biological wealth of the Earth and, as such, has intrinsic value in its own right.[5] It nourishes humans' spiritual and psychological well-being. Because we are embedded in the natural world, we are woven into the fabric of biodiversity. Taking a scientific perspective, biodiversity refers to the variety of life across all ecological levels, from the assortment of genes available within a species, to the different species within an ecosystem, to the planetary pool of ecosystems themselves.[6] The diversity of genes and species in an ecosystem has an impact on its functioning and, in turn, on the benefits that the ecosystem provides to humanity. A forest, for example, can store more carbon if it supports many different tree species. A stream can clean up more pollution if it hosts a greater array of microbial genotypes. Agricultural pests can be more effectively controlled if the organisms holding them in check are assortment of predators, parasites, and pathogens.

Biodiversity is also insurance against ecosystem breakdown when conditions begin to shift. It provides a buffer against fluctuations in temperature, humidity, or water availability, because different species respond differently to these changes, better preserving core functions of the ecosystem overall.[7] In the case of plants, all species in a given space might utilize the same resources (space, light, water, soil nutrients, etc.) but at different times during the growing season—for example, early and late season grasses in prairies. Increasing species diversity can influence ecosystem functions like primary productivity by boosting the likelihood that different species will use complementary but not identical resources, or will use the same resources at different times or in different ways.[8] This type of complementarity and mutual thriving applies to animals and microbes in an ecosystem as well as plants. Biodiversity, then, is critical for ecosystem stability.

Reciprocity is another model of beneficial coexistence in which different organisms support the growth and resilience of one another. Remarkable kinds of reciprocity are being discovered that border on science fiction.[9] Recent research indicates that trees are often linked to one another by an underground (mycorrhizal) network of fungi that resembles neural pathways in the brain. In one study, a Douglas fir that had been injured by insects appeared to send chemical warning signals to a ponderosa pine growing nearby. The pine tree then produced defensive enzymes to protect against the insects. The trees were essentially sharing information that was important to the well-being of the whole forest. Trees have also been known to share nutrients at critical times to keep each other healthy. This means that deforestation not only removes trees, but also impacts trees that are still alive by disrupting the mycorrhizal network that is critical for inter-tree communication. I include this example to demonstrate how complex unseen mechanisms are at work to ensure the mutual flourishing of individuals within living systems—mechanisms we are still learning about.

LOSING BIODIVERSITY: MULTIPLE STRESSORS PUT ECOSYSTEMS AT RISK

Not every threat to ecosystems comes from climate change, but all of the most destructive are caused by humans. These "stress multipliers" diminish the capacities of ecosystems, communities, and individuals to adapt to climate change. Figure 3.4.1 describes four of the major threats that add pressure on nearly all ecosystems already affected by climate change.[10]

Stressor 1: Changes to How We Use the Land and Waters

The way humans have reduced or fragmented habitats is the leading cause of terrestrial biodiversity loss.[11] For example, rainforests have been cleared to establish plantations of the African oil palm. These vast monocultures are expanding in many regions of Asia, Africa, and Latin America, the sheer scale

Figure 3.4.1 Threats to biodiversity

	Changes in land and waters use, including habitat loss, degradation
	Modification of the environment where a species lives by removal, fragmentation, or reduction in quality of key habitat. Common changes are caused by unsustainable agriculture, logging, transportation, residential or commercial development, energy production, and mining. Fragmentation of rivers and extraction of water are also threats.
	Species overexploitation
	Refers to unsustainable hunting and poaching or harvesting, whether for subsistence or for trade. Indirect overexploitation occurs when non-target species are killed unintentionally, for example as bycatch in fisheries.
	Invasive species and disease
	Invasives can compete with native species for space, food, and other resources, can turn out to be a predator for native species, or spread diseases that were not previously present in the environment. Humans also transport new diseases from one area of the globe to another.
	Pollution
	Pollution can directly affect a species by making an environment unsuitable for its survival. It can also affect a species indirectly, by diminishing food availability or reproductive performance, thus reducing populations.

of which is now pushing many plants and animals to the point of extinction. To be precise, of the 25,000 land-based species threatened with extinction, more than half are in jeopardy as a consequence of agricultural land clearing and degradation.[12] In urban areas, developers have drained and filled in wetlands in order to build housing. Increasing human populations have put pressures on water resources, and in many locations, agriculture, energy supply, industry, and tourism pose a threat to water resources. Restoration of natural systems by using green infrastructure, especially in wetland areas, can help protect people and nature from climate change impacts.[13]

Stressor 2: Species Overexploitation

Fishing, hunting, and harvesting can be done sustainably, but these same activities often overexploit a resource. Overall, people have been taking far more from nature than it can afford, and this, for example, is why world marine fisheries are in decline. An estimated 70 percent of fish populations are fully used, overused, or in crisis as a result of overfishing and warmer waters. Industrial, long-distance fishing fleets, mostly from developed countries, are largely responsible for the destruction of the marine food chain.

Stressor 3: Invasive Species and Disease

From the emerald ash borer in Michigan to the quagga mussels in Arizona, every state has invasive species that are disrupting ecosystems in costly ways. Global trade brings non-natives from their home ecosystems to other parts of the world, where there are often no predators to keep their numbers in check. The warming climate also allows dangerous species such as disease-carrying mosquitos to thrive in new latitudes. Some alien grasses and trees can significantly alter the natural role of fire to replenish the landscape, especially in areas that are becoming warmer and drier.

Stressor 4: Pollution

Pollution poses a serious problem to many ecosystems. For example, tiny bits of plastic suspended in ocean water build up inside birds, fish, and other marine species. Industrial toxins kill many species in rivers and lakes, not to mention poisoning human communities. Air pollution makes its way into soil, plants, and water. It all adds up to fewer species, less diversity, and weakened ecosystems. Pollution can also affect biodiversity indirectly, by negatively impacting food availability or reproduction, thus reducing populations over time. When we work with students on understanding stressors like these, it is easy to identify cases relevant to their local communities, no matter where they live.

ONLY THREE CHOICES: MOVE, ACCLIMATE, OR ADAPT

Ecosystems struggle to sustain themselves in the face of rapidly changing environments. This is made more difficult because of the limited choices individual organisms have in coping with transformed habitats. The root biological principle is this: every living thing has a finite amount of energy to use for reproduction, growth, maintenance or self-repair, and responding to the environment. So when organisms are stressed, it will cost them more to just maintain their core metabolism, and that's a problem. Imagine a pie chart representing how living things use energy. To survive climate-related changes in the environment, organisms must funnel more energy into one or two sections of the pie (like responding to new habitat constraints), thus shrinking the energy available for other life functions in the rest of the pie (like reproduction or self-repair). This rationing is unsustainable for a community of plants or animals, so for the sake of survival, species end up (1) moving in space or time, (2) acclimating to conditions, or (3) adapting genetically. If none of these are possible, species may die out in the region or go extinct altogether. Let's look at some examples.

If conditions where an organism lives are no longer suitable, it might move to where the climate is a better match for its traits—a phenomenon known as a *range shift*. In a warming environment, some species move to higher elevations or more-northern latitudes. One recent IPCC report indicates that approximately half of the species assessed globally have shifted poleward or up the sides of mountains. Mammals, birds, insects, and even forests are now found in different places than they have been historically, but the catch is that these relocations force other species that rely on those animals and plants to adapt as well, or deal with the consequences.[14]

Species can also *move in time* rather than space, shifting when important life events take place. Many plants time their leafing-out and flowering by using both temperature and day length as cues—raising the risk that some species could fall perilously out of sync with their pollinators, leading to a reproductive dead end.[15] Songbirds are arriving in California at different times than they have historically.[16] In one study, eight of the twenty-one species observed were arriving early, sometimes by weeks or months. Their off-cycle presence may be disrupting the ways in which this species interacts with others in the destination ecosystem.

A second response to climate pressures is that living things might stay where they are but *acclimate*. In everyday terms, acclimate means "finding a way to put up with conditions."[17] For example, a teacher in eastern Washington has her high school students studying the American pika, a tiny alpine mammal that normally lives exclusively in exposed boulder fields. But as the seasons in its habitat have warmed, the pika have changed their behaviors, spending more time in forests and under downed logs—places where they can escape high temperatures. In another example, salmon can survive in warmer streams, but the trade-off is they will produce fewer eggs (remember the pie chart?). Acclimation, whatever form it takes, is limited to an individual's lifetime and not passed on genetically.

Adaptation is a longer-term response that involves changes to the genetic makeup of a population. Over many generations, individuals that are genetically better suited to survive in a changed environment will be more successful and reproduce more offspring, slowly altering the species to better fit its habitat. The organisms in a population that can endure a wider range of temperatures, for example, will pass these positive traits to offspring. This evolutionary process can only be successful within a healthy and biodiverse community, where individuals have varied tolerances to environmental changes. Researchers found that some communities of mustard plants evolved to produce seeds earlier in the season so that they now finish their reproductive cycles before the rainy season in their habitat ends.[18] This is an example of how multiple responses to climate change can intersect—this mustard species has *adapted* in a way that *moves the timing* of its reproductive events to match favorable climate conditions.

Organisms that fail to respond sufficiently to climate change may perish. Although all natural communities change over time, rapid environmental change can challenge the ability of living things to adapt. While many short-lived, fast-reproducing mammals, for example, are able to expand their ranges, long-lived, slower-reproducing species are often trapped in dwindling windows of livability. If a species is unable to adapt or move, it may be stranded in an inhospitable environment, and populations may disappear locally or globally. Currently, the species extinction rate is estimated between 1,000 and 10,000 times higher than what would be occurring without human influence.[19]

Because living systems respond so fast to climate or other stressors, it makes them easier to study, and most students will relate to animals and plants more so than geophysical phenomena like the carbon cycle. We can feature familiar ecosystems within our communities and invite individuals, whose job it is to monitor these or implement restorative measures, into our classrooms. Consider all these as resources for an ecosystem unit—students' familiarity with local land, the place-based nature of investigations you could do, and community members who can share firsthand experiences of environmental change and resilience.

Weather Extremes and
the Human Niche

Weather is personal. It physically surrounds us to warm, cool, soak, and parch, to favor us with a gentle breeze or occasionally rip the shingles off our homes. We often remember the extremes of weather in our lives—the great flood or the tornado on the outskirts of town—but on the whole, we spend our days experiencing more typical weather conditions. Humans, like all species, occupy an environmental niche characterized by particular physical conditions we need to survive. For the last 6,000 years, most of us have lived within two narrow bands of the climatic envelope, one of which has annual mean temperatures that vary from around 11 °C to 15 °C (52 °F to 59 °F).[1] People in South Asia inhabit the second band, coinciding with regions that benefit from the Indian monsoon. The average annual temperature in that region is between 20 °C and 25 °C (68 °F and 77 °F). This dual range, referred to as the "human climate niche," is livable not just for us; the crops and livestock that we depend on are also adapted to these temperatures. Climate and weather in these ranges nurture a variety of ecosystems as well as human health, food security, water supply, and our livelihoods. For this reason, societies thrive when they stay within this zone and struggle if conditions begin to change.

We are all being pushed now to the edge of our niche. Compared with preindustrial times, the average human-experienced air temperature may rise 7.5 °C (13.5 °F) by 2070. This sounds more alarming than the 1.5 °C we're aiming to stay under, but here's the reason to take this seriously: land will be warming much faster than the oceans. The planetary mean might end up around 2 °C or lower, but terrestrial environments will be hotter. Already, about 0.8 percent of the Earth's surface experiences average annual temperatures above 29 °C (84.2 °F), mostly in the Sahara region of Africa.[2] But with the projected increases in global temperatures, this area will expand to cover about 19 percent of (now) inhabitable land, currently home to 3.5 billion people. For every

1 °C (1.8 °F) of average global warming, an additional 1 billion people will have to somehow adapt or migrate to stay within climate conditions that are best suited for food production and a sustainable outdoor work environment.

Imagine all the necessary human labor that happens outside—agriculture, construction, transportation, delivery, and so on. Some of the work that many of us take for granted will not be survivable under perilous combinations of heat and humidity. A wet bulb temperature of 35 °C sets the limit; when temperatures pass 35 °C (95 °F) and the humidity is above 90 percent, the body can no longer cool itself.[3] Does it matter if you sweat? If you are physically fit or work a lot in hot weather? None of this makes a difference, even in well-ventilated or shaded conditions. It is likely that climatic changes will place large cities and whole countries into temperature zones that current inhabitants would find unimaginable.[4] We simply don't know whether outdoor work can be adapted to these purgatorial conditions. Even if plant breeding technologies could expand the heat tolerance of corn, wheat, and soybeans, the required labor-intensive farming practices may not be possible.[5]

In the past, when climate conditions have fallen outside optimum ranges, regional upheaval has followed, including mass migrations, famine, conflict, and other disruptions that we need to plan for in coming decades.[6] People are already beginning to flee from some places in Southeast Asia where increasingly unpredictable monsoon rainfall and drought have made farming more difficult. More than 8 million people have moved toward the Middle East, Europe, and North America.[7] In the African Sahel, millions of rural people have been streaming toward the coasts and the cities amid drought and widespread crop failures. The flight from hot climates is already radically remapping the distribution of the world's populations.[8]

For educators, this raises familiar tensions: Do we share dire projections with our students in the name of transparency, or do we hedge on discussions about the future to avoid stoking climate anxieties? My imperfect answer is twofold. Prepare yourself to talk about the *range* of possibilities rather than a single extreme prediction. The second is to set up conversations about what's being done around the world in terms of mitigation and adaptation strategies. Above all, help students envision a more equitable and sustainable future, and don't forget to discuss the hard choices that will get us there.

LOADING THE CLIMATE DICE

Weather extremes require two key ingredients: energy and moisture.[9] Under the influence of solar radiation and the Earth's rotation, both the atmosphere and the oceans circulate heat around the globe in vast currents of air and water. Atmospheric circulation conducts heat from the equator, which receives the greatest amount of energy from the sun, to the poles, where more heat is radiated into space than is received. In the short term (hours to weeks), we experience such patterns as *weather*: rain, dry spells, clouds, hurricanes. Long-term patterns (occurring over years to decades and beyond) are known as *climate*. When I was visiting a seventh-grade classroom, one of the students suggested that "climate is like your wardrobe, weather is what you're wearing today."

As you may have already guessed, when excess heat is pumped into the system by climate change, it amplifies all kinds of weather phenomena, pushing them to extremes and reminding us how delicately balanced our atmosphere normally is. Even small increases in temperature can turbocharge Earth's naturally occurring weather processes.[10] For example, high temperatures accelerate the speed at which water evaporates from vegetation and the soil, amplifying drought. The downstream effect is that small wildfires quickly grow massive and move through desiccated terrain like locomotives. Warmer air can also hold more moisture, so when the rain finally does fall, it drops in a deluge. Floods are larger then, and their waters scour the landscape. As our atmosphere traps more heat, the oceans soak up that energy, fueling more energetic hurricanes.

A growing number of extreme events are now being labeled as "impossible" without climate change, yet natural variability still lays the foundation for such events to occur.[11] Natural variability refers to recurring conditions such as the seasons or El Niño years potentially adding intensity to specific weather events. Despite these foundations, the role of natural variation in Earth's temperature and moisture movement is diminishing in comparison to the growing effects of anthropogenic warming. Over the last few years, an unprecedented succession of off-the-charts events has unfolded around the world. In 2016, the hottest year on record, hundreds of people in India died during unrelenting heat waves. A gigantic blob of warm water formed in the Pacific, causing toxic algae to bloom off the coast of Alaska. This poisoned shellfish and caused seabirds to starve. December 2019 through February

2020 was the warmest and wettest period in recorded Russian history, causing melting permafrost to belch carbon and destabilize homes. In the summer of 2021, a dome of punishing heat descended on the Pacific Northwest, scorching crops, melting pavement, and cooking a billion sea creatures inside their own shells. More than a thousand people died. In my own Seattle neighborhood, the temperature spiked at 108 °F and remained above 80 throughout the night, but we were spared the worst of it. A few hours south, members of my family in Portland endured a blistering 116 °F. All these extremes were judged to be impossible without climate change, and more likely to happen in the future.[12]

Our students can better understand weather extremes if they grasp the differences between natural and anthropogenically influenced events. We need to find ways to represent this abstract idea, perhaps through data visualizations or analogies. A group of climate scientists came up with both in 2012. James Hansen, Makiko Sato, and Reto Ruedy decided to study how the frequency of extreme temperatures had changed after the Great Acceleration.[13] As a baseline, they examined data from 1951 to 1980. They mapped out small areas covering the planet (250 km x 250 km), then averaged their monthly temperatures, and calculated the standard deviation for each measurement to show how much variation there was from year to year. The baseline temperatures were very consistent, which was not surprising. Almost every measurement was within two standard deviations of the mean for that location. They then repeated the calculations for 1981–2010 and compared the results. Figure 3.5.1 shows that the graphs had shifted to the right for the most recent thirty years—the individual temperatures were warmer, as were the means for each land parcel. The eye-opener was that the graphs had also *changed shape*— the amount of variation (spread of temperatures) had increased dramatically. The authors reported:

> The distribution of seasonal mean temperature anomalies has shifted toward higher temperatures and the range of anomalies has increased. An important change is the emergence of a category of summertime extremely hot outliers, more than three standard deviations warmer than the climatology of the 1951–1980 base period.[14]

In other words, extreme heat waves that were almost nonexistent in the early decades of the Great Acceleration (1951–1980) had become more

Figure 3.5.1 Distribution of average global temperatures before and after the Great Acceleration

AN INCREASE IN MEAN TEMPERATURES

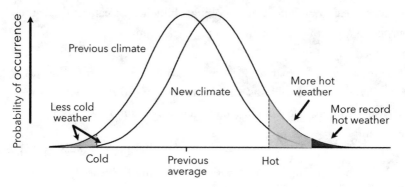

AN INCREASE IN VARIANCE OF TEMPERATURES

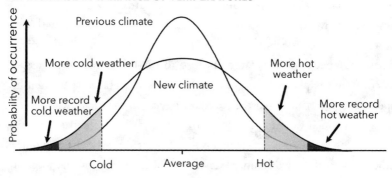

AN INCREASE IN MEAN & VARIANCE OF TEMPERATURES

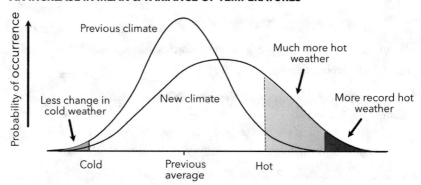

Source: Adapted from James Hansen, Makiko Sato, and Reto Ruedy, "Perception of Climate Change," *PNAS Plus* 109, no. 37 (2012): E2415–E2423.

frequent. The authors concluded "with high confidence that such extreme anomalies would not have occurred in the absence of global warming."[15]

To make their point in more everyday terms, they compared the two climate time periods to dice with colored faces. The die representing the baseline decades had two faces shaded red for hot, two shaded blue for cool, and two shaded white for near average. Rolling the baseline die would give you equal chances of any month coming up red, blue, or white. The die representing the years following the Great Acceleration, however, had become loaded: four faces were now red, meaning hot just comes up much more often.

But as climate writer Ian Angus observed, the analogy breaks down because we have to add another category—*extremely hot*. The climate is not just getting warmer on average, the whole climate curve now skews toward heat extremes (the bottom graph in figure 3.5.1). He cautions:

> Adapting to the new normal—if that is even possible—will require responding to extremes, not just averages. The issue is not just how much the average ocean level rises, but how high the biggest storm surges are, not just what the average daily rainfall is, but how long the droughts last; not just how much warmer it gets on average, but how long deadly heat waves will become.[16]

The most catastrophic weather events we experience are sometimes referred to as a "once in a hundred years" flood, drought, or hurricane. This labeling has become less meaningful, and any recalibration of how frequently high-magnitude disasters happen will certainly be confounded by the unpredictability of chaotic weather systems. What seem to be minor temperature increases globally—such as a 0.5 °C—actually push us into new and unwelcome territory. Imagine a farmer (it does not matter whether this person is in Iowa or Pakistan) whose crops were barely able to survive a stretch of extremely hot days that historically happen once every fifty years. How does she plan for the future if global temperatures increase by 2 °C and the chances of such extreme heat events become up to six times as likely?[17]

ENGAGING STUDENTS WITH WEATHER PHENOMENA

Most of your students will, if invited, share stories about the weather. Spend a day to find out what experiences they've had and how they think about the causes for patterns of temperature, precipitation, humidity, and winds. You could anchor a unit with a memorable local weather event, but in addition to having students develop explanations for it over time, you could also press them to find out how much the event deviated from historical norms in your region. There is abundant data available that students can search for and use, extending back decades or longer. Help students connect weather narratives back to the greenhouse effect and work with them to develop *explicit* links between the two.

When I was a middle school student, my teachers portrayed weather patterns as consistent, always falling within the typical. Needless to say, we now have to recast our key messages to include themes about changes in historical trends—"new normals" that keep getting pushed farther from the safe and comfortable. Perhaps most importantly, we have to engage young learners with ideas about who will be impacted, in what ways, and whether justice is reflected in global efforts to mitigate against further warming.

Coda

You've gotten an overview of the basic science behind five climate change domains, hopefully just enough to appreciate the big picture of what is happening now, especially in the more-than-human world. I hope this helps you identify additional information you need to seek and ask better questions about assembling a series of lessons on any of these ideas. The possibilities are endless.

Before moving on, however, we should take a moment to make sense of the links among the concepts we've just explored, beginning with what's happening in our atmosphere and ending with risks to human well-being. Figure 3.6.1 embodies the big theme of "everything is connected." I would never have dropped this into the beginning of chapter 3 because, at first glance, it is intimidating. But now you may find it decipherable, even useful for pulling ideas together into a whole that is more than the sum of its parts. As a teacher, you'll have to decide if or when some diagram like this helps your students analyze the big picture or perhaps they could recreate it for themselves, labeling all the connections in their own words. Depending on the grade level you teach, the diagram could be simplified for different purposes.

Because the figure is complex, I've included a walk-through here. Let's think our way from the top down. Setting everything in motion is the growing carbon dioxide concentration in the atmosphere. It's not an event, unless we acknowledge that humans are pushing these numbers in the wrong direction, adding CO_2 every day. This causes two things directly. One is that this amplifies the greenhouse effect in the atmosphere; the other is that much of this CO_2 is being absorbed into the oceans and causes them to become more acidic. Below the triangle is what happens in response to the greenhouse effect—the trapped energy warms the surface of the land as well as the atmosphere and increases the oceans' heat content. Energy from the greenhouse effect also melts parts of the cryosphere, meaning the continental ice sheets, ice caps, glaciers, and areas of snow and permafrost.

Figure 3.6.1 Map of climate change causes, impacts, and risks to human well-being

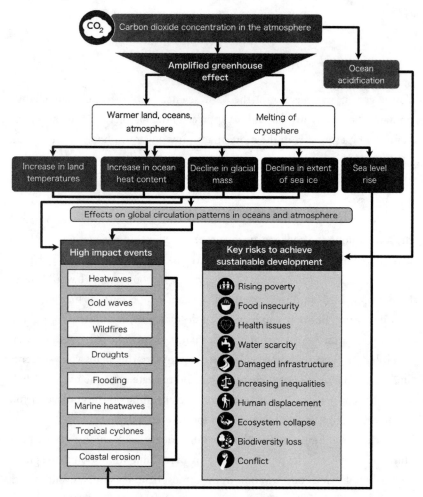

Source: Adapted from World Meteorological Organization, "State of the Global Climate 2020," WMO-No. 1264, 31, https://www.google.com/url?sa=t&rct=j&q=&esrc=s&source=web&cd=&ved =2ahUKEwjz2o3_-979AhW_FVkFHT1MCmwQFnoECDAQAQ&url=https%3A%2F%2Flibrary.wmo. int%2Fdoc_num.php%3Fexplnum_id%3D10618&usg=AOvVaw3g3RkrTde-o0Du_NMS12UU.

Some of these processes influence each other. For example, the fact that the oceans are warming means that the water in them literally expands. The oceans' heat combines with the atmospheric temperature increases to melt land-based ice and snow, which then adds to sea level rise. Beyond posing risks to humans, some of these processes also have the potential to release further greenhouse gases into the atmosphere in a feedback loop that can perpetuate warming. For example, rising temperatures can thaw permafrost, releasing more carbon into the atmosphere, and . . . you know the rest of that story.

You might think that the processes in the row with *Increase in land temperatures* and *Decline in glacial mass* cause events we are familiar with like droughts and floods, and that is true. But these processes also have an intermediate effect that is more widespread and less visible to us. Every process in that row, except for *Sea level rise*, has an impact on *global circulation patterns in oceans and atmosphere* (the row below). All life depends on these patterns being stable and predictable.

The stack of *High impact events* in the lower left is not the end of the story. These elevate *Key risks to achieve sustainable development* as described by the World Meteorological Organization. The WMO recognizes that ending poverty and other deprivations must go hand in hand with strategies that improve health and education, reduce inequality, and spur economic growth, while practicing stewardship of the environment. Climate change puts the achievement of many of these goals at risk.

None of these bodies of knowledge are isolated islands of content. In fact, it's impossible to deeply understand any one of them unless you understand how it fits with the others. At this point you may still feel confused, but the good news is you're likely perplexed about more important things than before you read this section. Professional learning happens gradually, not in a flash, and at this point you may still feel unsteady about climate change phenomena. However, with what you know now, you can likely be a better consumer of climate change teaching resources, asking: Can these lessons help my students build rich explanations of events and processes that are important in the larger climate change landscape? What is too trivial to include? Which science storylines can support conversations about social justice? Are these lessons sequenced in a way that will make sense for students? What examples or local community cases could we use to anchor units or illustrate key concepts? It wouldn't hurt to share with students how you continue to learn and grow.

CHAPTER 4

Solutions

Helping Students Envision
Sustainability and Resilience

WHEN CLASSROOM CONVERSATIONS turn toward climate solutions, students can feel the wind coming back into their sails. Reversing planetary warming abounds with possibilities like zero-emission buildings, clean cookstoves, solar farms, rights for Indigenous peoples to manage forestlands, and dozens of other regenerative strategies. These solutions are not always about innovative technologies or radical social reorganization; in fact, many rely on changing everyday human behavior, but all are about bringing the world back to life through compassion and transformative actions that students can be part of. Our job is to help young learners feel empowered by understanding what is possible and why.

We'll first need some conceptual categories to organize different strategies, and for this I borrow a framework from Project Drawdown, named after the future point in time when greenhouse gases in Earth's atmosphere peak and then begin to decline. Its team of experts poured over mountains of data from different disciplines to answer the question: "What can we do to decarbonize our world?" Led by environmental activist Paul Hawken, project members examined all known solutions for various climate challenges, with the caveat that they could operate at scale. They then determined the impact of each using a simple metric—the amount of carbon dioxide, or its equivalent, that a solution could take out of the atmosphere or prevent from going there in the first place.[1]

Every action described in this chapter, from the reduction of food waste to net-zero buildings, can be viewed through the lens of responsible engineering. The Next Generation Science Standards describe engineering as a set of practices designed to achieve solutions for human problems. Students are expected to define problems, specify criteria and constraints for acceptable solutions, generate and evaluate multiple solutions, build and test prototypes, and optimize outcomes.[2] *We must keep in mind that all solutions are only partial. We need hundreds that address different climate-related problems—there's plenty of work to go around. A note on my use of the term "solutions" in this chapter: I don't use it in reference to the restoration of land rights for Indigenous peoples or the redress of ongoing environmental racism. These are matters of justice and the affirmation of sovereignty for all human communities.*

REDUCE SOURCES OF GREENHOUSE GASES AND GET CARBON INTO THE RIGHT SINKS

The Drawdown team estimated how many gigatons of greenhouse gases a candidate solution could avoid or remove over time, as well as the costs of implementation. The team then compared each candidate's impacts and costs to the current practices or technologies it replaces. For example, the potential emission reductions from onshore wind turbines are based on comparisons with existing fossil fuel power plants—that's half the calculus; then costs for installing and operating those turbines were also compared with those of maintaining fossil fuel plants. This is more than you may need to know, but as with so much of the science in this book, the teachers I work with have found it helpful to see this broader view if their students' interests take them in these directions or they ask, "On what basis does this qualify as a solution?" Having the big picture also helps you determine what's fundamental to teach and what you can pass over.

Other research teams around the world also ran the numbers using similar analyses, and everyone arrived at similar surprising estimates. Some high-profile technologies like electric vehicles or solar farms sit in the top ten of promising solutions but are less impactful than the reduction of food waste, reforming how cement is produced, or controlling the chemicals we use in refrigerants.[3] Who knew? The solutions categories in figure 4.1 are labeled with the total weight of carbon dioxide or its GHG equivalent in gigatons (billions of tons: Gt) that could be reduced or sequestered between 2020 and 2050. Each number is the most *conservative* estimate of the carbon it can reduce. Just to give you an image for these enormous units of measure, a gigaton of carbon would fill over 400,000 Olympic-size swimming pools.[4]

Before we look at solutions, let's distinguish two terms that both refer to dealing with climate change.[5] *Mitigation* means reducing emissions of heat-trapping greenhouse gases entering our atmosphere or enhancing the sinks that accumulate and store carbon (oceans, forests, and soil). The goal of mitigation is to stabilize greenhouse gas levels soon enough for ecosystems to adapt naturally to the changes we are guaranteed to experience, avoid catastrophic weather, and restore Earth systems to health.[6]

Adaptation refers to adjustments humans make to current or expected conditions brought about by a warming world. These can help us reduce vulnerability to potential harms or, in limited cases, allow us to benefit from changing conditions. Adaptations might involve large-scale infrastructure changes, such as building shoreline defenses against sea level rise or behavioral shifts such as laborers changing their outdoor work schedules to avoid temperature extremes. You may have already guessed that adaptations do nothing to slow emissions—they really just buy time. As such, I won't refer to them as solutions in this chapter.

In classrooms, students often explore these solutions in depth, but teachers may not help them make clear connections to climate change, thinking they are self-evident. We have observed lessons where the topic is preventing deforestation and students understood what was involved in accomplishing this as well as the positive impacts on biodiversity. But links to climate change were not part of the conversation. I recommend that you help students *trace the solutions* to the effects they have on emissions or carbon sinks. Sometimes this storyline is direct and sometimes it is circuitous, but the connections can be motivating to figure out. These trace backs, we have found, generate a-ha moments for students in which an innovation or widespread changes in human behavior suddenly takes on new meaning because it is clearly coupled with the root causes of ecological harm and how they are held in check.

Figure 4.1 Solution categories with total weight of CO_2 or its GHG equivalent that could be reduced or sequestered between 2020 and 2050

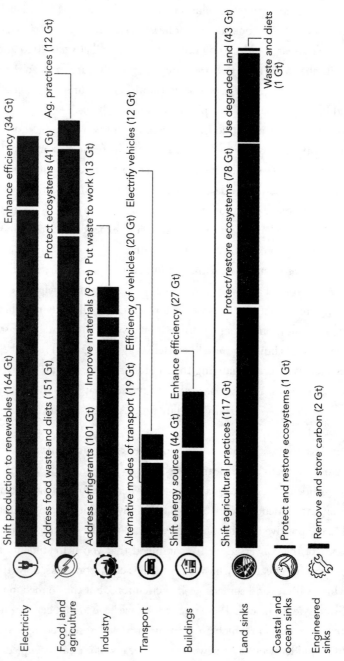

Source: Adapted from Jonathan Foley et al., *The Drawdown Review, Climate Solutions for a New Decade* (Project Drawdown Publication, 2020), 12–13, doi: 10.13140/RG.2.2.31794.76487.

Reducing Sources of Greenhouses Gases

Rethinking electricity. Most of the electricity we use for everything from cell phones to stadium lights starts its journey in generators powered by steam that is produced by burning coal, oil, or gas. This sounds antiquated, but until recently it was the only way to produce energy at scale. Our challenge today is to remove fossil fuels from that equation or, as climate writer Bill McKibben urges: "In a world on fire, stop burning things."[7] We have the technology to do this by harnessing the power of the sun, wind, and water. Two of the most well-known and efficient renewables are utility-scale photovoltaics (solar panels) and wind turbines, neither of which release any emissions.

Solar farms are second only to the Earth's own vegetation in harvesting the sun's energy to get work done. Photovoltaics depend on the property of some materials, like silicon, to absorb photons and release electrons. When these free electrons are captured, an electric current is produced. Solar installations can be found in deserts or on agricultural land, attached to highway sound barriers, embedded in roadways and bike paths, atop abandoned golf courses, and even floating on a reservoir outside London. Solar panels can provide a stable income for farmers, some of whom are also learning to grow shade-tolerant crops or to graze animals around and beneath the panels.[8] Utility-scale solar farms can prevent about 42 Gt of carbon from being released over the next thirty years.[9]

Wind farms convert the kinetic energy of moving air into electrical energy. Onshore installations rely on towering turbines to capture wind, but they also have small physical footprints, typically occupying no more than 1 percent of the land they sit on. This means that agricultural fields can support both crops and energy production. Electricity flows from the in-board generators of these turbines to cables below ground and into thousands of homes. We can also place more turbines off our coasts now, simply because of breakthroughs in how they are built; some can float rather than being anchored to the seafloor, and new advances in materials mean the turbine blades can be longer than a football field.[10] Hubs on the newest turbines are 479 feet high—as tall as a fifty-story building—and wind farms powered by these colossal structures will replace the energy from over 500,000 tons of coal per year. Ongoing cost reduction is a game changer. In many locales, wind power is now either competitive with or less expensive than coal-generated electricity.

The best part is these turbine installations can keep about 47 Gt of carbon out of our atmosphere.[11]

Students should know that wind and solar are *variable* sources of energy. There are times when the wind is not blowing or the sun is not shining. For these reasons, breakthroughs in energy storage are essential to renewable growth. When we think of storage, we often visualize chemical batteries, but even modern lithium ion versions have a limited capacity to hold energy. This is why scientists and engineers are now scaling up methods of energy storage that seem like Rube Goldberg contraptions or outsized toys. All of these work on the same principle: find ways to convert excess renewable energy when it is plentiful into some form of potential energy; then convert it back to electricity when needed.

Some innovators are experimenting with using electricity generated from renewable sources to compress air in tanks, just as fizzy drinks hold energy under pressure. Rather than vent the heat generated as the air is compressed, the most advanced systems capture it in a separate thermal tank and then use it to reheat the air as it's released and fed through turbines, which supercharges the flow and increases the electricity it can (re)generate.[12] Other projects focus on using excess clean energy to stack weights inside a forty-story building, giving them gravitational potential energy, and then later releasing that energy by using pulleys to lower them. One project manager said, "We can make that mountain every day, and unbuild that mountain every day."[13]

Other, less variable sources of energy may be relevant to your students, depending on the region they live in. These include geothermal power, wave and tidal energy from the ocean, and biomass. Burning biomass like switchgrass or woody plants releases a pulse of carbon dioxide into the air, but with only mild regret, because these materials replace fossil fuels. We can also burn methane that seeps from landfills or incinerate some forms of waste to produce power. These options are on the decline but remain important "bridging solutions" to achieving independence from coal, oil, and gas.

In addition to renewable modes of power production, we can also benefit from boosting electrical efficiency through technologies and practices that reduce demand in the first place. Widespread use of LEDs (light emitting diodes) can reduce emissions by more than 16 Gt over three decades. The common strategy of insulation reduces energy consumption and GHGs by increasing the efficiency of entire buildings. In new construction or retro-fits, it makes both heating and cooling more energy efficient, saving approximately 17 Gt in reduced emissions.[14] Net-zero buildings combine maximum efficiency through innovative materials like dynamic glass and design features like cool roofs (see the Building section), with on-site sources of energy like solar panels. They produce as much energy as they use annually, with low or no emissions.

To enable the transition to renewables at scale, the broader electrical system also needs to evolve. Flexible grids for transmission and effective energy storage make it possible to better balance electricity supply with demand. Science writer Matthew Hutson imagines a future in which some of these technologies become the norm, and society embraces a combination of renewable energy and renewable storage:[15]

> In such a world, wind turbines and solar farms will spread over fields and coastlines, while geothermal plants draw power from below. Meanwhile, in caves and tanks, hydrogen and compressed air will flow back and forth. In industrial areas, energy warehouses will thrum with the movement of mass. In rural places, water will be driven belowground and then will gush back up. When the sun comes out and the wind rises, the grid will inhale, and electricity will get saved. During the doldrums, the grid will exhale, driving energy to factories, homes, offices, and devices. Instead of burning dead things, in the form of fossil fuels, we'll create and store energy dynamically, in a living system.

Thoughts like this really help students imagine a desirable future.

Food, agriculture, and land use. Humans have repurposed a significant portion of the planet's land for growing crops, grazing livestock, and harvesting trees. Unfortunately, our consumption habits have disrupted or fragmented ecosystems. This is not just a displacement problem; agriculture and forestry activities generate nearly a quarter of greenhouse gas emissions worldwide. Cropland and pastures, for example, emit methane, especially when growing rice and raising ruminants like cattle or sheep; nitrous oxide is emitted from manure and overusing fertilizers; and carbon dioxide is released just by disturbing soils.

How can we become better stewards of the land, tending it in ways that decrease emissions from agriculture and forestry? To start with, eight of the top twenty ways of reducing carbon involve our food system.[16] If we address our own diets (especially those of us in the United States and Europe), we can prevent a lot of carbon from going into the atmosphere. Roughly a third of the world's food is never consumed, which means the land and resources used and greenhouse gases emitted for producing it were unnecessary. If we reduce this waste, we can keep over 91 Gt of carbon from entering the atmosphere. Going one step further, if we shift toward plant-rich diets, that will save another 65 Gt in greenhouse gases.[17] Favoring plant-based foods reduces demand for animal-based products, thereby reducing land clearing (intended for grazing or feedstock for animals) and fertilizer use. Eating lower on the food chain (more plant-based) and ensuring what's grown does not go to waste is a powerful combination that lowers the amount of energy put into farming, keeps land from being cleared, and does away with all associated emissions.

Our ecosystems also need protection. Peatlands probably don't spring to mind here, but they retain enormous amounts of carbon below ground—and we need to keep it there. Although peatland ecosystems cover just 3 percent of the Earth's land, they hold *twice* the amount of carbon as the world's forests, at a staggering 500 to 600 gigatons. Peatlands become prodigious greenhouse vents if disrupted by fires or excavation. Contrary to common sense, peat will rot if it dries out, and rotting happens to be a slow form of combustion. Thankfully, 85 percent of the world's peatlands are intact, but it will be critical to forestall degradation from forestry, fuel extraction, or farming before it starts, while restoring drained and damaged peatlands. The emissions that stay in the ground? About 26 Gt.[18]

The third pathway is to secure land tenure for Indigenous peoples around the world. This is a process that protects their rights to land stewardship. Indigenous communities are among those most dramatically impacted by climate change—despite contributing the least to its causes because of their land-based livelihoods and histories of cultural erasure as a result of colonization. These communities, in places ranging from Canada to the Amazon basin to the Indonesian Archipelago, have a long history of resistance to mining and other kinds of resource extraction, deforestation, and the spread of monocrop plantations. Nearly 20 percent of *all* land is Indigenous and community-owned, including over a billion acres of forest. New carbon analyses report a total of 293 Gt of carbon is held above ground, below ground, and in the soil beneath forests managed by Indigenous and local communities worldwide.[19] Growing the acreage protected under Indigenous land tenure can increase carbon stocks and reduce greenhouse gas emissions from deforestation. Indigenous land management not only secures carbon in biomass above and below ground, but enhances biodiversity while safeguarding vibrant cultures and regenerative ways of living.

Indigenous land practices include agroforestry in which trees, shrubs, herbs, and vegetables are planted together as a group, emulating a forest system in which each species benefits the others.[20] Another practice, controlled burns of forested lands, is taught by tribal elders in the American West. These small fires recreate a mosaic of landscapes, creating natural breaks that can slow down massive blazes. These practices open spaces where wildlife can flourish. One elder spoke of fire as "a kind of medicine for the land. And it lets you carry out your culture—it's why you are in the world."[21]

Industry: Curbing the waste and repurposing materials. The industries that furnish us with material goods of all kinds can be energy-intensive because of the chain of activities needed to create and deliver them. This includes extracting raw materials, manufacturing, packaging, delivering, dealing with disposal, and in rare cases, putting waste back to work. Absent the last step, this mode of operation is the unsustainable "take-make-use-trash"—a one-way flow to landfills that is energy inefficient and damaging to the environment. For these reasons, industry is responsible for about 21 percent of all heat-trapping emissions. The production of cement, iron, and steel top the charts, but even the fashion sector drives up atmospheric carbon.

Our challenge is reenvisioning industrial chains of production and how we consume these goods. We can start by improving materials. Plastic, metals, and building materials are prime candidates for improving how they are produced or replacing with alternatives that meet the same needs, but with lower emissions. An example is cement, a key component of concrete and a major contributor to global CO_2 emissions because of the thermal energy and electricity required to produce it.[22] Cement is made by firing limestone, clay, and other materials in a kiln. In the process, carbon dioxide is emitted from the combustion used to fire the material and from the reaction produced from the mixture when it is exposed to heat. Each pound of concrete releases nearly a pound of carbon dioxide.[23] To decarbonize, manufacturers could substitute fuels such as hydrogen or biomass for fossil fuels in heating the limestone and clay. Capturing the emissions that are released could also be part of the cement industry's transition process. In Sweden, for example, a company is aiming to recover 1.8 million tons of carbon dioxide from a cement plant and bury it in the North Sea.[24]

Refrigeration is another unlikely culprit. Keeping things cool is necessary for many industries, and in terms of potential reductions of GHGs, this category is a whopper. The fluorinated compounds used in refrigeration are lesser known but potent greenhouse gases, which often leak during use or disposal. Controlling these leaks can avoid emissions in buildings and later in landfills. Just this effort can save us 58 Gt of carbon. There are also alternative refrigerants. These include ammonia or, ironically, recaptured carbon dioxide, which is currently replacing fluorinated gases. This will save us another 43 Gt of emissions from going into the atmosphere.[25]

Changing how we get around. Trains, planes, and cars discharge 14 percent of global greenhouse gas emissions. Our challenge is to support the social good of mobility while ratcheting down our dependence on fossil fuels.[26] What's making headlines now is the availability of electric vehicles (EVs). These don't produce emissions themselves; however, the electricity they run on has to come from somewhere. It matters a lot if it is generated by renewables (solar, wind) rather than by fossil fuels like coal. When EVs come to dominate the transportation marketplace, they'll keep 12 Gt of greenhouse gases out of the atmosphere.[27] Your students will likely be able to share stories if their families own an EV and can give testimonials about the infrastructure needed (e.g., charging stations) to make these feasible for a wider range of consumers.

Other solutions within this group include walkable cities and infrastructure for bikes, high-speed rail, and public transit. Electric bicycles that use battery-powered pedaling assistance are also becoming more popular. In my own neighborhood, I see commuters who could not typically get to work using a traditional bike now able to zip up inclines with cargo or children along for the ride. Electrifying large semitrucks, ships, and planes are turning out to be a heavier lift, literally, but what seems out of reach today will soon become a reality.

Buildings: Improving the envelopes we live and work in. Buildings produce 6 percent of heat-trapping emissions worldwide. They are carbon intensive because of the materials they use and the processes of construction, renovation, or demolition. In day-to-day use, buildings release still more emissions by air conditioning, heating water, or cooking with gas.[28] Our broader challenge is to retrofit existing buildings and create new ones that minimize energy use. We can accomplish this through simple efficiencies, like keeping conditioned air inside and unconditioned air out, often by using insulation. Other, more high-tech solutions like dynamic glass and smart thermostats can optimize a building's energy consumption, depending on outside conditions and time of day. Heat pumps can be used to extract thermal energy from the air and transfer it, from indoors out for cooling or from outdoors in for warmth. Other solutions like green roofs use soil and vegetation as living insulation. Cool roofs also do their part by reflecting solar energy.

In every category of solution we've explored so far, there have been unexpected candidates for big drawdowns of emissions, and this category is no exception. The surprise here is improved clean cookstoves. Three billion people prepare meals every day with rudimentary stoves that produce heat but also smoke from fuels like wood, dried peat, animal dung, crop residues, or coal. Women, of course, are disproportionally exposed to health risks while doing these domestic chores. The stoves produce 2 to 5 percent of annual greenhouse gases worldwide through emissions, but there is a more immediate danger to human well-being. Burning these fuels emits carbon dioxide and other pollutants like soot and carbon monoxide. These fumes cause respiratory illnesses, heart problems, and even death.[29] The good news is that improved cookstoves already exist. These force gases and smoke from incomplete combustion back into the stove's flame, decreasing waste gases by up to 95 percent. Clean cookstoves would reduce emissions by a massive 31 Gt and protect human health in the process.[30]

Supporting Sinks

Land. The complementary project to reducing emissions is driving carbon into natural sinks—the land and oceans. Of these, the only sink we can enhance is the land, due in part because we can rejuvenate the soils we've degraded over centuries and allow trees, grasses, creepers, and climbers to flourish. The plants and the ecosystems we consider part of the land sink have an unparalleled capacity to absorb carbon through photosynthesis and store it in living biomass.

Healthy soils themselves are, in large part, organic matter, making them another enormous storehouse of carbon. Land sinks capture and return 26 percent of human-caused emissions back to the Earth. Our challenge is to sequester more carbon in living biomass and soil, and in the process, improve the capacity of the land to renew itself. Restoring ecosystems, especially tropical forests that have suffered extensive clearing, fragmentation, and degradation, can help them return to fully functioning carbon sinks. The numbers here are huge; healthy land-based ecosystems around the world can store up to 54 Gt over a thirty-year period.[31]

Coastal and ocean sinks. The oceans have already absorbed 20 to 30 percent of human-created emissions and eased the burden of surplus heat from the atmosphere. Humans cannot really enhance this capacity to take out more anthropogenic excess, in part because the oceans are so vast and already becoming saturated with carbon dioxide. Our efforts must shift to sequestering still more carbon in coastal environments. Coastal wetlands around the world have been degraded by agriculture, development, and natural disasters.[32] Fortunately, they can be restored by reducing pollution, replanting lost vegetation like seagrass, or simply repairing the natural flow of water.

Engineered sinks. The unabated flow of greenhouse gases into our atmosphere means natural processes can't do it all when it comes to carbon sequestration. Emerging technologies show some promise in removing carbon dioxide from the air; however, these prototypes are in the early stages of development. Removal has two meanings. It can refer to pulling carbon from the concentrated exhaust of a power plant or industrial process; this falls under the umbrella of "carbon capture." Removal can also refer to pulling carbon out of the open air, where it's much less concentrated. The world's largest facility designed to filter carbon dioxide from the air and turn it into rock has opened in Iceland. When operating at capacity, the plant will draw 4,000 tons of carbon dioxide out of the atmosphere every year and store it underground. Sound like a lot? Last year, global carbon dioxide emissions totaled 31.5 billion tons, meaning the facility would remove in a year what humanity emits in three or four seconds. Doing the math, we'd need 7 to 10 million of these installations, which is currently unfeasible by several orders of magnitude. This serves as an important lesson for our students; as they study the implications of these removal strategies for the global carbon cycle, they can come to appreciate the engineering involved and the scale at which natural and technological solutions must operate to have a significant effect.

Geoengineering, the deliberate large-scale intervention in our Earth's systems to counteract climate change, is controversial. Among the proposals is the injection of tiny reflective particles or aerosols into our stratosphere to reflect sunlight. Another is to add iron to nutrient-poor ocean waters to encourage the growth of algae that would take up carbon dioxide for photosynthesis. These both interfere with natural processes that has been evolving for more than 4 billion years—what could go wrong?

IMPROVING SOCIETY

The United Nations estimates the human family will grow from the current 7.7 billion to between 9.4 billion and 10.1 billion in 2050.[33] As we consider the future, it matters how many people will be using resources, consuming, and creating waste. People's choices about how many children to have should be theirs, and those children should inherit a livable planet. Providing equal access to education for girls and giving them the freedom and knowledge to engage in family planning throughout their lifetimes are fundamental human rights. These unquestionably just outcomes of access to health care and education, however, are in tension with assumptions about race, class, and the coercive history of ideas about population control. In so many ways, the challenge is not how many people will share the planet, but how they are living.[34]

To be more precise, high-income countries with a small minority of the world's population have been responsible for 74 percent of excess resource use in the past twenty years, driven mainly by the United States (27 percent) and wealthy nations in the European Union (25 percent). China ranks second and is responsible for 15 percent of that resource use. The Global South, on the other hand, is responsible for taking up only 8 percent of the world's resources. This means that the consumption of fifty-eight countries in the Global South, representing 3.6 billion people, remains within sustainable levels, unlike the

United States, Europe, and China.[35] Our students deserve to engage with these issues, but need to be fully informed of both the promise and potential injustices as they contemplate how different communities are being asked to sacrifice for the sake of a livable world.

BUILDING SOLUTIONS AND A SENSE OF EFFICACY INTO YOUR LESSONS

When we design a series of lessons based on solutions and the social good, a bit of structure can be helpful. Some of my K–12 colleagues start by identifying relevant standards, while others begin by considering how the lessons will fit into a unit or become a stand-alone series of learning experiences. These lessons will often integrate science content with solutions and engineering. The following sets of questions focus on important planning decisions, but this framework is adjustable, so you can address these design questions in an order that makes sense to you. Most of the teachers I work with start by going back and forth between the first two sets of questions—one about how they might embed a series of lessons within a curriculum and the other about lesson goals.

1. How can I integrate the science with solutions and engineering in my lessons?

There are four different strategies listed in figure 4.2. These are not the only possibilities, but they may spark your creativity for other designs that fit your students' interests.

Option A is a *science-to-engineering transition* model. It begins with students exploring, over a period of days, one or more climate-related science ideas that pose risks for human communities or the more-than-human world.

Figure 4.2 Four models for designing units on climate change solutions

Science to engineering A	Engineering deep dive B	Mitigation & adaptation survey C	Local challenge D
May be best place to start guided inquiry with students	Features systematic problem solving, design and testing	Fosters hope and knowledge of social change	Good for allowing students to exercise choice and agency

You could then introduce investigations into one or more possible solutions, transitioning to a series of lessons in which students might independently explore the practical and social bases for these mitigation or adaptation strategies, and how to feasibly implement them. For example, you could develop lessons on the greenhouse effect and the idea of albedo (reflectivity) to prepare students for mini-projects on urban heat islands in lower-income communities and the development of socially just solutions. Teachers often use this transition model, but a word of warning: the engineering phase is too often reduced to just a day or two, short-cutting students' ability to research and design meaningful solutions.

Option B is an *engineering deep-dive* model, in which you negotiate with students a climate-related challenge and then immerse them in the practices of designing and testing solutions. The challenge, for example, could be retrofitting the school as a zero-emissions structure. Regardless of the challenge, students would learn about the kinds of problems engineering can and cannot solve and the need of social action for some problems (such as community campaigns to help reduce food waste). State-level standards usually ask students to break down complex problems into more approachable challenges, which in turn helps them identify more tractable solutions. Students then test these under different conditions, deciding on their prioritized criteria for success, considering trade-offs, and assessing social and environmental impacts.[36]

Option C is a *mitigation and adaptation survey* model. Here students develop their own big-picture framework of many solutions, the challenges they address, and how they are implemented. You could explore mitigations or adaptations by posing a consistent set of questions about each, such as: What science or social action does this solution depend on for success? What does success look like? What are the trade-offs? How does this solution address human or community resilience? Whose interests are being served by these measures? Does the proposed solution create its own set of problems? Although we want students to explore a range of solutions, it might be best to draw some boundaries for discussion or for compare-and-contrast activities. They could focus, for example, on solutions related to enhancing local carbon sinks or creating more walkable cities.

Option D is a *local challenge* model. In these units, students would be introduced to several climate-related issues facing their community or region. They could choose one or two that interest them and find out what it's like to gather all the relevant information needed to start proposing changes. One of the big takeaways from doing this work is that context matters. If the challenge appears to be the restoration of local wetlands, then what seems reasonable and doable in one community may be too expensive or not aligned with the local values of another. Students will learn how challenging it is to follow through with a project, enduring setbacks and pushbacks on the way to their goals. A second takeaway is that new science ideas and resources that undergird solutions have to be continually sought out on a need-to-know basis, and that problem-solvers can never know enough. This is an opportunity to think about the scale of action—are we mobilizing the school, the neighborhood, community, or region? Rather than presenting what you think to the students, have them weigh in. Ask: "What level of action could *you* be part of?"

These four models differ only in their relative emphasis on science, solutions, engineering, and local context. Students should have access to all these experiences over the course of their K–12 education. Here is where coherence across grade levels matters and coordinating with colleagues in your school is important. If each of your science teaching peers could assume responsibility for part of this, the outcome would be a cumulative trajectory of learning that exposes students to deeper and more nuanced ideas over time, empowering them to be agents of change.

2. What are possible goals for a series of solutions lessons?

The sample standards below combine engineering practices with a specific kind of challenge (known as Performance Expectations in the NGSS). There are a few climate-specific engineering standards across the K–12 spectrum. We share four here, ranging from kindergarten to high school. A complete list can be found in appendix B. There are also generic engineering standards that can be applied to many climate solutions. At the end of the list is another possible goal for how traditional science and Indigenous science can work in complementary ways to help address climate problems.

- Communicate solutions that will reduce the impact of humans on the land, water, air, and/or other living things in the local environment (kindergarten).

- Generate and compare multiple solutions to reduce the impacts of natural Earth processes on humans (grade 4). Note: The phrase "natural Earth processes" can be changed to target anthropogenically altered Earth processes.
- Analyze and interpret data on natural hazards to forecast future catastrophic events and inform the development of technologies to mitigate their effects (middle school).
- Compare and contrast how different forms of energy production and other kinds of resource extraction have economic, social, environmental, and geopolitical costs and risks as well as benefits. New technologies and social regulations can change the balance of these factors (high school, adapted).
- Explain how both Indigenous science and traditional science can be used to define and solve climate-related problems (not in NGSS).

3. What should we consider in selecting or creating specific lessons?

These questions can help you plan the particulars of ambitious and equitable teaching:

- What experiences am I asking students to build on from previous grade levels or units?
- How will I elicit and represent students' initial ideas, experiences, and concerns?
- How can a solution be explicitly connected to climate change, risks, and human communities, rather than assuming our students will make these connections without support?
- What ideas should be emphasized or deliberately unpacked about the solution examples we explore?
- What key understandings will I assess along the way, how, and for what purposes that serve my students?
- What kinds of conversations will students benefit from that put solutions into a larger social perspective?
- What lessons will help students scale up from individual actions to those that engage communities?

This chapter makes clear our diverse opportunities to take action in our classrooms. The reality is that it's a big challenge, and no one can do it all, but coordinating our efforts with peers is a big step forward. The good news is that students are quite aware the world is changing, and they care about that. Using our professional capital as trusted public intellectuals, we can more purposefully cultivate climate-conscious and agentic youth.

CHAPTER 5

Dealing with Disinformation and Skepticism

STUDENTS ARE INFLUENCED by online climate change messaging more than any other topic we teach, and it's rarely neutral. Content rushes at them in the form of news feeds, tweets, and video, some of it accurate but alarmist and some slanting toward denial. Whatever their preferences, they can't avoid reading stories about environmental crises, some from sketchy sources and stitched together more by rumor than by science. Other posts are credible, but they obscure meaningful content within sensationalized storylines.[1]

Most of your students will likely be eager to find out more about the climate-linked phenomena that they constantly see in the news. Still, no matter what part of the country you live in, a few will feel that "climate change is a hoax," or just as problematically, "maybe this is happening—but why kick up such a fuss?" Attitudes can vary by state or by community; some of the teachers I've worked with even have class sections with climate beliefs that vary widely. As professionals, we're obligated to work with whatever ideas and experiences our students are willing to share, yet we are unsure about how their conceptions and beliefs, especially those not aired in public, will interact with the lessons we craft.

What *do* students believe? A 2020 national survey of over a thousand US thirteen- to eighteen-year-olds showed that eight of ten teens believed climate change is happening.[2] About 25 percent thought that human activities were the sole cause of increased warming, and another 60 percent thought humans were at least partially responsible. In another recent study of over 900 teens, 86 percent believed that human-caused climate change was happening, though just under half (46 percent) felt very certain of this.[3] The momentum is clearly shifting among school-age children toward wider acceptance of anthropogenic changes to the environment. We should seize this opportunity but go into it fully informed of how the worldviews students bring to climate conversations and the disinformation they are exposed to can affect classroom discourse.

STUDENTS BENEFIT FROM UNDERSTANDING THE SCIENTIFIC CONSENSUS

I'll start with the most straightforward suggestion for productive conversations. People are open to learning more about climate change if they are simply informed of the degree of consensus among scientists for human-caused atmospheric warming.[4] This tips the scales in favor of accepting the science but is only one part of a broader strategy. Students should hear how scientists, as a community, examine all kinds of evidence to determine what's currently happening with Earth systems and why. For us, these are low-risk strategies to get more of our students to suspend unfounded doubts about changes in our climate and focus more on the data.

The evidence pointing to anthropogenic climate change is incredibly robust. There are thousands of supportive studies and *multiple lines of evidence*— from ice cores, glacial melt, sea level rise, ecological shifts, ocean acidification, the unprecedented rate of temperature increases—that all converge on similar conclusions. The renowned geologist and historian of science Naomi Oreskes points out that "[i]n science, consensus doesn't refer to a discussion. It means knowledge that arises from independent research projects all achieve the same results."[5] For skeptics to challenge the consensus behind climate change, they would need to locate flaws with all the lines of supportive evidence *and* demonstrate how their own favored bodies of data can be explained using a different theory.[6] Don't hold your breath for this.

Most teenagers are unaware of how widespread the consensus is, estimating on average about 70 percent of scientists agreeing.[7] The actual numbers are very different. One study of 928 research papers published in refereed scientific journals between 1993 and 2003 found that *none* of them disagreed with the position that climate change is happening, and *none* argued that current changes in our climate are natural. More recent studies have consistently measured about a 97 percent agreement among the most published authors of climate-related papers.[8] All major scientific bodies in the United States, whose members' expertise bears directly on the climate, have issued statements stating unequivocally that nearly all Earth's systems are being influenced by human activity (US National Academy of Sciences, American Association for the Advancement of Science, American Meteorological Society, etc.).

Our challenge is to design experiences that unapologetically engage students with ideas that may conflict with their current thinking, while at the same time genuinely respect the diverse views they bring to the table. To thread this needle, we'll start by exploring the larger social context of climate rhetoric beyond the classroom, especially online disinformation and mischaracterizations of climate science.

MANUFACTURED DOUBT ABOUT CLIMATE SCIENCE

While we are hard at work preparing lessons about our changing climate, powerful voices are trying to discredit the science behind it. Educators need to be aware of how these actors work, and to develop strategies to deal with them.

How Public Opinion Is Manipulated

Well-funded and politically powerful corporations, most prominently the fossil fuel industry, keep their fog machines running at full tilt by funding media campaigns questioning and spinning whatever climate policies threaten their bottom line: Is climate change really happening? Can we be sure what is causing it? How can we really know the impact, especially the projections about the next few decades? Big Oil downplays its role in the climate crisis yet continues to undermine climate regulation—quite successfully—and dismiss activism as just so much theater.[9]

As educators, we need a working understanding of the political rhetoric behind all kinds of partisan messaging and manipulated media, starting with the vocabulary. *Misinformation* pertains to content that is false, inaccurate, or misleading, but inadvertently created or spread with no intention to deceive.[10] This can range from outdated news, initially thought to be true and disseminated in good faith, to oversimplified half-truths.[11] Misinformation is not typically aligned with any ideological position about human influences on the climate.

Disinformation is another beast. This is false information deliberately created and spread in order to mislead, influence public opinion, or obscure the truth.[12] There is no more apt example of disinformation than some of the public responses to COVID-19. A large swath of the adult US population refused lifesaving vaccines because their media sources warned against them as "unproven," rumored to have debilitating side effects, or containing miniature tracking devices. Many of these same folks flocked to websites that were touting sham cures with no grounding in scientific data. Doubt was merchandised and quack medicine itself went viral online, including my favorite—a deworming medication for livestock.

Many people who cling to unwarranted doubt about the science of anthropogenic warming self-label as climate change *realists* or *skeptics*, clinging to a veneer of principled objectivity and standing in contrast to those they refer to as *alarmists* (mostly people who tell the truth about what's happening and who's responsible; however, there are some who seriously go overboard with the doom). Realists and skeptics, however they self-describe, are in the *denialist* camp.

There are different aspects of climate change one can deny and different kinds of organizations that peddle their own brand of disinformation along these lines.[13] Four types are common: trend denial (no significant warming is taking place), attribution denial (humans are not causing it), impact denial (it will not have significant negative effect on us or the environment), and consensus denial (there is no agreement among climate scientists about anthropogenic climate change).[14] A wide variety of actors and organizations strategically use combinations of these to erode public understanding of climate science. These groups include political and religious organizations, industry (oil or coal extraction, also steel, mining, electric utilities, and car manufacturers), some media outlets, and governments.

The fossil fuel industry is the principal among several industrial players that set up front groups and Astroturf operations (online workers who create the illusion of widespread grassroots support for a person, policy, or product related to denial).[15] Doubt is also disseminated by a small number of contrarian scientists, who often exaggerate their expertise in the field of climate studies and spread their beliefs with assistance from conservative media and skeptical bloggers.[16] In the report *America Misled*, the authors describe how the fossil fuel industry's denial and delay tactics come straight out of Big Tobacco's playbook.[17] Just as tobacco companies were aware, early on, of the addictive nature of nicotine and the health hazards of smoking, scientists working for the fossil fuel industry knew about the potential warming effects of carbon dioxide emissions as early as the 1950s. Internal documents from Exxon indicate they were aware of the potential dangers to the climate caused by their products, but instead of warning the public, they initiated disinformation campaigns to water down these inconvenient realities. Through a network of collaborators they enacted these now familiar strategies:

- Casting doubt on the scientific practices used to study emissions and climate
- Making the public think scientists can't agree on anything
- Manipulating media to give attention to "both sides" of emerging climate findings
- Greenwashing to make it appear companies care about the environment
- Arguing for delay: "Let's wait and see before we act"
- Framing renewable energy as impractical and expensive

Some of the fossil fuel industry's recent messaging efforts include promoting natural gas as "clean energy." In truth it is mostly methane, a potent greenhouse gas, and certainly not clean unless you count the fact that you can't see it. The industry has also elevated its rhetoric about fossil fuels ensuring everyone's "energy independence" (a thinly veiled but illogical swipe at renewables) when in fact we are all dependent on profit-driven corporations providing us with that energy. The American public continues to be deceived about climate change, just as we were denied the right to be informed about the risks of smoking by the tobacco industry. It helps to know what we're up against.

Targeting Teachers

The fossil fuel industry has been increasingly concerned about the influence of high-quality education on young people's beliefs about the environment. Part of their multifront war plan is to directly influence teachers.[18] One example is a glossy book mailed directly to educators throughout the United States by the Heartland Institute, a conservative think tank. *Why Scientists Disagree About Global Warming* presents the false premise that evidence for human-driven climate change is deeply flawed and dismisses climate change as "another fake crisis."[19] A cover letter asks teachers to accept that the science is inconclusive and adds, "If that's the case, then students would be better served by letting them know a vibrant debate is taking place among scientists on how big the human impact is, and whether or not we should be worried about it." The authors assume the reader will take this at face value rather than checking the statements of hundreds of international science organizations that speak truth to power. A more recent publication from them, *Climate at a Glance*, cherry-picks data on nearly every page to shore up misleading claims about the state of the environment (see logical fallacies below).[20]

The fossil fuel industry also influences science teaching in more subtle ways. In 2004, British Petroleum hired a public relations firm to craft messages insinuating that consumers of oil and natural gas bear the responsibility for their own emissions, shifting responsibility for climate change away from itself and onto those who furnish their profits.[21] BP's brainchild was the *carbon footprint calculator*, which is still used in many classrooms to get students to calculate carbon emissions that result from their everyday activities. It's "about helping you to go carbon neutral—reducing and offsetting your carbon footprint," BP declares, without a hint of irony, on its website.

The foot in the door for most denialist agendas is not a direct attack on the facts; simple measures of global air temperature are now irrefutable. Rather, it is to insinuate doubt within the science education community where none exists. Curriculum publishers play a role in this particular deception. Some textbooks and online resources present climate change only as a probability. Human causation is left out or shrouded in terms like "uncertainty" and referenced as "one of the most debated issues in modern science." One study of thirty-two print and digital textbooks, most of which were released in 2015 or later, found that the topic of climate change was typically described on only one or two pages.[22] In a Texas middle school science text, a single paragraph was devoted to this topic. Of twenty-eight books that mentioned climate change, one-third failed to acknowledge the role of humans in causing it.

Only half of the science texts discussed the consequences of climate change—such as sea level rise, worsening wildfires, weather extremes, and species loss.

No one seems too young for curricular conditioning. As part of one curriculum, elementary students are introduced to Petro Pete, who stars in an online animated read-along. Pete realizes one morning that his sneakers are gone, his toothbrush is missing, and there is no bus to take him to school. Later in the story he wakes up and exclaims: "That was all a dream! All of my petroleum products are back!" Living without petroleum he concludes "is like a nightmare."

Because these efforts constitute deliberate attempts at miseducation, the National Science Teachers Association has directed unambiguous statements at bad-faith organizations. Its stance is that scientific explanations must be consistent with existing empirical evidence: "Ideas based on political ideologies or pseudoscience that fail these empirical tests do not constitute science and should not be allowed to compromise the teaching of climate science."[23] The authors of *America Misled* sum up the many pernicious effects of climate disinformation.[24] It confuses public understanding of climate issues, polarizes communities along political lines, weakens support for climate action, and perhaps most damaging, reinforces climate silence—the lack of public dialogue about anthropogenic environmental changes. Disinformation about climate change *does not drive people to act, but to sit on the sidelines.*

Recognizing Denialist Talking Points

Denialists rely on several strategies to misuse facts and theories about our changing climate.[25] I focus here on the use of logical fallacies because students may bring up some of these in your classroom; however, I am *not* advocating that lessons be centered on pseudo-arguments or having students figure out how some of the most common skeptical talking points can be rebutted. You may be teaching in a community where students simply want to know more about what they see in the media or in their own backyards and don't want to spend class time on claims they know are junk. This is where your professional judgment comes in—you know your students and your learning goals for them, so use discretion to guide if and how you address contrarian rhetoric. Regardless of your situation, becoming familiar with the most common talking points of denial may well deepen your knowledge of science as you uncover why these claims are mischaracterizations or patently false. Logical fallacies come in many flavors; I'll describe four of the most common next, with additional climate examples for each in figure 5.1.[26]

- *Cherry-picking* is the selection of only a limited subset of a larger body of data in order to support a claim. If a person takes daytime temperatures from only one city on Earth or one month in a decade, they can claim whatever they want about global temperatures going down; it just won't hold up when compared against the whole data set. Bottom line: we don't get to choose the data that gives us the answer we are hoping for and ignore the rest.

- *Having impossible expectations* is the demand for unrealistic standards of certainty before acting on the science. One of the most common examples here is claiming that scientific models predicting ocean warming or hurricane frequency can't be trusted because they are not perfectly precise. In reality, modern models represent sophisticated simulations of the Earth's past and present climate. Such models have already accurately predicted the loss of Arctic sea ice and geographic patterns of extreme weather.

- *Jumping to conclusions* is using a simple fact to segue into an unwarranted claim. This is also referred to as "overreaching the data." People sometimes blame volcanoes for adding to atmospheric concentrations of carbon dioxide, which is true. But they then leap to the conclusion that current climate change is due exclusively to natural causes like volcanoes. Volcanoes do indeed produce some carbon dioxide, but it is false to suggest they produce enough to account for measured increases over the past few decades. We know the larger cause, and it's us.

- *Oversimplification* is making a thing, idea, or process appear simpler by ignoring relevant complexities. Some denialists have claimed that increased carbon dioxide will benefit plants because "it is food for them." For starters, this is technically inaccurate, but more importantly, it fails to recognize the much larger negative impacts on agriculture and ecosystems through extreme weather, heat stress, drought, and flooding. In order to avoid this fallacy, we need to become comfortable with accepting complicated answers to what sound like simple questions.

Figure 5.1 Examples of logical fallacies

Myth	Fact	Logical fallacy
The Greenland ice sheet is thickening in the middle so it must be gaining mass.	Confusion caused by anecdotal stories of buildings being buried in accumulating snow on Greenland's ice sheet had led some skeptics to believe it is gaining ice. Evidence from several different measurement techniques suggests that not only is Greenland losing ice but that these losses are accelerating at a rapid pace.	Cherry-picking
It's cold outside, so global warming must be a hoax.	This confuses weather with climate. Climate trends are changes in weather over a long time span. Climate change doesn't mean cold days disappear; there are just fewer of them compared to hot days over time. Temperature data from the last 50 years show that new record highs occur nearly twice as often as record lows.	Impossible expectations
Natural climate change in the past implies that current climate change is also natural.	Paleoclimate data tell us that past concentrations of CO_2 have driven changes in temperature and precipitation. Today humans are the cause of vastly increased CO_2 concentrations, principally by fossil fuel emissions.	Jumping to conclusions
Human CO_2 emissions are tiny compared to natural CO_2 emissions into the atmosphere, so our influence on climate must be inconsequential.	For thousands of years, CO_2 in our atmosphere has been held in balance. The natural carbon cycle both adds and removes CO_2 to keep it in equilibrium. Humans have upset the balance. We add extra CO_2 without removing any. This fallacy ignores natural CO_2 sinks.	Oversimplification

Source: Adapted from John Cook, *Skeptical Science*, https://skepticalscience.com/.

It is unfortunate that we have to spend time informing ourselves about nuisance pseudo-arguments, but being familiar with these misguided talking points can help us shape our own messaging to students about how evidence is selected and used to make claims. We can also teach students to be better consumers of information when they inevitably run across print material or websites that pitch contrarian ideas from self-styled experts.

DO STUDENTS' WORLDVIEWS AFFECT HOW THEY PROCESS CLIMATE CHANGE INFORMATION?

Worldviews include one's beliefs, values, and social identity that evolve out of personal experiences and enculturation by others.[27] Some individuals hold a biospheric worldview, for example, which means they believe that humans are interdependent with other forms of life and that they consider the natural world as important in its own right. Many people with this perspective are also communitarian, meaning they believe society has an obligation to help ensure the well-being of all individuals.[28] People with these views tend to be more concerned about climate change and its impact on others as well as themselves. On the other hand, some people see the natural world as a collection of resources that humans have a right to exploit, regardless of the consequences. This worldview is often associated with individualism, the belief that everyone is responsible for their own well-being without interference from society and especially not from the government. Individualists generally perceive less risk from climate change and can downplay the vulnerability of impacted communities. This is a simplification of human reasoning but explains many behavioral trends and choices people make.

Worldviews can be activated in different situations and play an important role in how individuals respond to messages about climate change, as well as a range of other issues like gun control, wearing masks to prevent the spread of disease, or solutions for homelessness.[29] The climate-relevant part of this theory is that worldviews can also affect what content people choose to consume and how.[30] This selective filtering (staying in our bubble) may mean that some of us are more likely to be exposed to false or misleading claims, as long as they are consistent with our worldviews, and we may be less likely to expose ourselves to accurate information. When surveys ask people if they "believe" in climate change, their responses may say more about their values and their social identity than their understanding of climate science.[31]

Children also often bring ideologically driven viewpoints into the classroom.[32] These can be shaped by adults in their lives and may impact how they engage with climate change; however, they are still forming cultural worldviews and political ideologies that do not coalesce until early adulthood.[33] Still, worldviews are as influential in middle school and high school students as their knowledge of climate science. In a study of 357 students in grades 9 to 11, researchers found that those exposed to explanations of how the atmosphere is changing (i.e., the mechanism behind warming) were more likely to acknowledge, convey certainty, and/or express concern about climate change, compared to students who learned about climate variation without being exposed to these underlying mechanisms.[34] They found no evidence, however, that a mechanistic understanding of climate change actually prevented ideologically motivated reasoning in high schoolers. Adolescents with strong skills in analyzing data and individualistic worldviews tended to either avoid relevant data supplied to them—data that would contradict ideas associated with a politically conservative stance—or acknowledge the data but use them to support alternative explanations dismissive of anthropogenic influences.

One key to educating K–12 students might involve helping them understand how and why climate data are more consistent with anthropogenic explanations than other, more skeptical explanations such as "natural variation" theories for why the climate is shifting.[35] But for this approach to work, such instruction would need to be designed to not threaten students' identities in the process. Findings from students of varied ages offer hope that they may be able to think about and act on climate change in ways that are motived by the science, but indicate that their worldviews still play a role in how accepting they are of climate change and its risks. Biospheric worldviews influence climate change acceptance (positively so) regardless of age. The challenge for us is to cultivate an appreciation of the environment as sacred and life-sustaining, at the same time we are communicating academic ideas about climate change.

I note here a gap in the research. We currently lack an understanding of how students from nondominant racial and ethnic backgrounds respond to various messages about the climate change. Children of color and low-income respondents actually have a broader conceptualization of environmental issues than White and high-income respondents. We need to learn more from *all* our students about climate change teaching.

CULTIVATING OPEN-MINDEDNESS IN YOUR CLASSROOM

The following recommendations will help you manage a classroom in which students can learn about the evidence behind climate change while having their own ideas respected, and deal compassionately with the skepticism of some students that may shut down rather than open up conversations with peers. This is not quite as daunting as it appeared to be a few years ago. Teachers were concerned that refuting students who held inaccurate beliefs about climate change would backfire, that is, strengthen alternative conceptions rather than reduce them and create resistance. These effects occur only occasionally, and the risk of outright conflict is lower in most teaching situations than once thought.[36]

One of the first principles of climate change pedagogy is to treat students' ideas, values, and experiences as assets in the classroom. There will be times, however, when their ideas have to be unpacked and gently but firmly held up to known data and logical argument. This is the norm for a knowledge-building community. Even when you do this, it may not affect students' thinking in the moment, but over the course of a unit or the school year, it can cause them to revisit their own arguments and try out different stances about climate change.

1. Make the classroom a safe place to share ideas and change your mind. Make it a norm for students to revise their thinking in response to new ideas or arguments from peers. You can reinforce this by asking different versions of: "So, are you making some adjustments in your explanation? Can you share what might be changing your mind?" Don't single out or confront students, telling them they are wrong. This is a breach of trust and can silence them ("That was humiliating; I'm not going to open my mouth again"). Rather, acknowledge the legitimacy of the other's viewpoint (not necessarily the accuracy) and focus on a give-and-take dialogue because this creates more positive experiences that are influential in shaping students' knowledge and climate concerns.[37] Such dialogue

could still address misinformation by providing scientifically grounded facts, but you'd want to couch these interventions with genuine care for what others are thinking and feeling.

2. Understanding students' beliefs can also help you select instructive stories about how particular kinds of evidence (related to these beliefs) are collected and used to make claims about the current or past climate.[38] This is more purposeful than simply dismissing students' conceptions, patching one kind of knowledge on top of another, or worse, suggesting young learners are climate illiterate. This highlights the importance of using inclusive language and avoiding the stigmatization of groups for holding beliefs contrary to science.[39]

3. Lead off units by providing a context for the anchoring event in nontechnical language, without explaining it for students. This allows you to frame the initial climate messages and expectations for dialogue—without getting into someone else's talking points.

4. Be proactive about a few places where the skeptics like to argue. The most common are: (a) the role of carbon dioxide in amplifying the greenhouse effect, (b) attributing extreme weather to climate change, and (c) whether current climate cycles are simply part of long-term natural ups and downs. If you have to budget your prep time to gather additional preemptive evidence to share with the class, these three ideas may be good places to invest your effort. Students are far less likely to have denialist talking points ready about other downstream effects like ocean acidification or ecosystem disruption.

5. If a student disagrees with an explanation or the veracity of evidence being used, gently ask them to provide justification for what they are saying.[40] When you need to talk about what scientists think, use messaging that emphasizes how they arrive at their conclusions. This helps students understand how claims are supported and also signals to them that you respect their ability to understand the uses of evidence and argument. Cast this as sharing available knowledge and ways of knowing. Just don't fall into the trap of giving equal time to contrarian views.

6. Give your students multiple lessons to explore climate-related topics. The truth is always more complicated than glib snippets of disinformation and slack arguments. This will allow space for everyone to test and

develop a set of ideas and explanations, grounded in evidence, that reinforce one another. If you merely describe complex topics or rush through
them, students will perceive the message as "take it from me, this is the
truth."

7. Don't be a climate alarmist. You will have to be honest about climate-
related events like species extinctions or sea level rise; just don't harp on
the worst possible future outcomes. Help students understand what is
happening now, with facts, observations, stories, and data from the past
and present.

8. Many of our teachers have used a bit of forgivable misdirection when addressing climate change with students. They spend a few days exploring
the greenhouse effect, for example, without ever mentioning the phrase
"climate change." They have students analyze historical data on both
carbon dioxide and global temperatures over the past 200 years and
discuss how various gases in Earth's atmosphere re-radiate energy from
the sun. In most cases, students feel that the science sounds reasonable,
not realizing that they are co-constructing the foundational mechanisms
of atmospheric warming. There are no studies we are aware of that can
point to the effectiveness of this strategy, but even if anecdotal, it may be
worth considering.

I've not included lessons on media literacy, especially teaching students
to seek out scientific studies on their own to bolster arguments. Locating and
evaluating new information are crucial practices for science learners, but in
the case of climate change, students should be looking at synthesis studies
rather than individual investigations. They should be given reputable places to
search for these (NOAA, WMO, USGS, etc.) and explore within those carefully curated spaces. Several media literacy recommendations are not feasible
for K–12 students seeking climate-related studies. Among these are asking
yourself: "Are these authors experts in their fields?" "Was the data collected
in a way that allows their claims to be credible?" or "Are their claims valid?"
Even scientists reading outside their own subspecialties would have trouble
answering these questions.

Let's also be clear that old-school show-and-tell teaching strategies about
climate change will land on the floor with a thud. They set up the teacher as
an authority figure instead of a co-inquirer. They dismiss students' experiences

and discourage meaning-making. What the teaching strategies above do is help a larger proportion of your students entertain different ways of looking at why events and processes happen in the natural world. One teacher responding to a national survey said it best: "We must learn to balance 'validating' students' rights to speak their mind with the need to teach evidence-based reasoning. Understand that we are opening students' minds to consider [that] what they hear in media or at home may be only partly accurate."[41]

CHAPTER 6

It Matters How You Frame the Story

INTENTIONALLY OR NOT, we frame climate change lessons for our students as if we were positioning a movie camera, deciding what will be in the foreground and what will be left as a blur in the distance.[1] We also make decisions, often without realizing it, about the language we use or which examples we choose that send messages to students about the relationships between humans and the environment, as well as who or what is responsible for the mess we're in.

Some teachers rely exclusively on standards to shape climate-related instruction, which can lead them to portray Earth systems disruptions as mundane science problems, stripped of social context that can make abstractions like the greenhouse effect or deforestation more meaningful.[2] The science, by itself, does not explain what's happening to us. In other cases, teachers frame the crisis by saying that all of humanity is responsible for and equally impacted by climate change. This acknowledges the role of our species (the "Anthro" in Anthropocene) but forecloses on conversations about who contributes most to global carbon emissions and which human populations are most vulnerable to looming environmental risks.[3] Teachers refer to the notions of "industrialization" and "excess carbon dioxide" as root causes of atmospheric warming, without referring to human choices and corporate culpability, now or historically.[4] This framing situates humans outside and separate from the

113

climate system, which, in turn, keeps students from considering how social and political inaction perpetuates the multiple crises we face.[5] Speaking of exclusion, when traditional scientific inquiry is elevated as the only tool for learning about climate phenomena or sustainability, then other powerful ways of knowing, particularly Indigenous epistemologies, are left out. If we become more conscious of the frames we use, we can expand the range of meanings that students make of new ideas, including the way they think about historical causes and potential solutions for climate-related challenges.

Skeptics may trivialize framing as a teacher's preferred spin on various topics; however, the goal here is not to indoctrinate students. Rather, we want them to adopt critical habits of mind by looking at issues in versatile ways that allow insights into the climate crisis which would otherwise remain outside the frame and not part of the dialogue.[6]

This chapter lays out three frames for this work: (1) telling a human story, (2) connecting humans to the environment and the chain of life that affects us all, and (3) pushing toward explanations that integrate science with social justice. These are intended to be generative rather than constraining, fostering new points of view and occasionally challenging less critical perspectives that render invisible the experiences of certain groups of people. Productive framing is also about working with the many assets that students bring to class—their existing knowledge and values from previous instruction, friends, family, and community. These frames make clear whose ways of knowing and histories have been marginalized, and at what cost.

TELLING A HUMAN STORY

Teachers can be experts at unpacking dramatic climate change stories with students, but they're less comfortable asking questions about human impacts. It seems dicey to open a discussion in which there is lots of ambiguity, no right answers, and a few trapdoors. But I've also seen some teachers be up front about the difficulty of these conversations, which students appreciated and which motivated them to share their thinking.

There is no shortage of human stories that can make climate and sustainability more meaningful for students. One example is to incorporate narratives of how weather extremes take a toll on people's well-being. Documented accounts of these cases are now plentiful online; it's just a matter of strategic selection. Our example draws on the catastrophic California wildfires that consumed more than 3,500 square miles of forest in 2021, along with hundreds of homes. These fires can serve as a context for students to learn about weather extremes, ecosystem disruptions, and impacts on human communities. Almost all of California's ecosystems are fire-dependent or fire-adapted. Fire-dependent ecosystems need wildfires to maintain natural function and health, while fire-adapted ecosystems don't benefit from periodic burns but have evolved to survive them.[7] Despite these adaptations, when forests endure intense and repeated wildfires, it can undermine biodiversity through permanent loss of native vegetation, opportunistic invasions of non-native species, and long-term loss of habitat for native fauna.

I draw from a *New York Times* article published in 2020, to pivot from the enormity of those fires to the intimate human experiences of those living with risks that are literally "in the air."[8] Javier is a seventh grader who lives with his parents and two younger siblings in California's Central Valley. His neighborhood is surrounded by roads with lots of traffic and agricultural fields that churn up clouds of dust. The valley itself acts as a pool for emissions from cars and factories, trapped by a layer of warm air that is generated by the 3.5 million residents of Fresno and surrounding cities. This is bad news for Javier because he has asthma. There have been times when the air is so dense with particulates that he struggles to breathe or comes down with respiratory infections. Increasingly, wildfires are adding to his miseries.

The fires in his area were precipitated by successive summer heat waves as temperatures routinely peaked above 100 °F with no relief from rain. Then, in mid-August, fires erupted to the north and east, pouring smoke into the valley. Ash settled on every tree, and Javier thought the air smelled like charcoal. Even by mid-October, when the smoke had subsided enough for his mother to propose a family bike ride, all he could see of the horizon was a gray smear. Fresno County endured more hazardous smoke days than any other in California that year, capping a steady climb over the past decade, according to data collected from NOAA. Figure 6.1 shows that, for three months, there were only a few days when the air was healthy to breathe.[9] Soot generated by these fires added to the stress from the ever-present industrial pollution.

In the figure, PM2.5 refers to atmospheric particulate matter that has a diameter of less than 2.5 micrometers, which is about 3 percent that of a human

Figure 6.1 Fresno daily average: Fine particulate pollution (PM$_{2.5}$)

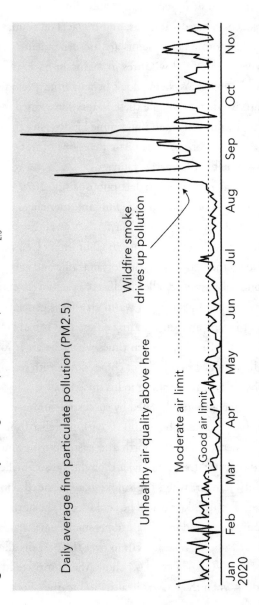

Source: Somini Sengupta, "Wildfire Smoke Is Poisoning California's Kids. Some Pay a Higher Price," *New York Times,* November 26, 2020, https://www.nytimes.com/interactive/2020/11/26/climate/california-smoke-children-health.html; California Air Resources Board; EPA Air Quality Index.

hair. These particles can come from power plants, motor vehicles, residential wood burning, dust storms, and of course, forest fires. Some pollutants are emitted directly into the air, while others are formed when gases and particles interact with one another in the atmosphere. For example, gaseous sulfur dioxide emitted from power plants reacts with oxygen and water droplets in the air to form sulfuric acid. Since they are so light, these particles tend to stay aloft for days, increasing the chances of humans and other animals inhaling them. Being exposed to air in the "unhealthy" range in figure 6.1 risks aggravation of heart or lung disease, premature death in persons with cardiopulmonary disease, and increased respiratory effects in the general population.[10] Children are advised against prolonged exertion or outdoor activity.

Javier's mother, who is studying public health, wants local officials to do more to mitigate the risks to children in the area by reducing traffic when wildfire smoke makes air pollution worse. She also wants improvements in the ventilation systems of local schools. For now, it's up to her to adapt in whatever ways she can. She closes the windows of their two-bedroom home so outdoor air doesn't get in. She changes the air-conditioner filter often and lugs an air purifier from room to room. Javier offered this advice: "If you had a child with asthma or any person in your house with asthma and you wanted to move into this area, it's not a good idea."

Cases like this, with all its humanizing details, make clear the serious downstream consequences of climate change events for people in ways that not many students—or adults—are fully aware of. I have seen teachers insert these kinds of accounts at the beginning of units on weather or ecosystems to draw students into initial conversations about the different ways they might be impacted by a changing climate. Alternatively, teachers can introduce a story like this in the middle of a unit, after students have learned about ecosystem responses to severe weather and drought. They then have them read about Javier's family and ask, "Who is being harmed, why, and what might some solutions be?" or "Can any of the impacts be mitigated or does Javier's family just have to adapt?" Some students have ended up focusing on the agency of Javier's mother and her efforts to reduce the effects of air pollution by pressuring local officials to reduce traffic at certain times of year or demand that the air in schools is healthy to breathe. Other students focus on climate conditions that lead to the wildfires and the level of action needed to prevent droughts or the accumulation of volatile tinder on the forest floors. Each of these conversations is like a sensemaking tool that helps students make sense of the others.

The science that is made relevant by this case can be found in the standards of most states, some of which deal with extreme weather, with ecosystem disruptions, and with the impact of climate change on humans. Stories like Javier's don't detract from these ideas; they give meaning to seemingly remote events. Teachers could ask: "What counts as a 'natural' hazard, given how humans influence drought conditions?" "Should we be focusing our attention on technologies to mitigate the effects of wildfires or on the human behaviors that make them more likely?" "Is it unjust that only certain communities bear the burdens of industrial pollution and threats from climate-induced wildfires?"

When searching for stories to use, don't wait until you find the perfect example. Observations of classrooms tell us that most narratives of people or communities connected to the science phenomena, even tangentially, are good enough to generate enthusiastic conversations among students. The human dimension makes students more invested in explaining what is causing the problem or helping redefine what they think the root causes are. And of course, some learners simply appreciate the opportunity to use science ideas for open discussions about families under stress.

In your curriculum, there has to be a balance between exploring climate change on the local level and linking back to planetary processes. This coupling is critical for students to grasp the scope of climate change and realize it is not affecting everyone equally. As these wildfires become commonplace in California, they are also ravaging Italy, Algeria, Turkey, and Australia. This list grows longer each year.

CONNECT HUMANS TO THE ENVIRONMENT AND THE CHAIN OF LIFE THAT AFFECTS US ALL

As we learned in the previous chapter, students come to us with worldviews about the relationship between humans and the environment that are still being formed. This means we have opportunities to challenge the taken-for-granted frames that dominate cultural discourses about human exceptionalism and nature simply as a place to visit or extract resources from. Viewing humans as superior among all species and distinct from nature has set the stage for unprecedented anthropogenic damage and its disproportionate effects on populations already on the margins of survival. In our classrooms, we can challenge these worldviews by foregrounding our kinship with animals, plants, and the larger environment.[11] Students can draw new understandings of these relationships and their role in generating more sustainable worlds from Indigenous knowledge systems that prioritize interconnections between humans, our more-than-human relatives, and future generations.[12]

To understand these worldviews, it is important to understand Indigenous histories. When settlers arrived in North America, they regarded it as terra nullius, or "nobody's land." Ignoring the fact that Indigenous peoples had been living here for thousands of years, settlers felt it was their land to colonize and "develop." Colonization is an ongoing phenomenon, happening around the world. It has come to mean any kind of external control, and it is used as an expression for the subordination of native peoples to those of wealthier nations. The colonial legacy is experienced through ecological damage that includes pollution, toxic waste, mining, desertification, deforestation, land degradation, and so on. These damages are a consequence of extractive capitalism and economic growth ideologies; they end up reproducing racial harms to entire countries in the Global South and communities of color in the Global North.[13] Climate coloniality now takes the form of land and water grabs, rare earth mineral mining, appropriating fossil fuel reserves, and so-called green revolutions for industrial-level agriculture—all of which benefit a few while dispossessing historically impoverished communities. To be colonized is to be made to feel less-than, to be told what the truths are, and ultimately to be dehumanized. Indigenous scholars refer to the colonial wound as engraved in bodies and minds, a slow violence. For many reasons, we should be listening to peoples who have lived in harmony with the land for millennia and we should be supporting the rights of Indigenous peoples to manage lands as well as sustain their cultures. Let's return now to the worldviews that can guide the restoration of our Earth systems.

Many Indigenous peoples consider themselves part of an extended ecological family that shares ancestry and similar origins. Within this view, environments thrive when humans treat the life surrounding them as relatives; these include not only animals and plants, but water, air, the land, and the sun. This "kincentric ecology" sustains all life and gives it purpose.[14] For example, the Laguna Pueblo of the southwest United States believe they could not have become part of the living world without the recognition that humans were "sisters and brothers to the badger, antelope, clay and yucca."[15] Their origin stories recount how it was not until they became aware of this that the Laguna people emerged into the world. From the kincentric perspective, humans have equal, not superior, standing with the rest of the natural world. All life, including us, are relations and in reciprocal obligation to one another.

Humans, then, are not passive recipients of the Earth's gifts, but stewards—active participants in its well-being.[16] The Pasto people of the Atriz Valley in Colombia see their land "as a living being, a being that, according to the law of origin, feels, listens, produces sounds, gets sick and is restored."[17] In some of the most biodiverse places on Earth, native communities are responsible for taking care of local ecosystems and have developed practices for making the land and life more resilient.[18] It is fortunate, in fact, that Indigenous peoples manage over 20 percent of the planet's land, including upward of 40 percent of protected areas. Indigenous communities everywhere have specialized knowledge of these interrelationships to revitalize the land with practices such as controlled burning and pruning vegetation to promote new growth, methods for carbon sequestration, the creation of new habitat, and agroforestry. These and hundreds of other specialized practices demonstrate how Indigenous stewardship of the land preserves biodiversity; without it, ecosystems fall apart.

When teaching our children, Western science is, by itself, inadequate to the imposing task of helping them learn to live in relation with ecologically damaged landscapes and taking action to restore them. As educators, we need to understand how different knowledge systems are used for these aims. Indigenous science is a "high-context" body of knowledge developed over generations by culturally distinct peoples living in close contact with the land.[19] Indigenous peoples pass down information-rich stories from one generation to the next using cultural languages and symbolism that are built into the oral tradition. Knowledge is put to use for sustainability and is specific to a tribal culture and environment, rather than being generalizable to all situations and places, as is the aim with Western science.

Indigenous science shares many of the same knowledge-building practices with Western science, including observing, interpreting, questioning, classifying, predicting, and problem-solving.[20] Indigenous science, however, focuses simultaneously on all relational connections that comprise the environment, within which humans are one species in the larger chain of life.[21] These knowledge systems are used to ensure the flourishing of their communities' health and to preserve self-determination of their future.[22] Māori communities in New Zealand, for example, have worked for generations to repair socio-environmental relationships through urban restoration projects, protecting waterways, regenerating forests, and rethinking food systems.

Teaching with this hybrid science lens and using authentic case studies of communities dealing with climate vulnerabilities can generate unexpected tensions in the classroom, but some tensions can foster new insights. In chapter 2, we were introduced to a middle-grades unit based on the book *My Wounded Island*, a story of an Inuit girl—Imarvaluk—living on the tiny island of Sarichef, which she refers to as "an ink stain near the Artic Circle." People in her village believe that a monster is slowly devouring the island, jeopardizing their relationships with the sea and with animals that sustain her people. Her grandfather despairs that "even winter is retreating." He means the sea ice that had protected their shoreline from powerful waves was now diminishing each year, leaving the land vulnerable to erosion and preventing hunters from venturing out on the ice to find seals for food. The two teachers who designed this unit, Jessica and Colleen, posed these essential questions for their students: "Why does Imarvaluk believe there is a monster?" "What is happening on her island that gives evidence for this and what is happening far away that ends up damaging the island?" The kinship and caretaking ethos of these Indigenous peoples is not sentimentalized in the book; there is disharmony in the environment, even threatening forces that have their origins thousands of miles away. The ties of interdependence the islanders have with the sea are being strained by long-term shifts in climate. Perhaps this is why the students were so invested in finding explanations.

The teachers found online video of other communities in Alaska and Canada that are impacted and who now publicly share how their cultures feel the strain of climate change. Students learned how these Indigenous communities developed deep knowledge of seasonal changes on land and in the sea. But the teachers also wanted them to dive deeper into the cultural knowledge shared in these communities, asking: "What roles do human memory and tradition play in this story?" Students were constantly looking for clues, from both Western science and Indigenous knowledge systems, even though they did not use these terms. Jessica and Colleen could see that this unit, more than any other, moved their students toward action they could take in their own communities. This included making their family and neighbors aware of the effects of climate change in faraway places, advocating for sustainable local practices, even encouraging the use of little free libraries in their neighborhoods so that people would not burn the fuel necessary to package the books and transport them to their doorstep.

We need to be vigilant about how classroom conversations on the environment unfold, perhaps even framing them differently. Too often, dialogue about the natural world begins with references to its value and the services it provides us from an anthropocentric point of view. Only then might the talk extend outward to include the interdependencies we have with nonhuman life and the land itself.[23] In contrast, Indigenous philosophy tends to work the other way around—it starts with the idea that everything matters in some way. The challenge then is to figure out *how things matter, how they fit together* within a network of relationships, how to navigate challenges that arise, and what decisions have to be made, given that the goal is to ensure that relationships among people are strengthened, as are the relationships between people and nature.

In our curriculum, we can likely find places to braid together Indigenous ecological knowledge and Western science in order to understand phenomena, but perhaps more importantly, we can model how to embrace Indigenous worldviews to frame our relationship with the environment. From the science perspective, we believe students could deepen knowledge of their interdependencies with plants and animals, but also with the land, water, sun, and air, blurring the boundaries between the living and nonliving. From a framing perspective, we could help students value the environment in different ways, not because it represents resources to extract, but because we have responsibilities to care for the well-being of the more-than-human parts of the Earth, just as it takes care of us.

If we could help young learners use the lenses of caretaking together with scientific inquiry for reformulating climate change problems and reimagining solutions, and give them different kinds of language to engage in dialogue with others about these issues, it could lay the groundwork for inspired and more informed restorative action by their generation.

PUSH TOWARD EXPLANATIONS THAT REFLECT SOCIAL JUSTICE

One of the widespread half-truths about climate change is that everyone will have their lives disrupted. Although this is accurate, the burdens of the crisis will not be distributed equally across nations or neighborhoods. The wealthy and well-connected will be buffered, at least temporarily, from life-changing impacts, while millions of others will struggle to survive. When teachers choose to connect science with human narratives of risk, we've seen that most students can anticipate who will be more vulnerable and who will have the means to protect their livelihoods. There are endless ways to weave together accounts of people who are subject to climate-related injustices—for example, losing access to fresh water, breathable air, or the energy resources to carry on daily life—with the science that explains how other people's carbon-intensive lives amplify the risks for everyone. You can probably tell how this frame overlaps with the previous two, but it explicitly addresses justice and further expands students' understanding about the kinds of problems that science, by itself, cannot solve.

We can start this by developing case studies of complex phenomena (natural or anthropogenically driven) in which our students build two kinds of explanations over time. One would be a causal story using concepts from biology, the earth sciences, chemistry, or physics. The other explanation would describe how certain groups of people are exposed to a variety of risks that can destabilize their lives. If you feel underprepared to tackle this, you are not alone. Most of us have a thin understanding of the conditions that put groups of people in danger; just search online for "climate justice" and you'll find enough material to construct a case, perhaps a local one, that your students will find compelling.

When exploring topics at the intersection of science and justice, students often lack ways to think about how systems and structures cause problems, and like many adults, they may blame individuals for their life choices.[24] When we assume that a social problem is the fault of those most directly affected by it, we become blind to the true root causes—limited health care, food insecurity, and lack of affordable housing; underlying much of this is racism. These structural conditions are like causal mechanisms for science phenomena—not always visible, but powerful in driving outcomes we can see and recognize. If these forces are dismissed as irrelevant, then potential solutions for redress or resilience will simply be misguided. Telling a human story about climate-disrupted lives must include the science, but also the experiences of marginalized communities that should have a voice in restorative action plans.

The following example is from a unit on extreme weather and human heat exposure. Heat kills more people in the United States than hurricanes, tornadoes, and other more spectacular weather events, contributing to over 12,000 deaths per year.[25] Higher temperatures can strain the heart and make breathing more difficult, increasing hospitalization rates for cardiac arrest and respiratory diseases like asthma. Even small differences can be dangerous. During a heat wave, every one-degree increase elevates the risk of dying by 2.5 percent.[26]

Urban areas have been known as heat islands since the early twentieth century. In the early morning of May 12, 1927, Wilhelm Schmidt began a three-hour journey by car through the streets of Vienna with a thermometer secured to a pole above his door. He recorded the time, temperature, and details of the local environment at hundreds of points along his route.[27] Then he mapped these data; the result was a visual portrayal of the urban heat field, showing higher temperature coinciding with "tightly built parts of the inner city," and then a "sea" of cooler surroundings in the woods, meadows, vineyards, and watercourses.

We now know that in urban neighborhoods, trees can lower air temperature by 10 lifesaving degrees Fahrenheit, in part because leaves and branches greatly reduce how much solar radiation reaches the ground.[28] In the summertime, only 10 to 30 percent of the sun's energy penetrates the canopy, with much of it absorbed for photosynthesis and some reflected back into the atmosphere.[29] But this is only part of trees' cooling power. They also evaporate water, pulling it from the ground and releasing it through their leaves into the air. That's why walking through a forest or just sitting in a park surrounded by large trees feels so refreshing. Tree cover reduces electricity demand for

air conditioning, sparing money and emissions as well as helping avoid catastrophic power failures during heat waves. If all that wasn't enough, trees also
filter out air pollution, absorb storm water, nurture wildlife, and even improve
people's mental health.

Not everyone, however, lives in a green neighborhood. Across the country,
in cities like Baltimore, Denver, Portland, and New York, sections of town
that are poorer and have more residents of color can be 5 °F to 20 °F hotter in
summer than wealthier, Whiter parts of the same city.[30] How does this happen? The science explanation includes the effects that tree canopies have on
shielding surfaces like houses, concrete, and asphalt from the sun's radiation,
and the cooling from evaporation. The social explanation for why communities of color have to endure hotter temperatures is a different kind of cause-
and-effect story. In the twentieth century, local and federal officials in many
US cities enacted policies that reinforced racial segregation and diverted investment away from minority neighborhoods in ways that created disparities
in the urban heat environment. Black neighborhoods, no matter their income
level, were mapped and then outlined in red, marking them as "hazardous"
areas for housing loans. In many cities, appraisers' notes made clear that race
was the key factor in downgrading these neighborhoods. White neighborhoods, on the other hand, were often outlined in blue or green and were given
priority for capital investment.

One hundred years later, formerly redlined neighborhoods remain lower
income and are more likely to have Black or Hispanic residents.[31] They have
far fewer trees and parks that help cool the air; they also have more paved
parking lots and nearby highways that absorb and re-radiate heat. Home appraisers in Richmond, Virginia, were especially transparent in their racism as
they mapped the city in the 1930s. Neighborhoods to Richmond's west that
were outlined in green on the old maps remained wealthier and predomi-
nantly White, with trees and parks covering 42 percent of the land. Neighborhoods in Richmond's east and south that were once redlined are today
still poorer and majority Black, with much lower rates of homeownership and
green space covering just 12 percent of the surface. This legacy is reflected
in figure 6.2, which shows these districts in bold outline and the differences
in their amount of tree cover (shaded in) as compared with other residential
neighborhoods in areas to the north and west of downtown.

Figure 6.2 Map of Richmond redlining and tree cover

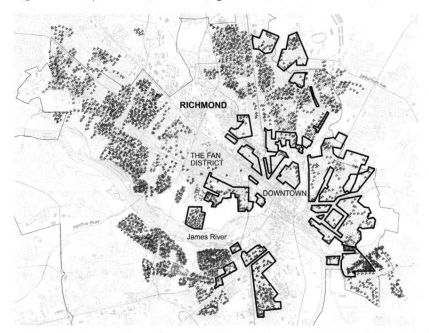

Source: Adapted from Brad Plumer and Nadja Popovich, "How Decades of Racist Housing Policy Left Neighborhoods Sweltering," *New York Times,* August 24, 2020.

To find tolerable temperatures in the summer, forty-year-old resident Imani James often takes her two young boys on a half-hour walk from her formerly redlined neighborhood across Richmond to a tree-lined park in an affluent section of town.[32] Her local playground provides little shade, leaving the climbing equipment and slides hot to the touch. James feels it's worth it to find a cooler play area, even if it means a long journey on foot with children in tow, because daytime temperatures regularly soar past 95 °F:

> The heat gets really intense, I'm just zapped of energy by the end of the day. Once we get to that park, I'm struck by how green the space is. I feel calmer, better able to breathe. Walking through different neighborhoods, there's a stark difference between places that have lots of greenery and places that don't.

In the places that don't have grass and tree canopies, there is little to shield people from the sun's relentless glare. Adding to the urban heat island effect are front yards paved with concrete, miles of asphalt roadways, and lots of commercial buildings. This also takes a serious toll on James's neighbors. Her

ZIP code has among the highest rates of heat-related ambulance calls in the city. Today, satellite analyses reveal that Richmond's formerly redlined neighborhoods, like James's, occasionally endure temperatures 15 °F higher than other parts of town.

Students seeking to understand why this is happening would have to address two interwoven explanations. One is the science behind urban heat islands, which would involve ideas about the absorption and re-radiation of different forms of energy as well as the cooling evapo-transpiration by trees that cycles water from the ground through their tissues and out into the air. The other explanation requires students to understand why people of color have less access to livable neighborhoods in terms of temperature, water quality, fresh food, and freedom from environmental pollution. Teachers are not always comfortable drawing these two kinds of explanations together with students, and for some of us, it is a sign of our privilege that we've been able to opt out of such conversations. But if we want science to mean something to young learners—like James's sons—we can't strip it of its social context.

SUMMING UP

The three frames explored in this chapter can foster students' more expansive perspectives and allow problems of injustice and limited eco-worldviews to come into focus (see table 6.1). These frames humanize the science and invite students to test out alternative ways of conceptualizing how the world works. The kinds of teaching proposed in this chapter represent transformative work, a way of co-creating with young learners a just and more sustainable future. It allows students to question, provoke responses from others, demand, listen, appreciate, and reflect on our (differently) shared realities.[33]

Teaching should be intentionally designed for such outcomes, yet we should approach these pedagogies with eyes wide open. Balancing science with justice means that we'll relate to our own students differently and have conversations that are difficult because of the unsparing candor required. Humility is essential in this effort—there will be fewer moments of satisfaction that some set of ideas has been "covered" or even understood similarly by all our students. For both you and your students, leaving the classroom puzzled and concerned about problems you had never thought about before are signs of learning and hope.

Table 6.1 Framing the climate story: What we should move away from and toward?

Key questions	Moving away from		Moving toward
What is the human relationship with the environment?	Environment is wilderness, a place to visit, or a collection of exploitable resources and services.	⇨	The environment is alive, inseparable from us, and critical for our survival; one of our primary roles should be respectful stewardship.
What knowledge about sustainability is valued?	Knowledge of natural systems generated by Western science is authoritative, sufficient unto itself, and can be universally applied to solve problems anywhere in the world.	⇨	Diverse forms of knowledge are needed to deepen our understanding of climate change and our role in it. Traditional science must be in dialogue with Indigenous science to work with place-based knowledge, built up over generations, and to think relationally about the environment.
Why are different people at risk?	Industrialization and GHG emissions are the root causes and put everyone at risk.	⇨	People and organizations with power make decisions that perpetuate the environmental crisis. Nondominant groups of people throughout the world are more vulnerable to climate risks due to being socially and politically marginalized. These forms of oppression are rooted in racism.
Where and who will solutions come from?	We will engineer our way out of this. Technology will solve ecological problems through innovation, efficiency, and managerial means. We have time to hold off on changes in how we live and can resist "radical" social initiatives aimed at sustainability.	⇨	Fundamental changes are needed in how we live, use land, work, eat, transport ourselves, and treat ecosystems. Solutions will be sparked by an informed and activist public, including children of present and future generations.

CHAPTER 7

How Do We
Know That Happened?

Reconstructing the Past to
Understand the Present

HERE'S A SIMPLE CHAIN OF LOGIC for teaching climate change: if we want students to understand what the future holds, they will have to grasp what's happening with Earth systems in the present. However, the present becomes meaningful and predictive only if we can find out how past climate conditions such as temperature, CO_2 levels, and precipitation influenced one another.[1] Because natural planetary changes unfold on immense time scales, scientists have to rely on evidence that was generated centuries or many millennia ago to make sense of the past and to offer conjectures about the future. The past, present, and future can be understood only in relation to one another.

I made a visit to Jessica's seventh-grade classroom to see firsthand how a little exposure to scientific models provokes student questions about the past. They were being shown an animated timeline graph that depicted global levels of carbon dioxide, starting at the present day—about 420 ppm—and slowly working *backward* in time. For starters, a close-up of only the last two years of emission levels rolled onto the screen (top panel of figure 7.1). Students could

Figure 7.1 Carbon dioxide levels in most recent two years, since 1970, and over past 800,000 years

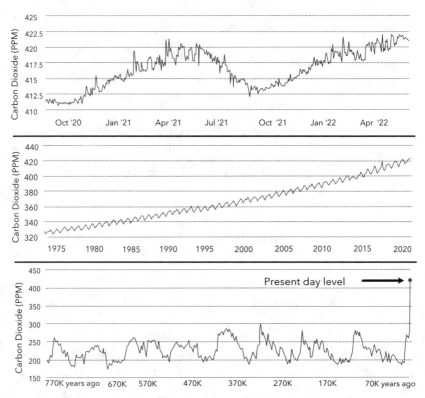

readily see CO_2 going up and down in seasonal cycles (more atmospheric CO_2 is present when forests experience winter in the Global North). Slowly, the view panned outward to show about 1970 to the present. Students noticed that it now looked like a different graph (middle panel), taking on a stairstep pattern with an unmistakably upward arc, while the seasonal ups and downs became less pronounced. After a few minutes, the view expanded to show 800,000 BCE (before current era) to the present. Again, it seemed to become a different graph. Students could now see cycles of extreme highs and lows that lasted hundreds of thousands of years (lower panel). They leaned forward to recheck the x-axis, and one boy shouted, "Where is that data from? There is no way to have data from that long ago!" Other students were puzzled. To put the present day back into historical context, Jessica reoriented her students, pointing out the tiny space where the graph had started, our most recent few years, in which the CO_2 level was now standing out as a towering, vertical line on the far right of the figure.

What kinds of evidence do scientists draw on to make claims about this world that existed hundreds of thousands of years ago? This chapter explains how we can know about a past that extends back before human records and before humans themselves. This knowledge is necessary for students to make sense of the ways today's climate cycles are anthropogenically skewed and to perhaps address the denialist argument that dramatic climate shifts we're seeing now are simply the product of natural variation, part of the Earth's up and downs that will swing back to normal in a human lifetime.

PALEOCLIMATOLOGY AS A TOOL FOR RECONSTRUCTING THE PAST

In the early 1990s, scientists began a series of unprecedented studies into the diverse physical, chemical, and biological traces that the ancient climate has left behind. Clues were found in caves, tree rings, coral reefs, lake sediments, and ice cores. Let's take glaciers as an example, in which ice (snow compacted over time) has accumulated in layers for hundreds of thousands of years. Researchers have developed methods of analyzing the contents of glacial ice that provide a wealth of new data about the history of Earth's temperature, atmospheric composition, ocean levels, and more. Some of the first samples were extracted in Greenland by drilling to a remarkable depth of 3,000 meters. Ice from these cores provided a record of climate conditions going back 100,000 years. Shortly after, a French-Russian team working in the Vostok region of Antarctica extracted and analyzed a core that was 420,000 years old at its deepest point. Climate writer Ian Angus described how data from the Vostok study were "arguably among the most important produced by the global change scientific community in the twentieth century."[2] More recent drilling has nearly doubled the reach of the climate record, back to 800,000 years. This research has revolutionized our understanding of Earth's past—and consequently of Earth's present and future(s).[3]

If we share these stories with students, they'll deserve more of the logic behind claims based on such exotic forms of evidence. After all, these ice cores and other traces of the past do not speak for themselves. How do we know that these artifacts tell us anything about the ancient conditions that existed and when? For this, we turn to paleoclimatology. Similar to the way archaeologists study fossils and other physical clues to gain insight into the prehistoric past, paleoclimatologists study different types of environmental evidence to understand what the Earth's past climate was like. This evidence comes from proxy data—indirect records of climate, imprinted on different parts of the biological and geophysical environment.[4] The word "proxy" is colloquially defined as an intermediary or substitute—often in reference to a person given the authority to speak on behalf of someone else. Proxy data, therefore, are pieces of information that substitute for direct observations of the Earth's ancient climate.

To do these kinds of analyses, scientists need to find material traces of the past that: (1) have survived, (2) can be dated, and (3) contain something they can measure that would have responded to a variable they are interested in (e.g., past temperature, precipitation). Scientists can use such records to estimate past *conditions* like rain or snow amounts, humidity, sea level, or the composition of our atmosphere. These extend our understanding of climate back hundreds to millions of years. Proxy data can also provide insights into a range of climate-relevant *changes*. These include sudden events like volcanic eruptions or major floods, and more gradual long-term trends such as warming and cooling, drought, cyclone patterns, monsoon seasons, fluctuating atmospheric carbon dioxide, or thinning ice sheets.

Knowing past climate conditions and how they changed helps us put current conditions on Earth in perspective. Proxies can tell us, for example, whether current rising air temperatures are on a long-term upward trajectory, or part of a regularly occurring up-down cycle, or simply an anomaly of the past century. Knowing the long-term picture is also the only way to test alternative theories about temperature shifts being caused by minor perturbations in the orbit of the earth (called Milankovitch cycles), the changing energy output from the sun, or a combination of these factors.

The study of paleoclimates has been particularly helpful in showing how the Earth can shift dramatically between different climate states in a matter of years. For example, tree-ring and lake sediment records from North America show that decade-scale "megadroughts" have occurred abruptly and multiple times over the last thousand years. Research has also revealed several periods of global warming alternating with several ice ages in Earth's history. Importantly, these data have cast doubt on the idea that the Earth acts as a self-correcting system, using different feedback mechanisms to periodically move itself back to a state of equilibrium after disturbances. Rather, records show that the temperature and chemistry of the atmosphere, as well as the oceans, can be thrown into chaos for extended periods of time without kicking in any type of magical self-righting processes.[5]

Organizations like NOAA retain enormous proxy data sets covering more than a dozen categories. A search for "proxy data" on its website will help you find projects in every US state involving these kinds of measurements; each paints a picture of what the Earth was like long before records were kept. For example, off the coast of Monterey Bay in California, bamboo corals have revealed the chemistry of the water in that region from 1888 to 2008. All across Florida, from the Ocala National Forest to the banks of the Choctawhatchee River, tree rings have been used to estimate ancient temperature and precipitation patterns going back to 899 CE. At Summit Lake near Mount Zirkel in Colorado, sediments from three lakes were used to infer fire events over the past 2,500 years, going back to 930 BCE.[6] Every school district in the United States has, within arm's reach, access to some type of local paleoclimate data project and the people who run them.

In contrast to proxies, more modern data are part of what we refer to as the *instrumental record*, collected by human observation or more commonly through some sort of technology. These tools range from simple thermometers to high-tech satellite sensors that constantly monitor sea surface temperature, the health of coral reefs, forest fires, volcanic eruptions, and changes in global vegetation. Combining proxy data with instrumental data has helped scientists understand how factors such as the sun's energy output, greenhouses gases in the atmosphere, and variations in Earth's orbit have all affected the climate over time. Although this instrumental record is now diverse and massive, from a geological perspective it's merely a snapshot in time.

TYPES OF PROXY DATA AND WHAT THEY TELL US

When talking with students about paleo-evidence, it helps to develop a shared vocabulary. *Proxies* are the specific substances that are described and dated. *Archives* are the sampled materials that contain proxies.[7] Archives generally fall into one of four categories—biological, chemical, physical, or historical (documents). Examples from these categories show how creativity and imagi-nation play central roles in climate science. The archives and proxies in figure 7.2 are commonly used, but the list is not exhaustive. The top row in each box names a type of proxy; the bottom row indicates past events or conditions it provides clues for.

Historical Documents as Archives

It may seem odd to categorize human-recorded documents with other types of proxies that extend back millions of years, but these qualify because they provide *indirect* clues to environmental conditions of the past, and as such, sci-entists count them as part of the paleoclimate archive.[8] These sources include diaries, photographs, and even paintings that contain references to climate information. For hundreds of years, seafarers have kept ship's logs with de-tailed notes about wind, precipitation, and sea ice. During the Middle Ages, many rural estates in England kept farming records on the success of crops and milk production. Scientists use these records to piece together evidence of droughts that impacted the region hundreds of years ago. Old photographs and sketched maps have been used to document changes in the size of glaciers, which over time give clues to longer-term fluctuations in the climate.

Great Plains Indians created pictographic calendars on buffalo skin or cloth called *waniyetu wówapi* or "winter counts" to record natural events im-portant to them, from roughly the seventeenth through the nineteenth cen-turies.[9] Memorable phenomena include unusual weather, meteor storms, and eclipses. The Lakota and Sioux also recorded the impacts of these events. For example, tribal elder Baptiste Good in 1711 documented a flood and reported "four lodges drowned." Long Soldier in 1824 recorded "no snow" and a "sand-blowing year." These winter counts, in conjunction with proxy climate records and other historical documentation, preserve a unique record of some of the most unusual climate events of the early American period.

Biological Archives

In the fifteenth century, Leonardo da Vinci noticed that the thickness of tree rings—the concentric circles found running through a tree's trunk—varied with rainfall during the growing season.[10] Today, scientists can drill into a tree to extract a cross-sectional core from its trunk; they know that each ring

Figure 7.2 Proxy types and what they tell us

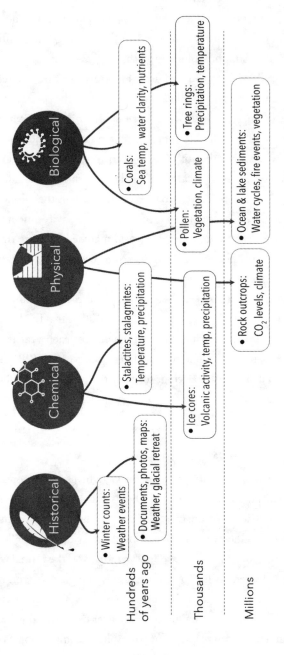

indicates a year of a tree's life and includes a light and dark part. The light part represents the rapid growth that occurs in the spring and early summer, while the dark part represents the slower growth of late summer and autumn. Rings will be wider in warm, wet years when the tree is getting sufficient sunshine and rainfall to support robust growth; rings will be narrower in response to stresses like drought, disease, damaging insects, or fire. The record embodied in these concentric rings will vary depending on the species of tree and where it is located—making it tricky to attribute their patterns to a single variable.

To draw out the climate data from cored samples, scientists first cross-date rings between a number of trees to identify the correct year for each ring. Then, using records of local weather data, scientists can calibrate the rings' widths against an observed climate record. This tells them how accurately that particular species of tree in that region reflects environmental conditions of the past. If the two data sources are well matched, the tree rings can be used to look further back, before the observed record began, to analyze the climate during the tree's full lifetime.

Using tree-ring analyses, scientists have created a record of drought frequency and intensity that covers the last 2,000 years. The longest continuous tree-ring record that includes measurements for each year is the astounding German oak-pine chronology that dates back to 10,400 BCE. But for most purposes, scientists use tree rings to study the past 500 to 2,000 years.[11] There are other bioarchives you could investigate, such as seal pelts or corals, but tree rings are the most versatile.

Chemical Archives

Perhaps the most revealing of all chemical archives are ice cores. At the Earth's extreme latitudes and altitudes, ice holds the only environmental data available for scientists to reconstruct the climate, hundreds to thousands of years ago.[12] Scientists have sampled ice from places as diverse as glaciers in the Andes of Peru, Mount Kilimanjaro in Tanzania, and the Himalayas in Asia. The cores are cylinders drilled out of ice sheets and glaciers, and can run several kilometers deep. This ice is built up from snowfall over thousands of years, with each layer compacting more tightly over time. Ice cores can tell scientists about temperatures, precipitation, atmospheric composition, volcanic activity, and even wind patterns. The thickness of each layer, for example, allows scientists to determine how much snow fell in the area during a particular year.

But how does this ice provide such a wide variety of clues? As snow accumulates, it also traps tiny bubbles of air or pollen from flowering plants—these are the actual proxies. The bubbles contain samples of the atmosphere captured over the life of the ice sheet or glacier. Analyzing along the depth of the core thus provides a centuries-long timeline of what's in these miniature gas pockets. This air contains different isotopes of oxygen, whose proportions can differ from year to year based on the surrounding environment. Isotopes are atoms of the same element, like oxygen, that are identical except for the different number of neutrons in the nucleus. Scientists are particularly interested in the oxygen isotopes ^{18}O and ^{16}O. The most abundant oxygen isotope is ^{16}O, which has a nucleus made up of eight neutrons and eight protons (all oxygen atoms have eight protons), giving it an atomic mass of 16. The isotope ^{18}O has two extra neutrons in the nucleus, giving it an atomic mass of 18. As a result, atoms of ^{18}O are very slightly heavier than ^{16}O. This seemingly small weight difference has implications when water is evaporated from the oceans and falls as snow at the Earth's poles, explains Dr. Robert Mulvaney, a glaciologist at the British Antarctic Survey: "Simply put, it takes more energy to evaporate the water molecules containing a heavier isotope [^{18}O] from the surface of the ocean, and, as the moist air is transported polewards and cools, the water molecules containing heavier isotopes are then more likely to fall to Earth as precipitation."[13]

The ratio of ^{18}O to ^{16}O in rain or snow then is controlled by temperature, humidity, and atmospheric circulation. Both evaporation and precipitation depend on the temperature, says Mulvaney, which means that the proportions of ^{18}O in ice cores can tell scientists how warm the climate was at that time in the past. The more ^{18}O in the sample, the warmer the atmosphere. Because isotopes can also provide climate information from any environment on Earth where there are archives of water or plant material, they are indispensable.

Physical Archives

Some of the most revealing physical archives are marine and lake sediments. Each year, billions of tons of materials from land surfaces are carried by wind and water into lakes and seas around the world. In the deep ocean, there falls a constant "marine snow," a mixed detritus of dead fish and plant bits, sand, soot, and excreta. These accumulate over time, adding layer upon layer with each year that passes. Here's where a familiar sampling technique comes in— drilling a core deep into the bed of an ocean or lake. Just as with tree cores or ice cores, what gets drilled out can show the makeup of time-matched sediments layered on top of one another. The size, color, density, and even magnetic properties of embedded materials can provide clues about where they came from (for example a volcanic eruption) and the environmental conditions at certain points in time.

In addition, all sorts of micro-fossils are found in these sediments. Foraminifera are a classic example, explains Dr. Paul Pearson from the School of Earth and Ocean Sciences at Cardiff University:

> Foraminifera are—mostly—microscopic shells secreted by single-celled organisms that live as plankton in or on the sea bed. In the right burial conditions, their shells can survive in virtually perfect condition indefinitely. These shells build up slowly on the seafloor producing a more or less continuous proxy record.[14]

Foraminifera build their shells from calcium carbonate extracted from the seawater. Isotope analysis that detects the amount of ^{18}O in these shells can reveal conditions in the ocean when the organism was alive and, by proxy, the climate. This type of proxy blurs the line between biological, physical, and chemical archives—these are fossil remnants of *living organisms* that are embedded in the *geological* sediment and analyzed at the *atomic level*.

Other types of micro-fossils, referred to as diatoms, are found in inland lakes. Diatoms are sensitive to changes in temperature, salinity, and other physical factors. Lake sediments, with their smaller footprint, are better suited than ocean sediments for reconstructing histories of local precipitation, and the diatoms they contain have been used to piece together historic records of extreme drought in the US Midwest.[15]

As any kind of proxy accumulates through natural processes, its records can extend back as far as that medium exists. The seabed has existed for a lot longer than trees, corals, or even ice sheets. Marine sedimentary records can reach back to the Cretaceous period—the time of the dinosaurs. For the isotopes in ice cores, they tell stories that go back as long as the ice sheet or glacier has been in place. To probe further back in Earth's climate history, paleoclimatologists resort to the oldest of proxies, explains Dr. Jessica Tierney from the University of Arizona: "To study climate changes before about 100 million years ago, we must work with rock formations on land, which contain marine or terrestrial sediments that have been lithified."[16] Lithification is the process by which sediments are compacted under pressure to form solid rock. This rock might naturally "outcrop" on the landscape, says Tierney, or scientists might drill into them to get a core. She adds: "In these ancient archives, we find evidence of truly extreme climate changes, like the end-Permian global warming and mass extinction (250 million years ago), and 'Snowball Earth'—a time when the Earth was totally covered in ice (635 million years ago)."

If you explore other sources of information about proxies, you may notice that scientists list some materials, like pollen, as either an archive or the proxy itself. Don't let these ambiguities keep you from seeking out more details and introducing these ideas to your students.

WHAT ARE OTHER WAYS THAT PROXY DATA CAN INFORM CLIMATE SCIENCE?

Proxy data also hint at how the climate might change in the future. They provide a key line of evidence that scientists have used to better estimate how much the Earth will warm if carbon dioxide concentrations continue to rise. Fifty million years ago, carbon dioxide concentrations were greater than today, and the planet was substantially warmer. One set of proxies allows scientists to quantify the former (carbon dioxide concentration), and another set of proxies allows them to estimate the latter (temperature). Scientists can use this information to estimate *climate sensitivity*, meaning how much the temperature will rise in response to a doubling of atmospheric carbon dioxide. This is not a trivial calculation, considering that the amount of carbon dioxide in our atmosphere recently crossed a troubling threshold—as of 2023 it had risen 50 percent above preindustrial levels.

Another way that proxies inform climate science is through modeling. Proxy records can be used to help *evaluate climate models that look back in time* rather than forward. Scientists create computer simulations based on data models that involve equations and built-in assumptions to see how well they reproduce past climate patterns. This is called "hindcasting" (in contrast to forecasting). Proxy data are needed to compare against the outcomes of these models. A model that successfully hindcasts what the proxy data tell us can then be used with more confidence to improve our understanding of that past time period and can provide credibility when the same models then forecast future conditions.

WHAT ARE THE LIMITATIONS OF PROXY DATA?

The process of interpreting proxy data to produce climate records of the past is anything but straightforward. Such complicated techniques have their limitations. Scientists need to take account of both the local conditions in which the archives were produced and any wider influences that might be at play. Tree rings, for example, are most prominent in locations where plants experience clearly defined seasons throughout the year. This means that trees in midlatitudes, including those in Europe, North America, and northern Asia, are more responsive to climate variations than trees in the tropics. Proxies like tree rings do not always indicate single variables like temperature or rainfall. Instead, they often reflect a combination of several. Thus, paleoclimatology involves disentangling different climate indicators represented in that proxy.

Another limitation is that some proxies may reveal a lot about the climate, but only for a relatively brief period in time. Historical documents only go back hundreds of years, and most data from tree rings only go back about 2,000 years, which seems like peering into antiquity, but this is a mere glance backward when you consider that ocean sediment and rock outcroppings reveal conditions from millions of years ago. Another time-related limitation is that a proxy may only provide very coarse estimates of climate variability, meaning that scientists can only detect climate-related changes every decade or longer, rather than every year. While the record from ocean sediments extends far back in time, the sampling interval can only detect climate changes from one century to the next. In contrast, data from tree rings and stalagmites that accumulate in caves can show changes from one year to the next. Even more fine-grained are historical documents such as diaries or ships' logs that record conditions hourly or from one day to the next. Finally, all proxies are subject to the vagaries of human documentation. With historical artifacts, for example, older records are generally less useful. There are weather logs preserved in Irish and Norse annals that go back to the middle of the first millennium CE, but their dating is imprecise and descriptions of weather and climate are often exaggerated.[17] For these reasons, scientists like to use multiple proxies together to determine climate conditions at a point in time. No single type of proxy, used by itself, is adequate for reconstructing large-scale patterns of past climate.[18]

TURNING RESPONSIBILITY OVER TO YOUR STUDENTS: "HOW *DO* WE KNOW?"

It's time again to think about your students being part of a knowledge-building community. To have them apprenticed into authentic intellectual work, they'll need to grapple with questions like: "What kinds of evidence do we have to make claims about the past?" "Why do certain kinds of proxy data count as evidence?" "What should be the limits of claims we make about the past or what proxy data indicate for the future?" You could help your students build a bigger picture, understanding how the past, present, and future of the climate are like interlocking pieces of a puzzle that, together, help explain how the Earth is responding at this moment in time and what is more or less likely to happen next. Conversations about environmental proxy data can be powerful for learning because they give your students practice in talking about the role of uncertainty in science, and how it can't be avoided but can be acknowledged and worked with to produce credible claims.

Before you get into epistemic discussions, students should become familiar with basics like how glaciers form, how trees respond to growing conditions, or what micro-fossils are. A key teacher task here is to estimate what is "just enough" content for students to master. If you work with sixth graders, you won't need to plumb the depths of oxygen isotopes in order for them to appreciate how the presence of ^{18}O in ice cores supports a story about prehistoric temperatures and precipitation patterns. If, on the other hand, you teach a high school chemistry class, pressing for more nuanced understandings of isotopes would be appropriate. Regardless of grade level, students will need a grasp of time scales that people don't usually reason with in everyday life. It would help to collectively interrogate graphs like those in figure 7.1. Understanding what isotopes are, for example, won't matter unless students also know that their relative proportions change on millennial time scales.

One starter activity teachers have used is pairing up students to do case studies of one type of proxy that interests them—it helps if you can connect this with data collection efforts happening in your community or region. You can engage student groups in this guided inquiry by posing questions that facilitate students' search for relevant information. These are middle school and high school expectations, but if you are an elementary educator, you can select a subset and modify them for your learners:

- What are the characteristics of this type of proxy?
- Is this type of data being collected in our area and for what purposes?
- How do scientists access the archive and extract the proxy data?
- Are these proxy data calibrated in any way; for example, can they be compared against any recent instrumental records?
- What, in general, can this type of proxy data tell us?

When students share with one another what they've found, it multiplies their exposure to authentic science. After you lay this groundwork, students can move into epistemic conversations, meaning dialogue about how knowledge gets constructed in a discipline. You and your students can wrestle with these questions:

- Why are these proxies indicators of past climate conditions?
- What science principles tell us that these proxies can "stand in" for climate conditions?
- What evidence and chains of logic allow us to make these claims?
- What are the limits of such claims; what can we assert and what is out of bounds?
- How can proxies help us anticipate future climate-related risks?

When students need to create or comment on claims and evidence, it helps to provide definitions. A *claim* is a statement about a process or event that helps explain patterns in observations or data—it is not just restating the trends in data. A claim can be a small part of a larger explanation, but it should not encompass the whole thing. Observations or data used to support a claim are referred to as *evidence. Justification* (sometimes called reasoning) serves a "joining function," describing why the evidence supports the claim.

A student offering an argument can use known scientific facts, concepts, or principles to make these links, as well as comment on the relevance and accuracy of the data as further support. A student contesting an argument can find weaknesses in the evidence, gaps in the justification, or problems with how the claim is stated.

All young learners love choice, so give them options for what to study and how, but with some structure. Many students who've done this work have found rich imagery to anchor their stories, ranging from photos of original winter counts on buffalo skin to colorful photo-microscopic pictures of foraminifera, to videos of researchers pulling up ice cores from a drilling site at the South Pole.

Scaffolding for this work is necessary. You might recall that scaffolding refers to ways of supporting students in doing an authentic task without oversimplifying the task itself—"Keep it complex" is what we remind our teachers. One strategy is for you to think out loud about which parts of the case study tasks are best done first, second, and later on. It is also helpful to show examples of previous students' responses to case study questions or presentations to peers, taking care to identify what was done well. If it is early in the school year and students are not familiar with the rhetoric of science argumentation, then you might provide a list of claims that are possible and ask students to select one they feel most comfortable justifying. Later in the year, students can be responsible for constructing their own claims and justifications. Table 7.1 describes more examples.

You can provide links to relevant online sites and then have students branch out to do some digging on their own, but first you should share why certain sites are more trustworthy than others. Students can help each other become more media savvy within their group, and groups can cross-share ideas for searching. It is helpful to provide authentic motivation for students, telling them, for example, that they will have to develop presentations or tutorials on their proxy for fellow students or to present some of these ideas to students in lower grades. These epistemic conversations help students feel that they know how science operates and supports their identities as inquirers into the natural world. This happens because they are the ones asking questions and finding things out for themselves.

Table 7.1 How teachers can support students' written and verbal arguments

Support students' writing and talk	Be explicit about the language of argument	Provide examples
• Provide a set of claims about an activity that students have just done and give them practice at identifying evidence and developing arguments that support or refute one of those claims. • Provide sentence frames to support written and verbal attempts at argument. • Let students create a public record of their argumentative reasoning so that peers can learn from them, respond to them, and provide feedback. This can be a poster or infographic, for example.	• Don't assume your students share common understandings of terms like *claims, justification*, etc. Be explicit about what they mean and define them. Use these terms in relevant contexts whenever possible and call them out as you use them. • Allow students frequent practice with these ways of using language, perhaps asking "what claims can be made" from individual lab activities. • Set up times for students to respond to one another's claims in whole-class settings. Provide specific roles for those who are in the audience.	• Begin the year by using examples of claims and evidence from events in students' everyday lives that they can relate to and comment on. • Use authentic but understandable cases of investigations where scientists gathered data to test a claim. Discuss how they gathered relevant data to use as evidence. • Model (think out loud) how you might select a claim to make from an investigative experience, what evidence might be useful, and how to reason about the links between claims and evidence.

CHAPTER 8

Our Possible Future(s)

*Data Visualizations and Climate Models
as Sensemaking Tools*

IN THE PREVIOUS CHAPTER, we learned how the Earth leaves behind traces of its distant past to help us understand climate cycles that typically last for millennia. Now we'll make the leap to the present. In the last few decades, climate scientists have accumulated a staggering number of observations of Earth's physical and biological systems. In its raw form, this vast repository of data is too complex for anyone to use, which is why visualizations have become indispensable tools for scientists and everyday folk to comprehend complex and globally distributed processes. You've seen such visualizations in the forms of charts, graphs, maps, and tables, some of which are animated or interactive. It's hardly possible for students to grasp what is happening with the climate now unless they are given opportunities to study these representations and, with support from you, use them as lenses to see phenomena differently and ask new questions about the world.

Later in this chapter, we turn to the future or more correctly to the many possible futures that lie ahead of us. Each version is constrained by the natural laws of science while also profoundly influenced by decisions humans make today. These decisions put us on pathways toward sustainability or chaos. To understand what might be happening over the next few decades, we must rely on a specific kind of visualization—the output from global climate models. When scientists forecast future trends for sea level rise or species extinctions, they are using data from the past and present, as well as mathematical equations that describe how different variables are related to one another and to downstream outcomes that determine the livability of the planet. These are global climate models. The implication for classroom teaching is that our students will need to develop more sophisticated forms of data fluency than we may be used to supporting.

VISUALIZATIONS OF DATA: WHERE DO THEY COME FROM?

Over the past forty years, scientists have vacuumed up data continuously using autonomous undersea drones, satellites in orbit, and hundreds of other technologies. They measure a lot of things. From the land, it is river discharge, snow cover, the extent of glaciers, conditions of permafrost, land cover, carbon in the soil, fire disturbances and soil moisture. From the oceans, it is surface temperature, ocean color (influenced by the presence of microscopic phytoplankton), waves and wind, the extent of sea ice, salinity, and the strength of ocean currents.[1] If that sounds like a blizzard of information, scientists are indeed trying to track everything that could possibly signal changes in our climate. A key late-stage step in this knowledge-building enterprise is to create visualizations of numbers and patterns that allow human minds to comprehend the state of the environment, or at least slices of it in space and time.[2]

Many of the visualizations that scientific communities are analyzing now can also be used to build lessons around in K–12 classrooms. The trove of data is an embarrassment of riches for us, but on the other hand, data displays are becoming increasingly complex, with multiple layers of information embedded in them. There are three basic families of visualizations, but digital tools have expanded what can be represented in each. The largest of these families is charts and graphs. We know these as scatterplots, bar or line graphs, and pie charts. The second family is made up of tables that display data in rows and columns. The third family, geospatial visualizations, is becoming more commonplace in scientific reports and in the media. These displays map a region of the Earth and use colors, shapes, relative sizes of objects, and other visual cues to show data of interest within a space. The map acts as a container, layering on selected measurements and their physical locations to open the door for insights about spatial phenomena. In digital form, the maps can be made dynamic, even interactive, showing changes in certain variables over time that help scientists understand trends, test theories, and forecast future changes. With the proper guidance, they can help our students to do much the same.

HOW VISUALIZATIONS CAN SUPPORT SENSEMAKING IN THE CLASSROOM

The graceful curves of figure 8.1 make up a hybrid representation that is part pie chart (showing categories as a proportion of a whole) and part flow chart (movement within a system). In this case, the "whole" on the left includes the varied sources of emissions that we put into our atmosphere, with each "arm" representing the fraction from different sources. On the right are the natural sinks into which some of these emissions are absorbed. The flow in the bigger picture is a one-directional movement of carbon from anthropogenic sources toward land and oceans, save for the 59 percent that remains in our atmosphere. Visualizations like this one are not the most complicated, but don't be fooled, the questions that teachers and students can ask about it can drive deep learning. Educators I've worked with have developed an adaptable five-part strategy: (1) provide or have students seek out context for the focal visualization (e.g., how were data collected, by whom), (2) support students' decoding of elements within the visualization (what they represent, including the title), (3) help students identify and make meaning of the patterns, asking their own questions and seeking answers, (4) figure out with them how these trends matter in the world and, if so, to whom, and (5) prompt students to ask what they want to know more about. This strategy can be used in the order above, but with practice, students will internalize these steps and learn to shift back and forth between them as they make meaning of what they see. With practice, students will also transition from spending their energies decoding what visualizations mean to using them for asking and answering questions they find compelling.

Students we've observed have gradually taken ownership of these sensemaking strategies, asking themselves and their peers these questions without prompting from the teacher. Table 8.1 shows actual examples of questions and supports teachers provided their students, along with sample responses from middle school students examining the emissions figure.

Figure 8.1 Emissions sources and natural sinks

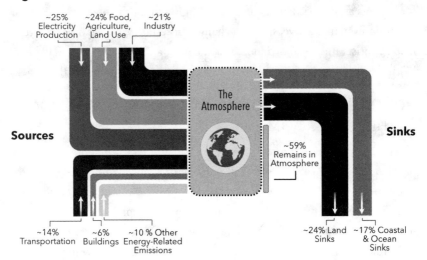

In a K–12 earth science class, a visualization like figure 8.1 might be the object of inquiry for lessons in which students explore the composition and dynamics of the atmosphere. Or the story behind these sources and sinks could be investigated in a chemistry class, serving as context for understanding how chemical reactions release greenhouse gases and conversely how the molecular machinery of sinks work to sequester carbon. This leads us to a good lesson about models and other visualizations—they represent how the world works, but in making complex phenomena accessible, they have to simplify things. In this case, there is a lot that this model does not show but that students could easily unpack. In some classrooms, teachers ask students to choose parts of diagrams like this and dive deeper into that science. Students working with this visualization have asked, "Can carbon dioxide ever come *out* of a sink?" It opened the door to conversations about ecosystems like the rain forests of the Amazon, where clear-cutting and burning of biomass are flipping its role from carbon sink to carbon source. It now accounts for more than 1 billion metric tons of emissions every year, mainly due to burning trees that are leveled to make room for beef cattle to graze.[3] The margins of this ecosystem are also shifting to become grassland, a nearly irreversible transition that leaves the land far less capable of storing carbon.

Table 8.1 Samples of teacher and student questions, over two days, to support sensemaking of emissions visualization

I. Teacher provides some context and prompts for checking trustworthiness	
T: "We have a good understanding of the greenhouse effect now, so this representation will help us understand the primary sources of emissions and whether they can be drawn out of the atmosphere by natural means. Here's a bit of background on how these data were collected . . . "	S: "Is this showing the US or the whole world?" S: "Why does CO_2 have to be measured in Mauna Loa?"
T: "Who created this visualization? Is it trustworthy?"	S: "It says *Project Drawdown*, so maybe we should look up if they are climate scientists." S: "Let's compare what we see here with data from other websites."
II. Students decode elements of the visualization	
T: "To understand what this representation is telling us, let's start with the title. What clues are there? Are we sure we know what the key terms mean?"	S: "It says 'emissions.' Does that mean carbon dioxide or other stuff too?"
T: "What's being measured here?" (If a graph, ask about the axes. What are they? What is the scale? Are either of the axes a set of categories? Of what?)	S: "Looks like sources and sinks should each add up to 100%." S: "Industry is supposed to produce 21% of the total carbon dioxide emissions, but how many tons is that?"
T: "What do these 'arms' on either side of the atmosphere block represent?" (If there is a key, what do the symbols represent? In a geospatial representation, what kind of area is represented?) "What kinds of data are contained in these areas?"	S: "Not sure what the big block of 'Atmosphere' represents."
T: "Is change over time represented? If so, how?"	S: "It's not showing change over time, but could it if we got the same data from 30 years ago?"
T: "Can we point out the most/least in a category? Are there trends we can identify?" (These could be some measure that is rising, falling, cyclic, random, or correlated positively or negatively with another variable's patterns.)	S: "Wow, agriculture and electricity make up half of all the carbon dioxide released. Transportation is only 14%—then why are we hyping electric vehicles?" S: "There's only two sinks; that's not fair!"

continued

continued

| T: "What do we need to know more about before we can identify patterns?" | S: "What counts as a land sink?" |

III. Students identify and make meaning of the patterns

| T: "What do the conditions or patterns in this visualization tell us about the future? Can we make any claims?" (What will happen if these trends continue?) | S: "We think that sinks can only hold so much, like a kitchen sink, so unless sources slow down, carbon dioxide will, like, back up into the atmosphere. It sounds bad. Can that happen?" |

IV. Students figure out why these patterns matter

| T: "To whom might these trends matter and why?" | S: "It will matter for extreme weather and because there are no borders in the atmosphere; the whole world will feel it." |
| T: "Why should we care about these trends?" | S: "Because it affects the oceans with heat and acidity, and that will cause bad domino effects around the world." |

V. Teacher prompts for metacognition (what students feel they need to know more about)

| T: "What would we like to know more about? What questions are we left with? How has our thinking changed after this discussion?" | S: "What sources should we cut first and how?" S: "We need to know if the sinks will still work if more and more carbon dioxide gets into the atmosphere." |

Teachers have used several strategies in addition to the questions in table 8.1. We know that learners can better interpret data if they can imagine the conditions under which they were collected. This can be done, for example, by showing a video of scientists in the polar regions pulling ice cores from glaciers or showing satellites and how they gather data about drought conditions. It doesn't take much for students to link a data capture technology with a part of the world being studied, and to feel a beginning acquaintance with how the representations are produced.

USING VISUALIZATIONS TO MOTIVATE KNOWLEDGE-BUILDING ACTIVITIES

Once students can make sense of data in visualizations, they can venture further into knowledge-building activities by using them to create claims and formulate arguments.[4] We share here a series of four linked activities from a professional development project that was designed by learning sciences researchers Lynne Zummo and Sara Dozier. They used these activities with high school educators who taught underserved students.[5] With minor modifications, this could translate into a dynamic multiday sensemaking opportunity for students.

Session 1: Eliciting what learners know and want to know. For the first session, researchers posted a number of climate-related newspaper headlines, quotes from public figures, and photos on the walls of a classroom. Teachers were asked to circulate for ten minutes; then each was given five stickers to place on artifacts they felt were particularly meaningful. Teachers then shared with a partner why they made these choices; later in the whole group, each teacher revoiced what their partner had told them. Teachers described trends they noticed in the artifacts and what additional climate ideas they were familiar with that were not represented. In groups, teachers then came up with their own questions and sorted them thematically on a public board. Examples included: Why is the climate changing? Why is there so much controversy and doubt about it? When will it get really bad?

Session 2: Making meaning of different climate data sets. In the second session, teachers began interpreting data-based visualizations. They worked in groups of three, with each assigned a climate-related topic that would further their understanding. Topics included atmospheric gases, temperature, species populations, precipitation, sea and land cover, and energy resources. Each group was given a set of data representations from trusted scientific websites regarding their topic and a tool for organizing their analyses. Each group analyzed a set of five visualizations and had access to additional representations that they could investigate.

For each representation, a written guide prompted teachers first to identify the variables or elements that were shown. Then, teachers made observations about specific data on the visualizations of their choosing. The guides prompted participants to ask: "What do I see?" and "What do I think it means?" When finished, they reviewed their findings and selected what they felt were the most useful data to share with others. They were asked to record each of these observations on an evidence card. Teachers discussed these within their groups and then posted the cards to a public board.

Session 3: Assembling and sharing evidence for why climate change is happening. The whole teacher group was asked to collaboratively construct an explanation for one of the main questions on their board: *Why is the climate changing?* They began with a gallery-viewing of all groups' evidence cards, paying attention to their findings. Then they joined jigsaw groups, made up of one expert from each of the six topic areas. Each jigsaw group created a poster using data representations and evidence cards on the public board. They also indicated connections they noticed between the selected evidence cards. Jigsaw groups then circulated to one another's posters and took notes about interesting or puzzling ideas. To synthesize these ideas, a whole-group discussion followed.

Session 4: Creating and evaluating arguments together. In the final session, teachers were randomly assigned to groups of three or four and given a skeptical claim about climate change. For example: *The climate has always been changing and now is no different.* These claims had all appeared during the Session 1 activity, in quotes from public figures or in newspaper headlines, and had generated substantial interest from participants. In groups, teachers used the handwritten evidence cards to evaluate their assigned claim. They first sorted the cards, deciding which ones supported, contradicted, or were unrelated to the skeptical claim. They were then asked to select evidence cards to create an argument in support of the skeptical claims (for example, how natural variations in climate could be causing a temporary increase in global temperatures). After piecing together an argument as best they could, they were asked to repeat the process to design a counterargument, refuting the skeptical claim.

Finally, they evaluated the two arguments, centering on which was more credible and why. To conclude, researchers led a whole-group discussion about the full sequence of epistemic conversations held during the four sessions, as a way to build knowledge about climate change. Teachers were asked to write journal responses to the following: What did you learn from this activity? What do you understand about climate change now that you did previously did not? What would your students get out of this experience? The researchers who hosted this professional development collected data on the teachers' experiences and found that the activities supported the same kinds of learning we would want for our students: increased attention to variation in climate data, the integration of several science concepts—socially contextualized—into causal explanations, enhanced ability to link concepts about variation to explanations of climate change, and more nuanced understandings of argumentation in general.

The purpose of studying data visualizations is not data literacy, or at least not the decoding of representations as an end in itself for students. It is more powerful for them to use these tools for *fluency*, understanding the ways data are produced in different science domains, being able to locate data in diverse locations, bring them together in ways that generate new understandings, and if relevant, asking if equity was considered in how the data were collected.[6] In the classroom we want our students to discover unexpected relationships, to argue their underlying cause, to seek new information beyond what is provided, and to make room for not knowing. Fostering these habits of mind will lessen the chance that climate change becomes yet another science abstraction disconnected from students' lives, happening "somewhere else, to somebody else."[7]

HOW DATA SHAPES NARRATIVES ABOUT THE FUTURE
What Are Climate Models?

None of us can see the future, but there are ways of rendering it imaginable.[8] Students have big questions about what lies ahead and how likely it is that restorative benchmarks will be achieved (e.g., the point of drawdown) or whether the Earth will slide toward catastrophic tipping points like the collapse of ocean circulation. The science community is helping us imagine multiple possible futures by using *global climate models* or GCMs, to create visualizations of what may be in store. Unlike the data in hand from the past and present, future conditions on Earth are dependent on choices we make now, which means the projections of GCMs have to be recalculated constantly as social, political, and technological trends evolve. Most visualizations generated by GCMs show how outcomes like air temperature or sea levels will change between the present day and the year 2100. Your students can do the math, and some will realize, "I will be alive to witness where we end up on this graph."

The following descriptions of what goes into a global climate model may, again, seem more than a K–12 teacher would have to know. Your students, however, will wonder how the future can be forecast and how trustworthy the process is. They deserve some age-appropriate explanation, even if it means you are just pointing out what is considered in creating such models and how to make sense of different future scenarios. Knowing about GCMs more deeply than you would teach about them also helps you to recognize what is important *about* climate models to insert into your curriculum, how you describe their value in science knowledge-building, and their crucial role in decision-making by nations and communities. Let's start by identifying the building blocks scientists use to construct such models.

Why are these models used so widely? Scientists cannot study the global climate system using experimental methods because there is no way to manipulate parts of it while controlling others for the purpose of isolating the effects of single variables.[9] It is simply too big and radically entangled. The time scales of change are also problematic. Geophysical processes happen over centuries or millennia, and who's going to wait around for those data? Scientists instead rely on climate models that simulate essential mechanisms of Earth's systems. Climate scientists agree, in fact, that most of what we know about the world's climate—the past, present, and future—is through models.[10]

A comparison will illustrate the complexity of global climate models. Everyday weather forecasts incorporate only the circulation of the atmosphere and properties like local temperature and humidity into their short-term predictions. Modern climate models, however, even in their simplest form, need to also build in the effects of subsystems like the ocean, the cryosphere, the marine and terrestrial biospheres, and even soils.[11] Because all these subsystems influence one another, and the climate system is shaped by the many feedback events among them, global climate models are the only reliable tool that can help us grasp the dynamics of the whole Earth system.[12] For this reason, I'll limit the amount of technical detail in describing how these models are created and used.

A planetary climate model consists of a set of seven equations that together emulate how the atmosphere acts like a heat engine. All these equations are derived from experimental and observational data—mountains of it.[13] When all the subsystems mentioned above are added in, these models can simulate future conditions and produce predictions for changes in atmospheric chemistry, large-scale patterns of precipitation, changes in sea ice, global mean temperature, and the amount of heat our oceans will absorb over time. It's important to understand that there aren't separate global climate models simulating past, present, and future.[14] Rather, all GCMs attempt to replicate mathematically how natural climate mechanisms work together, and these relationships are no different for the purposes of projecting the future than they are for characterizing the past or present—the same models are used for each.

Evaluating Climate Models: Hindcasting and Forecasting

Scientists are compulsive about evaluating climate models for accuracy and reliability. The most common test is to "run the model" (the equations) on supercomputers and then compare output such as global temperatures, carbon dioxide concentrations, and so on, with actual observations from the past few decades. Another test is to set conditions in the model, such as greenhouse gas concentrations to correspond with known paleoclimate conditions, before the era of recorded observations, to see how accurately the model will *reproduce* the ancient climate profile.

Teams of modeling experts have become remarkably accurate in predicting the movement of average global temperatures.[15] In figure 8.2, the thin lines represent direct measures of the Earth's average air temperature over time from five different research teams. Because they are straightforward recordings of temperature from modern times, we would expect these to trace out similar paths, and they do. More importantly, however, the average output of several global climate models (thick line) tracks these observations very closely. The models were created and run around 2006. Note how closely they *forecasted* the next seventeen years or so. The same models were also tested by *hindcasting* the temperatures of the recent past. As you can see, the model equations are able to reproduce temperature patterns very similar to the observed record of 1970 to 2006.

Today's climate models can reproduce more than average global temperatures; they virtually generate several features of the past and present climate, such as the location and strength of the jet stream, changes in the seasonal cycles of precipitation, and the natural occurrence of extreme weather events, such as heat and cold waves, droughts and floods, and hurricanes or cyclones.[16] They can also reproduce longer-term historic cycles, such as past ice ages and interglacial warm periods. Modelers are confident in their projections of how

Figure 8.2 Projected warming (mean projection by multiple models is thick black line; actual temperature readings–thin lines

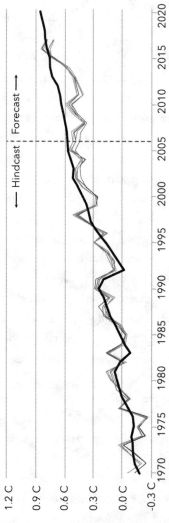

Source: Adapted from Zeke Hausfather, *Analysis: How Well Have Climate Models Projected Global Warming?* Carbon Brief, May 10, 2017, https://www.carbonbrief.org/analysis-how-well-have-climate-models-projected-global-warming/.

climate is likely to change in the future in response to key variables, chief among them anthropogenic emissions, in part because of how accurately they have been able to represent past climate changes.

Uncertainties will always be part of modeling. One kind of uncertainty arises from not being able to predict tipping points, in which some natural processes suddenly become so chaotic that the equations modeling them are no longer valid. A second kind of uncertainty surrounds climate sensitivity—a measure of how the planet will warm in response to a doubling of carbon dioxide in the atmosphere. This basic sensitivity relationship is key to accurate modeling and is still being refined with new data.

Using Social Scenarios to Project Possible Futures

Climate modelers are now developing projections for a range of plausible futures that involve social, economic, and political scenarios. Because modeling teams need to compare their predictions with one another for accuracy, everyone has to agree on what these scenarios might be. The different futures are referred to as *shared socioeconomic pathways* (SSPs). The pathways take into account "what if" factors like urbanization, economic conditions, population growth, new technologies, and even social movements.[17] As you can tell, these are not climate inputs, but they have everything to do with the direction in which we may be headed. Some future scenarios are characterized by continued dependence on fossil fuels, while others assume the widespread adoption of renewable energy. Different combinations of these factors are plugged into climate models to estimate how they would impact emissions and global temperatures.

There are five scenarios; each reflects a plausible mix of conditions. They have cryptic labels, but for our purposes here I'll simply mention them without a technical explanation. Two of the scenarios, SSP1-1.9 and SSP5-8.5, represent relatively positive trends for human development, with global investments in education and health, rapid economic growth, and well-functioning democratic institutions (we can always hope). Remember that we are not just referring to the United States here, but the world. The two pathways differ in that SSP1-1.9 assumes there is a gradual shift *toward sustainable practices and renewables*, while SSP5-8.5 assumes development will be *driven by an increasingly energy-intensive, fossil fuel-based economy*. SSP1-2.6 and SSP3-7.0 are more pessimistic in terms of inequitable futures for economic and social development, with little investment in health or education in poorer countries, accompanied by rapid increases in world population. They differ in that SSP3-7.0 includes high emissions, doubling by 2100. SSP2-4.5 represents a "business as usual" scenario in which historical patterns of development and energy use are continued throughout the twenty-first century. Figure 8.3 shows the estimated warming trends for each scenario—remember that a difference of a half a degree, up or down, may not look like much, but these destinations at the end of the twenty-first century represent very different worlds.

What's not figured into this representation are the possible but improbable jumps *between* pathways as the future unfolds. Improbable because the moves would require radical upheavals of social and economic trends. What's more to the point is that, as time moves forward, climate consequences increasingly become an irreversible reality, the range of places where we could end up in 2100 narrows each year, and if we don't cut emissions now, we'll be closer to the perilous upper reaches of this graph. Even SSP1-1.9 is costly for the Earth and us.

Though you may not choose to show students this particular representation, they would benefit from conversations about future-oriented scenarios as something imaginable, a virtual space they could shape through actions in the present. In research with high school students, teachers who scaffolded these kinds of conversations both widened students' perspectives and made the future seem more approachable.[18] Specifically, these students described a sense of their future as closer in time and conceivable as a set of possibilities. They also imagined their future as closer to themselves, in the sense that the fate of the world moved within their reach, and they came to see themselves as agents in shaping their own futures. This is important because the influence of choices we make now have *far* more of an effect on the magnitude of future warming than do choices made later in time.

For our students to choose futures that require changes in how human communities live and choose to exercise agency to move the world in that direction, they have to be able to imagine the social and political scenarios that they should work toward. This will inevitably mean fighting for social justice and more robust forms of democracy, even when their efforts don't directly target the environment. This is another reminder that science, by itself, cannot solve our problems.

Figure 8.3 Global surface temperature changes relative to 1850–1900, by shared socioeconomic pathways

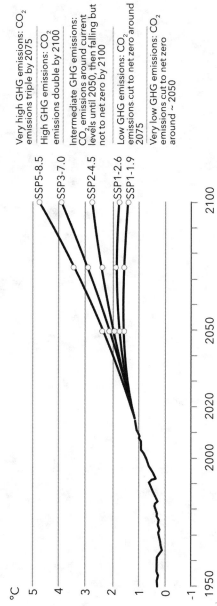

Source: Valérie Masson-Delmotte et al., "Climate Change 2021: The Physical Science Basis," *Contribution of Working Group I to the Sixth Assessment Report of the Intergovernmental Panel on Climate Change: Summary for Policymakers,* 2021, 22, doi:10.1017/9781009157896.001.

CHAPTER 9

Helping Students Show
What They Know

Building Models and Explanations

AMBITIOUS PEDAGOGY REQUIRES us to *work on and with students' ideas*—
which means we need to find out what they already know and how they
think. Specifically, we need ways for students to show what they know at
different points along the curricular trajectory. One practice that serves this
purpose is modeling. We are not talking about the abstract mathematical
models that climate scientists use, but rather models that pictorially represent specific events and processes related to climate change or solutions.[1]
For example, middle school students could represent how the biodiversity
in a local wetland habitat rebounds after invasive plants are removed. High
school chemistry students could depict how safer refrigerants, such as ammonia, interact less problematically with the atmosphere than hydrofluorocarbons do. These kinds of conceptual models can include representative
images, connections between them, and labels to indicate what is changing
over time. The middle school students could sketch a "before the restoration"
drawing and an "after" version that include components of a wetland—bi-
otic, abiotic, and human-made features—then add labels and causal links
among these to show how invasives stress a habitat already at risk from climate change and how those stresses are reduced post-restoration. When

students construct models like this and add explanations, they not only reveal what they know. The process helps them construct deeper and more interconnected understandings of the phenomenon.

Student modeling is not just about individual reasoning; it also supports a knowledge-building community in the classroom.[2] Teachers typically ask learners to sketch out an initial model after being introduced to an anchoring event. They frame these drafts as "our beginning ideas, which we can learn from and improve upon as we go through the unit." These teachers are also careful to remind students: "There are many ways to show what you know. I don't expect all your models to look the same." Let's explore one example.

In Jessica's seventh-grade classroom, students worked on initial models of how the greenhouse effect is impacting the people of Sarichef Island in Alaska. She gave students a template showing an outline of the island on the left and an image of the Earth on the right. Jessica wanted to know what her students already understood about links between what is happening with fossil fuel emissions at the global level and the loss of sea ice near the Arctic Circle. At the top of the island side, she asked: "What is happening to the island of Sarichef? Show the changes that Imarvaluk and her people can see or feel. Use zoom-ins to better explain the unseen causes of the changes to the land, air, ice, water, and living things." On the Earth side of the model template, Jessica asked: "What is happening far away from Sarichef that might be causing the island's problems? Zoom out to show a bigger view of planet Earth. You can use zoom-ins to show molecules of water, air, ice, and land as needed." At the bottom, Jessica put spaces for writing and asked students to "explain your thinking."

Figure 9.1 focuses on the right side (only) of an initial model by Lilah. Her handwritten text is transcribed exactly for legibility. In the previous unit, the class had explored the carbon cycle. Lilah made good use of what she'd learned by filling in commentary about sedimentary layers in the oceans being one of the world's largest carbon reservoirs (upper-right text box). She included a mini-model of the greenhouse effect (far left) and then added text about the thermal expansion of gases and liquids when heated (upper left), even the fact that "heated air will start trying to achieve thermal equilibrium with water" (bottom left), meaning that it causes ocean warming. Lilah included a paragraph on plastics (lower right), even though she was not sure if this was related to climate change or just another polluting product of fossil

Figure 9.1 Portion of Lilah's initial model

Initial Model: What is the Monster in the Story "My Wounded Island" and Where Did It Come From?

What is happening far away from Sarichef that might be causing the island's problems? "Zoom out" to show a bigger view of planet Earth. You can use "Zoom-ins" to show molecules of water, air, ice, and land as needed.

Thermal expansion. Molecules take up more space due to movement. They speed up when they gain energy. Such as heat, light. With solids they just vibrate, no pushing. Gases and liquids push or expand when they are colliding.

CO2 traps light. The energy is absorbed as it passes through the molecules. Like sound is molecules being moved by energy. The CO₂ is heating the air. Heated air will start trying to achieve thermal equilibrium with water. The water will be subject to thermal expansion.

Land forms are affected too. They are submerged sometimes under rising sea levels. The sedimentary layer is the largest carbon reservoir. For climate change to continue, presumably, it relies on the carbon cycle which occurs throughout the whole planet.

Plastics are made primarily of fossil fuels and chemicals which is what makes the bonds strong. They have tons of carbon contributing to pollution in the sea. They also have cellulose. If plastic is broken down by UV light and chemicals, then the carbon may form H₂O following the cycle.

Explain your thinking in two or more sentences. Make sure to explain what is happening that we can't see.

Fossil fuels, full of carbon are burned for energy. CO₂ is released into the atmosphere. The CO₂ collects in the atmosphere, trapping the heat from the sun, raising the Earth's temp. The heat is preventing ice from forming, and probably causing issues with animals and plants like the moose population.

fuels. She chose not to draw anything directly on the earth graphic that Jessica had included.

You might look at Lilah's draft and ask, "Is this really an *initial* model?" The reason for all her ideas is because this middle school science department has coordinated its curriculum so that different aspects of climate or mitigation strategies are addressed at least a couple of times per year at each grade level, building on one another with few redundancies or gaps. Because this was a beginning model, Lilah just wanted to get any relevant ideas on paper. Jessica had assured students that the model was a safe space to try out theories because they would sort these out, borrow ideas from one another, and improve the models over time. This is exactly what you want to encourage—students showing everything they think might be connected to the anchoring event, including their puzzlements. The left side of Lilah's model had, for now, a few facts from an introductory video Jessica showed students, mostly about where Alaska is located.

When I interviewed Lilah and her table partner about their models, they explained yet another event that never made it onto the paper: that ocean warming could stop undersea convection in the future "because there's no hot or cold anymore—just hot." There is indeed a modest probability of this happening. They hadn't included the convection collapse in their models because, as they saw it, the idea didn't contribute to the essential question. This reminds us that no model can represent everything a student knows. A few weeks later, Lilah filled in many of the missing pieces to complete a connected causal narrative in her final model: the effects of infrared radiation on different surfaces that contribute to atmospheric warming, feedback loops, the role of sea ice in ecosystems, and how the Inuit community was planning to adapt to climate changes caused in faraway places. This is a good place to note that the second-most common comment I've heard from teachers who try out modeling for the first time is "I never knew my kids had those kinds of ideas." The most common comment? "I had kids participate that I've never heard from before." These are two of the reasons ambitious teaching is worth the effort.

SCAFFOLDS TO HELP STUDENTS SHOW THE MOST OF WHAT THEY KNOW

Scaffolding means structuring the modeling endeavor for students, such as giving them a pre-drawn template or using written prompts to help them understand what is expected in models and explanations. Some teachers give their students a blank page, while others include questions or prompts. While some students may be eager to draw on the unstructured expanse of empty paper, many learners can become confused and frustrated by the open nature of the task. This can marginalize those who are not yet skilled at representing their scientific or everyday knowledge visually. This can also disadvantage students who are unfamiliar with modeling expectations in your classroom or students with Individualized Education Programs for writing. We need to offer supports that allow students to make their own choices of how to represent ideas and explanations to others and, in the process, show the most of what they know.

I'll outline a three-layer approach to designing these kinds of model templates.[3] Before discussing examples, I'd like to note that teachers should *not* use templates to funnel students toward representing concepts or connections in particular ways. The teachers I work with have found that these structures support a wider range of students to reason scientifically, use their everyday experiences as assets, and represent ideas in diverse ways.

Layer 1: Keep the Essential Question in View

The model template should be based on the event you have already selected to anchor the unit. The essential question that goes with the anchoring event clarifies what students should explain. Remember, even the smallest tweak of an essential question can make the explanations and models more challenging and better support learning. The essential question goes at the top of the template or is projected at the front of the room during modeling, but either way, students need to be reminded that it frames the problem they are trying to solve.

Layer 2: Select a Layout

Next comes the base pictorial layout. This layer includes the visual outlines of just a few objects related to the anchoring phenomenon that you don't want students to spend their time drawing. Base pictorial layouts are minimalist structures. They include outlines of people, animals, the atmospheric layers of the Earth, technologies, whatever is relevant to the phenomenon. When creating a layout for a climate change phenomenon, you really have to be creative about representing things like scale in the layout, the passage of time, or different views of the same structures. You'll even have to pay attention to the white space left available for students to draw in. It really helps if the template is printed on eleven-by-seventeen paper—trust me, you'll get more drawing and writing from students in this larger format. Why? If we ask students to model complex phenomena, which often are systems interacting with other systems, then they must have room to represent multiple events, processes at different scales (micro- and macroscopic), and connections.[4] There are three versions of base pictorial layouts; the choice depends on the modeling experience your students have and the nature of the anchoring event.

Before, during, and after. This first type of layout divides the template into three sections in which students are prompted to explain an event or process before it starts, as it unfolds, and after it has ended or changed. These layouts may include labels for each section indicating specific time increments (e.g., "preindustrial era" or "after deforestation").

Comparing two cases. This layout divides the paper into side-by-side panels for a contrast between cases representing a phenomenon that can occur in different ways, in different places, or can cause different impacts depending on the situation.

Big picture. This format is a single frame with an image or ensemble of images. There is significant white space surrounding an image or within it for students to add ideas about what is happening. This layout naturally lends itself to climate change phenomena about the earth and atmosphere, the ocean, extreme weather events, and even the inner workings of a wind turbine or the failure of a region's energy grid. Large-scale geographic events or engineering topics frequently require students to model using spatial reasoning or to depict changes over long periods of time. These can best be supported through big-picture layouts or a combination of big-picture frames from varying perspectives (e.g., cross-section *and* bird's-eye view in same layout). The layout can also be blank if your students have experience with modeling and know how to use explanation elements (see below).

Layer 3: Explanation Elements

The final step for creating model templates is to prompt students to add their own explanation elements to reveal the details of their thinking or even personal responses to the anchoring event. We've seen learners include:

- Zoom-in or zoom-out bubbles
- Drawings of cross-sections where none were provided (of the Earth, ocean, skin, battery)
- Mathematical equations or graphs
- Molecular models
- Sketched-in instruments like oxygen meters or thermometers showing their readings
- Short comic strips and characters narrating action about the phenomenon
- Graphic organizers like mini–flow charts, tables, food webs, life cycles, Venn diagrams
- Maps or other geographic representations, terrain mini-models
- Timelines
- Choice boxes, which can be anything the student wants, such as dates, notes that specify connections between two parts of the model, a key or legend

Teachers who've used prompts to insert elements have been excited to see what learners include and how effectively the inscriptions represent important ideas. In some AP classes, students have used molecular models, graphs, equations, zoom-ins, and keys, and written explanations, all in the same model, for heat transfer. This provides enormous freedom for students, but the explanatory elements, as in the chemistry case, have to work together, contributing to a coherent story. They shouldn't just be eye candy.

WHAT MODELING LOOKS LIKE OVER THE ARC OF A UNIT

Student involvement with modeling and explanation follows a characteristic arc in a knowledge-building classroom. Teachers start by sharing a video or story of a phenomenon that engages students. After inviting students to relate the phenomenon to experiences in their own lives and then asking for observations or theories about "under what conditions would something like this happen," they have an opportunity to model what they think is going on. As students work on initial models, usually in pairs, the teacher visits groups to listen and prompt thinking. Each visit takes about three minutes, and the teachers select from a repertoire of gentle probes as they look over the shoulders of their young learners:

- "So I'm hearing you talking about [aspect of phenomena]. Can you share some of your thinking with me?"
- "I see that you've drawn this [pointing to feature of model]. Can you tell me what this represents? How did you decide to show the ideas in this way?"
- "What might be going on here that we can't see?"

You should always ask follow-ups to whatever students say; these generate a lot more thoughtful responses than you might imagine:

- "Can you say more?"
- "Do you agree with what your partner said?"
- "What are some things we're not sure about?"
- "What kinds of information or experiences do we need to learn more about?"
- "How would we test the idea you just mentioned?"

The initial models make student thinking visible to peers and teachers, who get a quick overview of the proto-theories everyone is working with. Public sharing of the models expands the range of ideas available to the entire class for refining explanations as the unit moves forward. This reveal can be helped along by a gallery walk in which the teacher is careful *not* to suggest that some versions are more complete or correct than others. Here are some questions that have worked well for teachers to use during and after a gallery walk:

- "What ideas in some of these models make you think about how you've drawn your own model or what you might add?"
- "Can there be more than one way to represent parts of this phenomenon?"
- "Are there parts of these models that bring up questions for you?"
- "What might we need to find out more about?"

After several lessons, students realize they have new ideas that require adjustments to their models. Teachers ask students to make one of four changes, with handwritten sticky notes placed on their original versions: (1) "add a new idea or feature to your model," (2) "get rid of an idea," (3) "make changes to an existing idea," (4) "pose a question that your model makes you think about."[5] Here again, the teacher can circulate as students work on revisions to foster deeper reasoning with carefully selected questions. This round of table visits is different, however, in that teachers are challenging students to make changes that are consistent with what they've recently learned. Rather than simply probing their thinking, teachers are asking pressing questions:

- "What parts of your model seem consistent with evidence and ideas we've explored in the last few lessons? Check your notebook!"
- "Can you tell me how [science idea X, lab experience Y, or peer argument Z] influenced changes in your explanation or model?"
- "How does [this part of your model] fit in with the rest of it? Is [this element] contradicting another idea embedded in your model?"
- "Does your explanation or model account for how unobservable processes caused the phenomenon to happen in this way?"
- "Is something causing this part of the phenomenon that goes beyond science, perhaps to choices that humans have made?"

This revision process helps students see that changing one's ideas is a sign of astute reasoning rather than making mistakes. It also helps us formatively assess our students' learning early in the unit. It only takes a few minutes at the end of class to look across these sticky notes and get a sense of where the gaps still are, who has provocative ideas that need to be elevated to the whole class, and even how effective or confusing your recent lessons have been.

Over the arc of the unit, teachers weave in epistemic conversations about "how we know what we know," questions about stability and change, and metacognitive prompts for students about the information they need to fill gaps in their evolving explanations. If students have opportunities to put together the individual pieces to represent the whole, they will better understand natural systems, feedback loops, and how to explain phenomena at different scales of time and space.[6] Near the end of a unit, students create a final model that is always accompanied by explanatory writing that elaborates on what is happening. The day before this happens, teachers negotiate with students which key ideas should be in a "gotta-have" checklist. This is a set of concepts that have to show up in all models, regardless of the forms they take. One final caution here is that modeling and explanation, if focused exclusively on canonical climate science ideas, may divert student thinking from the social and political dimensions of climate change.[7] Sensemaking about why climate change is such a crisis won't get very far if students focus exclusively on natural systems.[8]

TWO MORE CASES OF MODELING

Third Graders Model Ecosystem Disruption

A couple of weeks into their unit on rainforest ecosystems and deforestation, Carolyn's third graders were eager to show what they had learned about the relationships between trees and carbon. Figure 9.2 shows how Mateo's model uses words and drawings to convey important ideas. Consider the variety of actors he shows—trees, clouds, the forest, birds, rain, humans, carbon dioxide, and oxygen. He also represented their naturally supportive interactions: rain that hydrates the trees (A), trees taking in carbon dioxide and releasing oxygen that animals depend on (B). But this is also a model of disruption. Humans are pictured using heavy machinery to devastate the landscape, and Mateo makes note of how this prevents trees from carrying out their life-supporting role of gas exchange. Equally problematic are the felled trees that, whether burned or left to decompose, will give up their carbon to the atmosphere (C). There are other inscriptions that adults may consider "cute," such as the clouds reassuring a tree: "don't worry, we help!" or a toucan who implores the viewer to "think of me." These convey emotional messages that should not be dismissed as whimsical additions but rather adding an element of both giving and asking for compassion.

Carolyn routinely asks students to include the question "Why do we care?" on their models and journal entries (which are also filled with spontaneous mini-models). This is something that all of us should consider standard practice, especially when teaching about climate impacts. Mateo tries out a phrase used by Carolyn to sum up his concern: "I care because when we cut down trees, we are *putting a risk* in the Rainforest" (D). If you are an elementary teacher, you know that children often communicate profound ideas using creative grammar and stick figures. You also know that if you sit down with young learners and listen as they narrate their model, gesturing here and there, they can add texture to ideas that are only partially represented on paper and, in the process, reaffirm to us what young minds can do.

Ninth Graders Model the Roles of Water and Energy in Disrupted Ecosystems

Molly taught an interdisciplinary unit centering on a small mammal–the pika—that depends on the local snowpack in the winter to provide insulation

Figure 9.2 Mateo's model of deforestation

against freezing temperatures. They also depend on snowpack runoff in the summer, which cools the surrounding environment just enough for them to avoid heat exhaustion. They can only live in a narrow temperature band, and climate change is now stressing them. Over the course of this integrated physical sciences unit, her students explored topics like the greenhouse effect, the role of freezing and thawing cycles that create the fractured stone fields pikas inhabit, and the conservation of energy as water vapor becomes snow and melts again. Near the end of the unit, Molly negotiated with students the "gotta-have" checklist for their final models:

> So, your models may end up very different from one another, but can still be scientifically accurate. This means we have to decide what ideas are so important that they should be in *everyone's* model or explanation in some form. Let's think about the past few weeks and come up with a list of four or five ideas. Turn to your neighbor and talk for about five minutes. Then we'll come back together and start a list.

This strategy gives students ownership over their own assessments. The conversation can raise controversies about why some ideas are more central or have more explanatory power than others, but airing these arguments is an additional learning opportunity. The dialogue also allows students to recognize whether their current models and explanations might still be "gappy," and if they'll need to seek out more information. Here are ideas that made it into the gotta-have checklist:

- ☐ Pika background information
- ☐ Take into account North Cascades geology or habitat
- ☐ How mountains dictate weather and climate
- ☐ The role of freeze-thaw cycles in creating habitat for pikas
- ☐ The role of hydrogen bonds in water
- ☐ What GHGs do in the atmosphere with different wavelengths of electromagnetic radiation
- ☐ Humans' roles in GHG emissions

Molly's final instructions for her students were to: (1) work together to show and explain how changes in heat energy in the atmosphere are causing pikas in the Cascades to be stressed, (2) think deeply about feedback between different earth systems (geosphere, hydrosphere, atmosphere, biosphere), and (3) follow the gotta-have checklist. Because her students model several times a year, they are comfortable representing their ideas without a template.

One pair of students decided to split their poster paper into different Earth systems. Figure 9.3 shows the hydrosphere corner of their drawing to illustrate how these students used modeling elements to connect phenomena at different scales. At the top they provide historical context, with one graph showing the decline of snowpack over the past fifty years (A) and the other showing the current sparse snowpack across the western United States (B). Zooming in on the habitat, the students use three separate drawings to depict how snow insulates pikas against freezing temperatures in the winter, and summer runoff from the snowpack carries away potentially deadly heat in the summer (C, D, E). The students reference these processes at the molecular level in another part of their model (not shown): "Because of the cohesions and water's polarity, there is a lot of empty space in snow. This means that no energy can escape through the snow through radiation, and that the pika's body heat warms temperatures below the talus [broken rock]." They added that without snow, there would also be no runoff in the summer to cool the pikas: "There would be no hydrogen bonds to absorb heat. Because of this, the pikas would be exposed to extreme temperatures and would die as a result."

The molecular-scale events they refer to are shown in the "raindrop" images. Just in this part of the overall model, the students have used several explanation elements to show their thinking—graphs, mini-models, and molecular zoom-ins. The rest of their model explains other natural systems and, most importantly, shows how they interact. In the center of this poster paper is their summary (italics are in original text):

> The *biosphere* is impacted by many outside factors. As GHGs are added to the *atmosphere* the temperature of the Earth warms, and pikas have less time to forage for food. This also causes less snowpack (*hydrosphere*) which decreases thermal insulation in the winter and reduces runoff in the summer, which in turn warms temperatures in the *geosphere*. Increased temperatures will be detrimental to the freeze-thaw cycle. To combat these effects of climate change, pikas migrate to higher elevations, increasing competitions among pikas. Overall, pikas are being negatively impacted by global warming. The future of pikas and other inhabitants of the North Cascades depends on our choices.

Figure 9.3 Portion of high school students' final model showing how hydrosphere helps explain pika stress

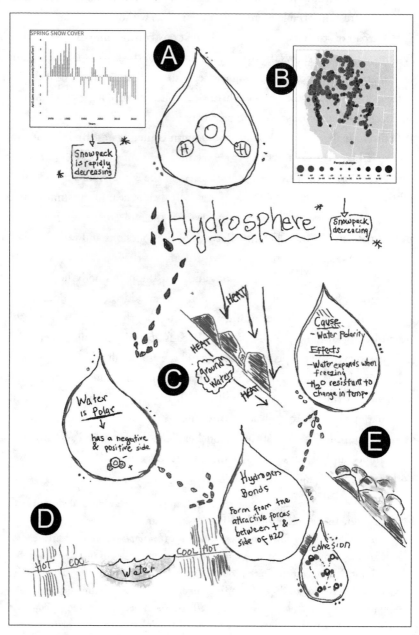

Used with permission.

This model, and others in this class, are the result of sustained knowledge-building work with peers over time and a focus on systems thinking. This type of sensemaking could not be done in a couple of lessons.

ASSESSING MODELS

When Jessica's seventh graders constructed their final models and explanations for how the greenhouse effect is impacting the people of Sarichef Island, they were given a rubric ahead of time so they could clearly understand the criteria they'd be graded on. Around the margins of the rubric, Jessica included five big data sets her students had analyzed during the unit: temperature and CO_2 levels over the past 800,000 years; the percent of greenhouse gases that each sector (electricity, transportation, etc.) contributes to the global total; the percent of people who support renewable energy in the United States; the increase in extreme weather incidents in the world since 1900; and the different greenhouse gases given off by various human activities. Next to each graph, Jessica included the summary by her students of what the trends meant after each of the lessons. For example, next to the data on CO_2 and temperature, the takeaway by students was: "For the last 800K years BCE, the level of CO_2 cycled between 180 ppm and 280 ppm. As CO_2 increased, temperature also increased."

Jessica designed the rubric in table 9.1, which she used to assess students' final attempts (there was a column on the far right indicating that the student did not address this criterion, which I've left out). Rubrics used to assess models and explanations have a criteria column. There should be four or five criteria to capture the various features of models and explanations that make them high-quality representations of knowledge—i.e., the big ideas. More criteria than that and you are likely assessing characteristics of the models that are not critical; fewer means that you've likely missed key features. In Jessica's rubric, she is not just asking for a "good explanation" but a *why* explanation. The breakdown of *what*, *how*, and *why* explanations follows. She uses these terms throughout the school year, so her students know what they mean.

"Why" explanation
- Student traces a full causal story for why a phenomenon unfolded the way it did.

Table 9.1 Rubric for student models of greenhouse gases impacting the Arctic

Criteria	Distinguished (WHY) 100% Includes unseen forces and shows relationships between ideas and synthesizes systems level.	Proficient (HOW) 85% Includes unseen level but may lack synthesis of multiple ideas, application, or big picture.	Approaching (WHAT) 75% Facts-based but lacks connections or unseen elements.	Novice 65% Observations only.
1. Human impacts on climate change	Makes evidence-based claims that clearly explain HOW and WHY increased resource consumption causes global warming.	Makes evidence-based claim that clearly explains HOW increased resource consumption causes global warming.	States that there is a relationship between population size, standards of living, resource consumption, and climate change.	Makes an observation about changing population size, wealth, resources consumption, and climate change.
2. Effects of climate change on earth systems	Explains and visually represents HOW and WHY increasing atmospheric CO_2 levels lead to increasing global temps, which lead to the disruption of multiple Earth systems, and that these disrupted systems often interact, making life on Earth increasingly difficult.	Explains and/or visually represents HOW increasing atmospheric CO_2, and average temps disrupt Earth systems, making life on Earth increasingly difficult.	Describes the effects of global climate change on Earth systems.	Lists an effect of global climate change on Earth systems.
3. Evidence of the causes and effects of climate change	Analyzes and uses data in two or more graphs to explain HOW and WHY human activities have caused the rise in global temps over the past century.	Analyzes and uses data in two or more graphs to explain HOW human activities have caused the rise in global temps over the past century.	Describes the data presented in two or more graphs.	Makes an observation about the data presented in two or more graphs.
4. Solutions that could reduce atmospheric carbon	Explains HOW and WHY one or more solutions could work.	Explains HOW one or more solutions could work.	Describes one or more solutions to reduce carbon in the atmosphere.	States that solutions exist. May or may not include specific solutions.

- Student uses science ideas that have unobservable or theoretical components that influence observable events.

"How" explanation
- Student tells a one-step cause-and-effect story.
- Student predicts the way some natural systems will behave based on previously collected data, but without talking about unobservable events or processes.
- Student describes but does not explain relationships between variables, differences between experimental groups, trends over time, or qualitative observations.

"What" explanation
- Student describes only what is observable or measurable in a phenomenon. Even if the description includes meticulous detail, it is still a "what" explanation.

The rubric tells us that Jessica is less interested in whether students include a prominent title or key and does not have vague criteria like "model clearly illustrates idea X." Rather, these criteria reflect her broad goals for the whole unit, in terms of what students understand. She and a teaching partner, Colleen, designed the rubric long before the unit began and then made sure that their instruction provided ample opportunities for students to construct the knowledge needed to address each criterion. All her students have a shot at excellence, and it can be demonstrated in many different ways.

IMPLICATIONS FOR MODELING IN YOUR CLASSROOM

The models in this chapter exemplify a mantra repeated throughout this book: let students show the most of what they know. Models aren't just an accumulation of facts thrown onto paper; they represent students' efforts toward sensemaking and tell a causal story about complex events. These are also stories of interconnected systems, of stability and change. We want to assess students in additional ways, perhaps using short-answer responses to questions, multiple choice, and the like. But these more conventional measures cannot, by themselves, reveal the breadth of what students have learned. Modeling and explanation also teach students that the "right answers" for authentic questions are not out there; rather there are only more evidence-based and coherent accounts that can still be revised as we learn more. Even so, there may be more than one credible explanation for the same event. It's real science. And speaking of real, when knowledge-building communities try to explain climate change phenomena, the questions they should always return to are "Why should we care? To whom does this matter?"

CHAPTER 10

Activism and Self-Care
for the Long Haul

IF YOU ARE HELPING your students reconsider their relationships with the environment, then you might be part of a social movement. It's understandable if you don't think of yourself this way, but what counts as activism is defined more by purpose and commitment than how many people you can assemble for a rally against single-use plastics. Social movements of the last hundred years have always gained a foothold in public consciousness slowly and on many fronts at once, with everyday folk marching, writing letters, attending meetings, getting candidates on the ballot, and exposing injustices with the status quo.[1] Just as with civil rights, women's rights, and LGBTQ rights, the frontlines of climate action are everywhere, including in our schools. The empowered view is that this gives educators many ways to make a difference.

Successful climate activists mobilize others to change individual or group behaviors for the sake of sustainability and equity, and they pressure economic and political actors toward the same ends—to use their influence for the common good. Young people across the world are protesting overconsumption, dependence on fossil fuels, and unethical exercises of power in decision-making about the climate. These messages interweave concerns about social injustice with environmental issues such as pollution and biodiversity loss.

Not all forms of dissent are alike. One type aims for *awareness and education* of others. This is often expressed through activities that schools and community organizations sanction to resist climate-damaging practices, such as overdevelopment or unrestrained resource extraction from sensitive habitats, and to promote alternative ways of thinking and being. One example of awareness and education dissent is students using their voices to highlight climate change solutions to their peers, younger children, or community members. Another is bearing witness to the scope of a local climate-related problem and sharing this with the public. Then there is *disruptive dissent*, in which youth and adults seek to change existing political and economic structures, often through protests and collective action.[2] They may start petition campaigns and boycotts or interrupt climate meetings to draw attention to environmental hypocrisies and the exclusion of important voices. Working against society's continued dependence on fossil fuels is frequently a goal of disruptive dissent, which is aimed at changing the system rather than working within it. In the context of K–12 schooling, student activism includes both types of dissent and can blur the lines between awareness or education efforts and disruption.

Diverse examples of activism demonstrate that none of us has to work alone. We can be individuals yet also find new purpose and leverage within human networks. Climate writer Paul Hawken explains:

> Each of us is multitudes. We have different skills and potential, including sharing, electing, demonstrating, teaching, conserving, and diverse means of helping leaders, cities, companies, neighbors, co-workers and governments become aware and able to act.[3]

Collectives that change the world begin with one person, and then another. A working space coalesces where commitment, talents, and action bond people together to accomplish what could not be done individually—drawing together a group, a team, a movement.

Here is another place where you might think, "Wow, I was not trained for this." You are in good company, meaning 99 percent of educators are not graduates of the "activism academy." However, the work can take many forms, and as Hawken notes, even students and teachers with no experience in environmental movements can still choose how to participate in meaningful action for a sustainable Earth. Activism has benefits for students beyond social transformation; it builds their sense of self-efficacy and agency. Both are important for young learners. There is room for everyone in this movement, and the truth is that there is one generation left—the children we are now teaching—that will determine which climate future becomes reality. Room for everyone means that the recommendations for action in this chapter are an invitation for you to get involved. We can't wait; legions of high schoolers across the world are already in this fight, and our elementary students will be voters in the blink of an eye. We are those valuable trusted messengers that other activists hold up as key to the cause—we are influencers. Sustaining ourselves for the long haul, therefore, is not an indulgence but a necessity, as we'll learn in the next section.

SELF-CARE TO MAKE THE WORK SUSTAINABLE

It is appropriate that the last chapter of a book on planetary challenges draws us back to our own fragility and the need for self-care in this fight. Climate change education rarely accounts for students' (or teachers') emotional lives, even though research shows that emotions have a substantial influence on our attention and capacity to continue learning.[4] This makes it as critical for students to address their feelings as it is for them to engage with environmental disruption and injustice. Training an emotional lens on efforts to restore the health of the Earth gives us a better chance to help students attend to the social inequities of climate change, cultivate new relationships, and take action.

In her book, *A Field Guide to Climate Anxiety*, Sarah Jaquette Ray warns readers about four features of activism that can undercut personal resilience.[5] First, the culture of activism can valorize working beyond one's capacity, assuming that our bodies and minds can sustain constant crisis in the name of justice or sustainability. This is a recipe for burnout. As a long tradition of social activism demonstrates, self-care is a tool for political engagement. Ray argues that cultivating relationships and restoring energy through sleep, exercise, silence, mindfulness, timely inaction, and the pursuit of activities that generate passion and creativity are essential for us to maintain the human capital needed for the work of change. Any behavior that protects emotional and physical resources counts as resistance.

Second, some social activists have done a lot of hand-wringing over whether certain kinds of resistance or support of a cause are worth pursuing when it is not clear whether those efforts will achieve an immediate and recognizable outcome. Why sacrifice so much, they wonder, when there's no guarantee that the vision will be realized? Too many people seek high-visibility payoffs for their actions, which neglects the tidal power of relentless and diverse means of resistance that don't make the headlines. We have to start by shifting our perception of what "impact" is. Environmental humanities scholar Nicole Seymour believes the climate movement cannot afford to overlook actions like expressing dissatisfaction with the environmentalist status quo, raising activist morale, caregiving, going to meetings, serving as cultural analysts by helping others understand our current eco-political moment from nonprivileged perspectives, and modeling flexibility in the face of turmoil.[6]

These choices broaden our notion of what counts as meaningful action and make it apparent that we indeed have the capacity to play pivotal roles. In certain situations, action taken might not seem to be enough—but it may be all that is possible.[7] Seasoned activists' ideas about social change can relieve us of "big and right now" expectations for success, which just ramp up our anxiety. Social change can be slow, unnewsworthy, and unspectacular. Triumphant moments, on the other hand, are a result of behind-the-scenes work by unnamed idealists and of subtle social maneuvers impossible to track. Being an agent of social change, therefore, requires humility.

Third, the illusion of rugged individualism, especially the American version of it, undermines personal resilience by making us think we are alone in our efforts and alone with periodic episodes of despair. The reality is that climate action demands social capital as much as funding or other material resources. We need interpersonal trust as much as we need changes in infrastructure. A growing body of evidence shows that the keys to enhancing human resilience are building robust social support networks and close collaborations within and among local organizations.[8] For educators, this can be a difficult mind-set to embrace. We are used to being solely responsible for making things happen in classrooms. But everything valuable about climate action happens in relation with other human beings, often outside of school. It takes us out of our comfort zones, but that's where the work is.

Fourth, a focus on hope is not as valuable as a focus on efficacy. Hope is often tagged onto otherwise disturbing stories as a silver lining, which can be a distraction from action. Your work with students should instead cultivate a sense of efficacy and agency; these two capacities roughly translate as "I believe we can make a difference" and "We've got the plans for making it happen." You can start by routinely framing problems and futures as things that students can influence. This sounds like rhetorical sleight of hand on your part, but the message is accurate and students have to feel empowered. Feeling as if you have the capacity to accomplish something, including the most important task—preserving yourself and your students for a lifetime of thriving in a climate-changed world—*is* the point.

The best way to resist burnout, Ray sums up, is to stop "performing busyness as a badge of commitment," and cultivate a daily practice of self-care, the kind that helps you heal and prioritize what's important in your life so you can stay in the game. The following adapted list has examples of her self-care strategy:

- Avoid self-sabotaging habits like doom-scrolling on social media or perfectionism in creating climate lessons for students.
- Get enough sleep and exercise; try mindfulness practices.
- Focus on tasks you find fulfilling and in line with your priorities; don't say yes to everything.
- Foster a support network for yourself; seek out family, friends, fellow educators, and community members who share visions of sustainable and just futures.
- Visualize positive outcomes for your work and the local environment.
- Celebrate small successes, perhaps an unexpected conversation with students who want to take action in their neighborhood, or an email from a parent who expresses appreciation for your instructional emphasis on a changing climate.
- Seek beauty in your everyday life and get out into nature.

ECO-ANXIETY AND ACTION IN THE WORLD

There was a time when most of us were unaware of how intimately our mental health was linked to the state of the natural world, but we are now living through a wave of destructive spectacles that can traumatize us in unexpected ways. Over the last few years, terms like *eco-anxiety, environmental grief, climate depression*, and *pre-traumatic stress* have become common vernacular, even among youth. Being nervous or afraid is an understandable reaction to uncertain and uncontrollable ecological threats that, for some people, become the core angst in their lives and lead to a sense of hopelessness, even the denial of one's anxiety. For others, it is a chronic background unease that can exacerbate more acute distresses, such as concern about one's health or local injustices. Mental health experts now recognize troubling links between climate change and depression, sleep disorders, substance abuse, and even suicide.

But there are glimmers of hope that educators can help learners deal with these emotions, even redirect such feelings to take action in the world.[9] Current research indicates there can be a "practical" side to eco-anxiety that motivates a person's cognitive engagement—information gathering, deliberation, and reflection—aimed at helping one come to better, more informed decisions on what to do about environmental threats. In this way, eco-anxiety can be used to foster agency and even a sense of well-being, but all this would take intentional planning on your part.[10]

How might we address eco-anxiety in our classrooms? First, give voice to what students (and you) are experiencing. This is why asking some version of "How do you feel?" is important when leading into climate change discussions with children or adolescents.[11] As part of this dialogue, naming emotions helps people channel their energies more constructively and understand their own unique experiences of eco-anxiety. Because children and adults alike often struggle to recognize or name their own emotions, this entry into climate conversations requires preparation, perhaps in consultation with school counselors or colleagues who have skills in supporting socio-emotional well-being.[12] For most students, something as simple as acknowledging those feelings (likely a mix of anger, helplessness, fear, guilt, loneliness) allows them to unpack what is happening to them, then move on to solutions and actions because they're no longer investing emotional energy in suppressing, denying, and deflecting problems that could consume them.

Second, students need to be reassured that they are not alone in experiencing fear and the impacts of environmental disruption. Part of our depression and anxiety comes from feeling isolated. And when people feel alone, they don't feel like taking action. Encouraging a sense of inclusivity and community is essential in coping with eco-anxiety. Promoting solidarity among children and having them engage in neighborhood events or other forms of activism are ways to help reduce their feelings of isolation and disillusionment, which brings us to the final recommendation. The final classroom coping strategy echoes one of the central themes of this book—to frame climate challenges around solutions. By trying to solve problems, especially those at the local level, students are more likely to become informed, share information with others, and feel empowered to make changes. This framing engenders constructive hope (a sense of efficacy) that, in turn, lays the groundwork for resilience.[13]

HOW MANY PEOPLE DO WE NEED TO INFLUENCE? HOW DO WE START THE WORK?

Occasionally students will wonder how many people they have to reach to initiate widespread change. The sweet spot for climate action is between 10,000 and 100,000 people.[14] Christina Kwauk and Rebecca Winthrop of the Brookings Institution point out that this is equivalent to focusing efforts at the school-district level (the range does not represent the number of people that have to be directly engaged by activists, but rather the number impacted by implementing an intervention). School districts are administrative networks that exist across the world and usually have enough community connections to scale up climate learning and activism efforts. Kwauk and Winthrop argue that focusing efforts at this level enables action to be community-driven, which is aligned with what we know about effective climate change education: it needs to be customized for local culture and circumstances, and tied to local environmental issues.[15]

Another reason that schools are so well positioned to change social norms around climate issues is that children can have a strong influence on their parents' climate views. This is referred to as *intergenerational learning,* and researchers have said that children "are arguably best equipped to navigate the ideologically fraught topic of climate change with older generations in ways that inspire action."[16] Five key principles of classroom work can promote child-to-adult intergenerational learning around climate action. These include *staying focused on local issues, teaching longer-term and more in-depth lesson sequences* (preferably with repeated revisiting of big ideas, lasting a few weeks or more), *engaging students in hands-on projects, encouraging parental participation,* and *enthusiastic teaching.* These conditions are all consistent with the broader vision of classrooms as knowledge-building communities. Girls, in particular, have strong effects on their parents' thinking and actions, especially on those adults who are ideologically conservative.[17] The effect extends to changes in environmental behaviors like energy conservation, waste reduction, and flood education. If children are also equipped with strategies to engage with their parents about their community's climate challenges, they can work around adults' political entrenchments that can act as barriers to recognizing climate risks and taking action.[18]

WHAT DOES THE WORK LOOK LIKE?

Students readily take ownership of climate awareness projects that are interest-driven and build important communicative or organizing skills through pursuits they perceive as relevant. Just as with other climate activists, students benefit from a focus on producing things—creating objects, tools, and designs for performances through iterative cycles of consulting with others and revising plans, and then delivering those works to stakeholder audiences.[19] Students like to play the roles of both teachers and learners, regularly calling on one another as sources of expertise and mentorship. While this description makes activism seem a bit intimidating, we should remember that small efforts often catalyze greater involvement and impact. When a student puts together a website showing how her school could decarbonize by shifting to renewable sources of energy, she may be uplifted by the attention the website receives from classmates and teachers. She might then realize she's not the only person who feels that change is needed.[20] Modest successes build confidence as well as students' sense of belonging within a community of similarly concerned others, which then creates momentum for more involved work.

When you start working with students on climate-related issues, it helps to use high-level organizing principles to guide decision-making. The following framework has five touchstones drawn from the writings of experienced activist organizers who work with youth.[21]

1. Cultivate climate literacy among students and their audiences. On most activist websites, the first recommendation is to build climate literacy. This involves a bit more than knowing the science. Older students especially should have at least a basic grounding in the social, economic, and political forces at play. If audiences perceive that activists don't comprehend the basis for climate problems or solutions, their messaging will be seen as less credible. If students do not have entry-level knowledge, they may put all their efforts into addressing imagined environmental harms or promoting causes unrelated to climate change. On the other hand, with basic literacy comes an understanding of the social justice implications of climate change, specifically how it is disproportionately impacting marginalized communities. This awareness is necessary for purposeful action.

2. Plan for action and open up pathways for everyone's participation. Teams of students can help you develop a plan to take action in the school or community. Student leaders can either be creative and collaborative problem-framers or encourage peers who have these skills to take the lead in figuring out challenges and solutions.[22] The eventual plan should allow for a wide range of peer interests and talents to be part of the activity (some students are interested in graphic design, humor, numbers, public speaking, artful confrontation, food, etc.). One mistake to avoid is being too science-centric in how we reach audiences. For example, we don't pay enough attention to the environmental humanities with its focus on storytelling, creative expression, and emotion. Including the humanities can facilitate breakthroughs for planners and, later, for audiences. Tools for the work of public persuasion and enlightenment are plentiful. Students can use combinations of videos, infographics, poetry, street art, letters, personal appearances, podcasts, emails, blogs, and social media posts.

3. Start with what the community cares about. This means grounding activity in the concerns of the neighborhood or region, and reaching out to local organizations that are already working on climate change resilience (or want to). Learn more about proposals circulating in your community that are working toward sustainability, but take care to filter out those that are simply "covers" for powerful groups looking out for their self-interests. It is critical for everyone to understand climate change impacts happening in their own community and how climate change is affecting them directly; this helps make solutions genuinely restorative and meaningful. We, especially White educators, have to listen and learn. Climate justice writer Mary Annaïse Heglar provides this advice: "The next time you want to 'educate' communities of color about climate change, remember that they have even more to teach you about building movements, about courage, about survival."[23]

4. Let solutions become the bigger story. Focus on sharing ideas about solutions. These can take many forms; some will be about mitigation, some about adaptation, and some about just cleaning up the mess. Simply making local conversations about climate change impacts and solutions more commonplace is a powerful form of activism.

5. Orient the work around justice and compassion. Understanding that climate change impacts people differently is critical. Youth, particularly young people of color, feel this more than anyone. Just as with our classroom teaching, connections should be made explicit between risk, racism, and environmental change. This does not have to be a lecture; it can be an opportunity to share stories and connect with audiences on a deeply personal level. Here are just a few examples of topics that could be explored in most parts of the United States:

- Climate-related health concerns like water safety, air quality, or urban heat islands
- Indigenous sovereignty of local lands
- Land use and preserving carbon sinks
- Protecting local biodiversity
- Food insecurity and food waste
- Disaster relief from climate-related events
- Transitioning to renewables

Figure 10.1 shows examples of activism that are squarely in the wheelhouse of K–12 students and teachers. In the left column are suggestions that aim for climate literacy and awareness of risks as well as local solutions. In the right column are suggestions for actions that would fall under the category of disruptive dissent because they seek to change existing political and economic structures through protests and collective pressure. Placement of actions in either category is not set in stone. Projects in one can be reconfigured in their means or goals to make them fit in the other. Both forms of dissent are necessary for widespread change in the world.

Figure 10.1 Types of awareness and education, and disruptive dissent appropriate for secondary students

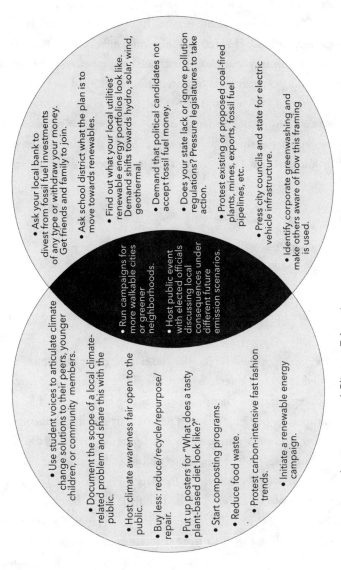

- Use student voices to articulate climate change solutions to their peers, younger children, or community members.
- Document the scope of a local climate-related problem and share this with the public.
- Host climate awareness fair open to the public.
- Buy less: reduce/recycle/repurpose/repair.
- Put up posters for "What does a tasty plant-based diet look like?"
- Start composting programs.
- Reduce food waste.
- Protest carbon-intensive fast fashion trends.
- Initiate a renewable energy campaign.

- Run campaigns for more walkable cities or greener neighborhoods.
- Host public event with elected officials discussing local consequences under different future emission scenarios.

- Ask your local bank to divest from fossil fuel investments of any type or withdraw your money. Get friends and family to join.
- Ask school district what the plan is to move towards renewables.
- Find out what your local utilities' renewable energy portfolios look like. Demand shifts towards hydro, solar, wind, geothermal.
- Demand that political candidates not accept fossil fuel money.
- Does your state lack or ignore pollution regulations? Pressure legislatures to take action.
- Protest existing or proposed coal-fired plants, mines, exports, fossil fuel pipelines, etc.
- Press city councils and state for electric vehicle infrastructure.
- Identify corporate greenwashing and make others aware of how this framing is used.

Awareness and Climate Education   Disruptive Dissent

A HIGH SCHOOL MOBILIZES FOR CLIMATE AWARENESS AND EDUCATION

At a Bay Area high school in California, faculty and students started an event billed as a Teach-in for Climate Justice. This gathering was held to educate the entire school, as well as interested community members, about climate change solutions. Students referred to their created space as a resiliency village, consisting of four quadrants: (1) Science for Survival, (2) Civic Engagement, (3) Visual Arts, and (4) Voice and Performance. The village was intended to educate the community in a fun and friendly way about living sustainably. Erin, a biology teacher at the school, led this effort by drafting a compelling rationale in four bulleted points, which she and other teachers presented to the administration:

> Why are we proposing this?
> - Young people are powerful agents of social change.
> - Young people need accurate information about the reality of the climate crisis.
> - Young people need our support to remember that they are powerful and can take action to stop climate change.
> - Adults can encourage young people to think and take action. They can take young people's leadership seriously.

Erin's biology students planned and ran the event (determined the exhibits, created materials, interacted with visitors, etc.). They partnered with several local organizations that provided training around ideas like solar power, electrification legislation, and food justice. Participating students had to create a booth and offer an interactive presentation for passersby. On the day the village opened, tables were lined end to end around the central campus of the high school, with students in groups eager to corral visitors and talk about their projects. Exhibits helped audiences understand the role of pollinators, sustainable makeup, cleaner fuel for airplanes, the different kinds of eco-friendly lighting used in their school, environmental racism, and other topics. Teachers found that interactive exhibits were more compelling to audiences. For example, one exhibit involved building your own sustainable city using small models of homes, offices, solar panels, wind turbines, and green spaces, which audience members could move around on a tabletop landscape. Other participatory exhibits allowed visitors to play a game or do eco-artwork.

A fast-fashion exhibit prompted visitors to spin a cardboard wheel with different types of clothing represented, just to see how much water is used to create items that will be worn typically no more than seven or eight times before being discarded. Any kind of interactivity drew more visitors and sustained longer conversations.

Erin noticed that some of the projects were about biodiversity or human impacts on the environment without being explicitly connected to climate change. She recalled, "Like litter, doing beach cleanups, pollution, and buying reusable straws. I'm not sure that they were actually able to relate them to climate science." This was something she wanted to change for the following year. The highlight for everyone, Erin observed, was the enthusiasm of students:

> There was a ton of engagement, like even our kids who traditionally might not appear motivated in a classroom all day, they were interacting with people that came to their booth, they were all speaking about their project in some way. And I think the most exciting thing is that it really involved all different groups on our campus to come and visit.

Erin added that, early on, teachers weren't sure how much they would have to facilitate interactions between exhibit hosts and visitors: "But we had a moment where all the teachers were just like standing on the sidelines, watching it happen. And it was very much like, the students were running it. They basically took it over, it was a really cool moment."

This example of young people stepping up and exercising agency is an appropriate way to close this book. Education for dissent and action on climate change can be a profound learning experience for our students and should be a more common outgrowth of climate literacy that we can foster in our classrooms. Participating in civic activism and more radical forms of resistance can help youth revitalize our democracy, perhaps motivating adults in their lives to stand in solidarity with them and make the sacrifices to ensure a livable future for all members of the human and more-than-human communities. We cannot overestimate how much we will end up depending on our children to heal the world, and this responsibility will be passed to them more quickly than we can imagine. But not before we do our part.

Unit Trajectories in a Third- and a Ninth- Grade Classroom

Below are two trajectories of units described in chapter 2. Figure A.1 represents a third-grade unit on ecosystems and deforestation. Figure A.2 represents a ninth-grade unit on how pikas are adapted to geophysical conditions in the Cascade foothills that are now changing. In both units, the teachers elicited students' ideas and had them represent their current thinking in models and explanations. Each of the lessons listed extend over two or three days. Later in these units, students' initial representations were revised based on new ideas and evidence, and then finalized at the end of the unit. Both classrooms worked as knowledge-building communities with these opportunities threaded throughout their units:

- Epistemic conversations
- Modeling
- Revising ideas
- Making meaning of data
- Metacognitive reflection
- Students' ideas as part of the curriculum
- Conversations about who is doing harm and who is being impacted

Figure A.1 Lesson trajectory for a third-grade unit (ecosystems and deforestation)

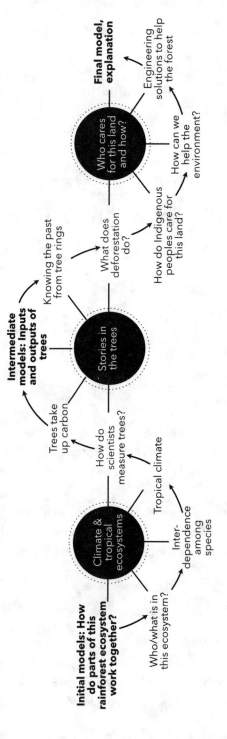

Figure A.2 Lesson trajectory for a ninth-grade unit (why pikas are stressed out)

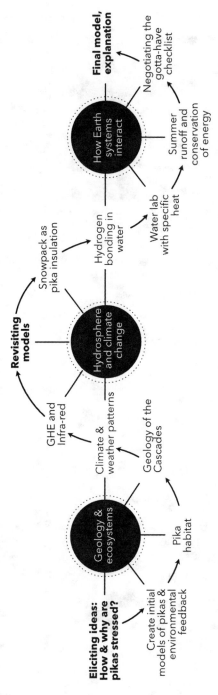

Climate-Specific Engineering Standards

Below are all the climate-specific engineering standards across the K–12 spectrum in Next Generation Science Standards. Some of these are performance expectations (PEs), and others are disciplinary core ideas (DCIs). There are also generic engineering standards, not listed here, that could be applied to nearly any type of climate-related mitigation or adaptation solutions.

Grade level: K

Energy (K-PS3)
PE: Use tools and materials to design and build a structure that will reduce the warming effect of sunlight on an area. (K-PS3-2)

Earth and Human Activity (K-ESS3)
DCI: Things that people do to live comfortably can affect the world around them. But they can make choices that reduce their impacts on the land, water, air, and other living things. (ESS3.C)

PE: Communicate solutions that will reduce the impact of humans on the land, water, air, and/or other living things in the local environment. (K-ESS3-3)

Grade level: 3

Earth and Human Activity (3-ESS3)

DCI: A variety of natural hazards result from natural processes. Humans cannot eliminate natural hazards but can take steps to reduce their impacts. (ESS3.B)

PE: Make a claim about the merit of a design solution that reduces the impacts of a weather-related hazard. (3-ESS3-1)

Grade level: 4

Earth and Human Activity (3-ESS3)

DCI: A variety of hazards result from natural processes (e.g., earthquakes, tsunamis, volcanic eruptions). Humans cannot eliminate the hazards but can take steps to reduce their impacts. (ESS3.B)

PE: Generate and compare multiple solutions to reduce the impacts of natural Earth processes on humans. (4-ESS3-2)

Grade level: Middle school

Matter and Its Interactions (MS-PS1)

PE: Gather and make sense of information to describe that synthetic materials come from natural resources and impact society. (MS-PS1-3)

Biological Evolution: Unity and Diversity (MS-LS4)

DCI: In artificial selection, humans have the capacity to influence certain characteristics of organisms by selective breeding. One can choose desired parental traits determined by genes, which are then passed on to offspring. (LS4.B)

Earth and Human Activity (MS-ESS3)

PE: Analyze and interpret data on natural hazards to forecast future catastrophic events and inform the development of technologies to mitigate their effects. (MS-ESS3-2)

Engineering Design (MS-ETS1)

PE: Define the criteria and constraints of a design problem with sufficient precision to ensure a successful solution, taking into account relevant scientific principles and potential impacts on people and the natural environment that may limit possible solutions. (MS-ETS1-1)

Grade level: High school

Energy (HS-PS3)

PE: Design, build, and refine a device that works within given constraints to convert one form of energy into another form of energy. (HS-PS3-3)

Waves and Their Applications (HS-PS4)

DCI: Solar cells are human-made devices that likewise capture the sun's energy and produce electrical energy. (PS3.D)

DCI: Photoelectric materials emit electrons when they absorb light of a high-enough frequency. (PS4.B)

Earth and Human Activity (HS-ESS3)

DCI: All forms of energy production and other resource extraction have associated economic, social, environmental, and geopolitical costs and risks as well as benefits. New technologies and social regulations can change the balance of these factors. (ESS3.A)

DCI: Scientists and engineers can make major contributions by developing technologies that produce less pollution and waste and that preclude ecosystem degradation. (ESS3.C)

PE: Evaluate competing design solutions for developing, managing, and utilizing energy and mineral resources based on cost-benefit ratios. (HS-ESS3-2)

Notes

Chapter 1

1. "Global Energy-related CO2 Emissions," International Energy Agency, https://www.iea .org/data-and-statistics/charts/global-energy-related-co2-emissions-1990-2020, October 26, 2022.

2. Ilona Otto et al., "Social Tipping Dynamics for Stabilizing Earth's Climate by 2050," *Proceedings of the National Academy of Sciences* 117, no. 5 (2020): 2354–65, doi:10.1073 /pnas.1900577117.

3. Liz Hamel et al., *The Kaiser Family Foundation/Washington Post Climate Change Survey*, Kaiser Family Foundation, 2019, https://www.kff.org/report-section/the-kaiser-family -foundation-washington-post-climate-change-survey-main-findings/.

4. Connie Roser-Renouf, Teresa Myers, and Edward Maibach, *American Adolescents' Responses to NASA's Climate Change Website* (Fairfax, VA: George Mason University, 2020), https://www.climatechangecommunication.org/all/nasa_teens2018_2/, doi: 10.13021 /ya48-qt30.

5. David Wallace-Wells, *The Uninhabitable Earth* (Harlow, England: Penguin, 2019), 3.

6. Matt James et al., "Communicating the Climate Health Connection," Climate Reality, March 9, 2017, video, https://www.youtube.com/watch?v=7SRTLsUo9D8.

7. Andrew Volmert et al., *Just the Earth Doing Its Own Thing: Mapping the Gaps Between Expert and Public Understandings of Oceans and Climate Change* (Washington, DC: FrameWorks Institute. 2013).

8. Roser-Renouf et al., *American Adolescents' Responses*.

9. Ed Maibach, "5 evidence-based messages that help people reach appropriate conclusions re CC climate change: It's real. It's us (i.e., human-caused). Experts agree (about human-caused CC). It's bad (for us). There's hope (there are helpful actions we can take)," @MaibachEd, June 25, 2018, https://twitter.com/maibached/status/10112678 83664662529.

10. Per Espen Stoknes, *What We Think About When We Try Not to Think About Global Warming: Toward a New Psychology of Climate Action* (White River Junction, VT: Chelsea Green Publishing, 2015).

11. Paul Hawken, *Drawdown: The Most Comprehensive Plan Ever Proposed to Reverse Global Warming* (Harlow, England: Penguin, 2018), 217.

12. Amitav Ghosh, *The Great Derangement: Climate Change and the Unthinkable* (Chicago: University of Chicago Press, 2017), 62.

13. Priyadarshi Shukla et al., *Summary for Policymakers: Climate Change and Land: An IPCC Special Report on Climate Change, Desertification, Land Degradation, Sustainable Land*

Management, Food Security, and Greenhouse Gas Fluxes in Terrestrial Ecosystems (Geneva, Switzerland: Intergovernmental Panel on Climate Change, 2019), 10.

14. Ghosh, *The Great Derangement.*
15. Glenn Althor, James Watson, and Richard Fuller, "Global Mismatch between Greenhouse Gas Emissions and the Burden of Climate Change," *Scientific Reports* 6, no. 1 (2016), https://doi.org/10.1038/srep20281.
16. David Schlosberg and Lisette Collins, "From Environmental to Climate Justice: Climate Change and the Discourse of Environmental Justice," *Wiley Interdisciplinary Reviews: Climate Change* 5 no. 3 (2014): 359–74.
17. Manjana Milkoreit et al., "Defining Tipping Points for Social-Ecological Systems Scholarship—An Interdisciplinary Literature Review," *Environmental Research Letters* 13, no. 3 (2018): 033005.
18. Timothy Lenton et al., "Climate Tipping Points—Too Risky to Bet Against," *Nature* 575, no. 7784 (2019): 592–95.
19. Otto et al., "Social Tipping Dynamics"; Damon Centola et al., "Experimental Evidence for Tipping Points in Social Convention," *Science* 360 (2018): 1116–19.
20. Centola et al., "Experimental Evidence," 1117.
21. Naomi Klein, *This Changes Everything: Capitalism vs. The Climate* (New York: Simon & Schuster, 2014), 459.
22. Ming Lee Tien et al., "Predictors of Public Climate Change Awareness and Risk Perception Around the World," *Nature Climate Change* 5, no. 11 (2015): 1014–20, doi:org/10.1038/nclimate2728.
23. Roser-Renouf, Myers, and Maibach, "American Adolescents' Responses."
24. Hamel et al., *The Kaiser Family Foundation/Washington Post Climate Change Survey.*
25. Eric Plutzer et al., *Mixed Messages: How Climate Is Taught in America's Schools* (Oakland, CA: National Center for Science Education, 2016), 30.
26. Plutzer et al., *Mixed Messages,* 10.
27. Klein, *This Changes Everything,* 462.
28. George Lakoff, "Why It Matters How We Frame the Environment," *Environmental Communication* 4, no. 1 (2010): 70–81, doi:org/10.1080/17524030903529749.

Chapter 2

1. Jacques Pasquet and Marion Arbona, *My Wounded Island* (Victoria, BC: Orca Book Publishers, 2017), 16.
2. Christina Kwauk and Olivia Case, *A New Green Learning Agenda: Approaches to Quality Education for Climate Action* (Washington, DC: Center for Universal Education at The Brookings Institution, 2021), 14.
3. Frameworks Institute, *Expanding Our Repertoire: Why and How to Get Collective Climate Solutions in the Frame,* 2017.
4. Martha Monroe et al., "Identifying Effective Climate Change Education Strategies: A Systematic Review of the Research," *Environmental Education Research* 25, no. 6 (2019): 791–812, doi.org/10.1080/13504622.2017.136084.
5. Brian Reiser et al., "Storyline Units: An Instructional Model to Support Coherence from the Students' Perspective," *Journal of Science Teacher Education* 32, no. 7 (2021), 805–29, doi.org/10.1080/1046560X.2021.1884784.
6. Marlene Scardamalia and Carl Bereiter, "Knowledge Building and Knowledge Creation: Theory, Pedagogy, and Technology," in *Cambridge Handbook of the Learning Sciences,* 2nd ed., eds. Keith Sawyer (New York: Cambridge University Press, 2014), 397–417.

7. David McCandless, *Knowledge Is Beautiful* (London: William Collins, 2014), 1.

8. Marcia Linn, "Designing the Knowledge Integration Environment," *International Journal of Science Education* 22, no. 8, (2000): 781–96.

9. Laura Zangori et al., "Student Development of Model-Based Reasoning About Carbon Cycling and Climate Change in a Socio-Scientific Issues Unit," *Journal of Research in Science Teaching* 54, no. 10 (2017): 1249–73.

10. Mark Windschitl, Jessica Thompson, and Melissa Braaten, *Ambitious Science Teaching* (Cambridge, MA: Harvard Education Press, 2018).

11. Devarati Bhattacharya, Kimberly Steward, and Cory Forbes, "Empirical Research on K–16 Climate Education: A Systematic Review of the Literature," *Journal of Geoscience Education* 69, no. 3 (2021): 223–47, doi: 10.1080/10899995.2020.1838848.

12. Monroe et al., "Identifying Effective Climate Change Education Strategies."

13. Nicole Holthuis et al., "Supporting and Understanding Students' Epistemological Discourse About Climate Change," *Journal of Geoscience Education* 62, no. 3 (2014): 374–87, doi:10.5408/13-036.1.

14. Mageswary Karpudewan, Wolff-Michael Roth, and Kasturi Chandrakesan, "Remediating Misconception on Climate Change Among Secondary School Students in Malaysia," *Environmental Education Research* 21, no. 4 (2015): 631–48, doi:10.1080/13504622.2014.891004; Holthuis et al. "Supporting and Understanding."

15. Bhattacharya et al., "Empirical Research on K–16 Climate Education."

16. Laura Bofferding and Matthew Kloser, "Middle and High School Students' Conceptions of Climate Change Mitigation and Adaptation Strategies," *Environmental Education Research* 21, no. 2 (2015): 275–94, doi:10.1080/13504622.2014.888401.

17. Monroe et al., "Identifying Effective Climate Change Education Strategies."

18. Kwauk and Casey, *A New Green Learning Agenda.*

19. Susanne Moser, "Not for the Faint of Heart: Tasks of Climate Change Communication in the Context of Societal Transformation," in *Climate and Culture: Multidisciplinary Perspectives of Knowing, Being and Doing in a Climate Change World*, eds. Giuseppe Feola, Hilary Geoghegan, and Alex Arnall (Cambridge, UK: Cambridge University Press, 2019), 141–67.

20. US Environmental Protection Agency Office of Resource Conservation and Recovery, *Municipal Solid Waste Generation, Recycling, and Disposal in the United States: Facts and Figures, a Methodology Document* (Washington, DC: US Environmental Protection Agency Office of Resource Conservation and Recovery, April 2014).

Chapter 3

Chapter 3.1

1. "Solar Irradiance," NASA, November 27, 2017, https://www.nasa.gov/mission_pages/sdo/science/solar-irradiance.html.

2. Veerabhadran Ramanathan, "Climate Change," in *Bending the Curve: Climate Change Solutions Digital Textbook*, eds. Veerabhadran Ramanathan (Oakland: University of California, UC Office of the President, 2019), 1–53.

3. Holli Riebeek, "Global Warming, " NASA, June 3, 2010, https://earthobservatory.nasa.gov/features/GlobalWarming.

4. "Carbon Cycle," Science Mission Directorate, October 28, 2022, https://science.nasa.gov/earth-science/oceanography/ocean-earth-system/ocean-carbon-cycle.

5. Kerry Emanuel, *What We Know About Climate Change* (Cambridge, MA: MIT Press, 2018).

6. "The Carbon Cycle," https://earthobservatory.nasa.gov/features/CarbonCycle.

7. "Why Does CO2 Get Most of the Attention When There Are So Many Other Heat-Trapping Gases?," Union of Concerned Scientists, August 3, 2017, https://www.ucsusa.org/resources/why-does-co2-get-more-attention-other-gases; "The Causes of Climate Change," Earth Science Communications Team at NASA's Jet Propulsion Laboratory, October 26, 2022, https://climate.nasa.gov/causes/.

8. Ramanathan, "Climate Change," 1–11.

9. "The Causes of Climate Change," Earth Science Communications Team at NASA's Jet Propulsion Laboratory, October 26, 2022, https://climate.nasa.gov/causes/.

10. Susan Bales, Julie Sweetland, and Andrew Volmert, *How to Talk About Climate Change and Oceans* (Washington, DC: FrameWorks Institute, 2009).

11. Devarati Bhattacharya, Kimberly Steward, and Cory Forbes, "Empirical Research on K–16 Climate Education: A Systematic Review of the Literature," *Journal of Geoscience Education* 69, no. 3 (2020), doi: 10.1080/10899995.2020.1838848.

12. Eric Plutzer et al., *Mixed Messages: How Climate Is Taught in America's Schools* (Oakland, CA: National Center for Science Education, 2016), 21, http://ncse.ngo/files/Mixed Messages.pdf.

Chapter 3.2

1. Lori Bruhwiler et al., "Chapter 1: Overview of the Global Carbon Cycle," in *Second State of the Carbon Cycle Report (SOCCR2): A Sustained Assessment Report*, eds. Nancy Cavallaro et al. (Washington, DC: US Global Change Research Program, 2018), 42–70, https://doi.org/10.7930/SOCCR2.2018.Ch1; Andrew Watson et al., "Revised Estimates of Ocean-Atmosphere CO_2 Flux Are Consistent with Ocean Carbon Inventory," *Nature Communications* 11 (2020): 4422, https://doi.org/10.1038/s41467-020-18203-3.

2. "Carbon Cycle," Science Mission Directorate, October 28, 2022, https://science.nasa.gov/earth-science/oceanography/ocean-earth-system/ocean-carbon-cycle.

3. Bruhwiler et al., "Overview of the Global Carbon Cycle."

4. "The Carbon Cycle," https://earthobservatory.nasa.gov/features/CarbonCycle.

5. Bruhwiler et al., "Overview of the Global Carbon Cycle."

6. Bill McKibben, *Falter* (Melbourne: University of Melbourne. Black Inc., 2019), 49.

7. Katja Fennel et al., "Chapter 16: Coastal Ocean and Continental Shelves," in *Second State of the Carbon Cycle Report (SOCCR2): A Sustained Assessment Report*, eds. Nancy Cavallaro et al. (Washington, DC: US Global Change Research Program, 2018), 649–88, https://doi.org/10.7930/ SOCCR2.2018.Ch16. 2018.

8. Valerie Masson-Delmotte et al., "IPCC, 2018: Summary for Policymakers," in *Global Warming of 1.5°C,* eds. Panmao Zhai et al. (Cambridge, UK: Cambridge University Press), 3–24, doi:10.1017/9781009157940.001.

9. "Carbon Cycle," https://earthobservatory.nasa.gov/features/CarbonCycle.

10. Kerry Emmanuel, *What We Know About Climate Change* (Cambridge, MA: MIT Press, 2018), 14.

11. Valerie Masson-Delmotte et al., "IPCC, 2018: Summary for Policymakers," 15.

12. Berrien Moore, "Challenges of a Changing Earth: Towards a Scientific Understanding of Global Change," *Earth Science Frontiers* 9, no. 1 (2002): 41–47.

13. "Trends in Carbon Dioxide," https://gml.noaa.gov/ccgg/trends, NOAA Global Monitoring Laboratory, October 5, 2022.

14. "Increase In Atmospheric Methane Set Another Record During 2021," NOAA, April 7, 2022, https://www.noaa.gov/news-release/increase-in-atmospheric-methane-set-another -record-during-2021.

15. Laura Zangori et al., "Student Development of Model-Based Reasoning About Carbon Cycling and Climate Change in a Socio-Scientific Issues Unit," *Journal of Research in Science Teaching* 54, no. 10 (2017): 1249–73.

16. Beth Covitt et al., "Understanding and Responding to Challenges Students Face When Engaging in Carbon Cycle Pool-and-Flux Reasoning," *Journal of Environmental Education* 52, no. 2 (2020): 109, doi: 10.1080/00958964.2020.1847882.

17. Lindsey Mohan, Jing Chen, and Charles Anderson, "Developing A Multi-Year Learning Progression for Carbon Cycling in Socio-Ecological Systems," *Journal of Research in Science Teaching* 46, no. 6 (2009): 675–98, doi.org/10.1002/tea.20314.

18. Daniel Shepardson et al., "Conceptualizing Climate Change in the Context of a Climate System: Implications for Climate and Environmental Education," *Environmental Education Research* 18, no. 3 (2012): 323–52, doi.org/10.1080/13504622.2011.622839.

Chapter 3.3

1. David Reidmiller et al., *Impacts, Risks, and Adaptation in the United States: Fourth National Climate Assessment, Volume II* (Washington, DC: US Global Change Research Program, 2018), 1515, doi: 10.7930/NCA4.2018.

2. Kalila Morsink, *With Every Breath You Take, Thank the Ocean*, Smithsonian, July 2017, https://ocean.si.edu/ocean-life/plankton/every-breath-you-take-thank-ocean.

3. Fiona Harvey, "Atlantic Ocean Circulation at Weakest in a Millennium, Say Scientists," *Guardian*, February 25, 2021, https://www.theguardian.com/environment/2021/feb/25 /atlantic-ocean-circulation-at-weakest-in-a-millennium-say-scientists.

4. Valerie Masson-Delmotte et al., *IPCC, 2021: Summary for Policymakers, Climate Change 2021: The Physical Science Basis, Contribution of Working Group I to the Sixth Assessment Report of the Intergovernmental Panel on Climate Change*, (Cambridge, UK: Cambridge University Press,2021) 3–32, doi:10.1017/9781009157896.001.

5. Reidmiller et al., *Impacts, Risks, and Adaptation in the United States*.

6. Reidmiller et al., *Impacts, Risks, and Adaptation in the United States*.

7. Masson-Delmotte et al., *IPCC, 2021: Summary for Policymakers*.

8. William Sweet et al., *Global and Regional Sea Level Rise Scenarios for the United States: Updated Mean Projections and Extreme Water Level Probabilities Along U.S. Coastlines*, NOAA Technical Report NOS 01. (Silver Spring, MD: National Oceanic and Atmospheric Administration, National Ocean Service, 2022).

9. E. J. Payne et al., "Coastal Effects," in *Impacts, Risks, and Adaptation in the United States: Fourth National Climate Assessment, Volume II*, eds. David Reidmiller et al. (Washington, DC: US Global Change Research Program, 2018), 322–52, doi: 10.7930 /NCA4.2018.CH8.

10. Ian Stewart and Lulu Garcia-Navarro, "Building for an Uncertain Future: Miami Residents Adapt to the Changing Climate," NPR, March 31, 2019, https://www.npr .org/2019/03/31/706940085/building-for-an-uncertain-future-miami-residents-adapt -to-the-changing-climate.

11. Xiaoqing Peng et al., "A Holistic Assessment of 1979–2016 Global Cryospheric Extent," *Earth's Future* 9, no. 8 (May 2021), https://doi.org/10.1029/2020EF001969.

12. American Geophysical Union, "Earth's Cryosphere Is Shrinking by 87,000 Square Kilometers Per Year," July 1, 2021, https://phys.org/news/2021-07-earth-cryosphere-square-kilometers-year.html.

13. Mika Rantanen et al, "The Arctic has warmed nearly four times faster than the globe since 1979," *Communications Earth Environment* 3, no. 168 (2022), https://doi.org/10.1038/s43247-022-00498-3.

14. Kristen Pope, "Things You Should Know About the Arctic and Antarctica," *Yale Climate Connections*, July 3, 2019, https://yaleclimateconnections.org/2019/07/things-you-should-know-about-the-arctic-and-antarctica.

15. Sarah Kaplan, "Climate Change Has Destabilized the Earth's Poles, Putting the Rest of the Planet in Peril," *Washington Post*, December 14, 2021.

16. Masson-Delmotte et al., *IPCC, 2021: Summary for Policymakers.*

17. Oswald Schmitz, "Why Drilling the Arctic National Wildlife Refuge Will Release a Double Dose of Carbon," *Yale Environment 360*, February 18, 2022, https://e360.yale.edu/features/why-drilling-the-arctic-refuge-will-release-a-double-dose-of-carbon.

18. Fiona Taber and Neil Taylor, "Climate of Concern: A Search for Effective Strategies for Teaching Children About Global Warming," *International Journal of Environmental & Science Education* 4, no. 2 (2009): 97–116; Daniel Shepardson et al., "Students' Conceptions About the Greenhouse Effect, Global Warming, and Climate Change," *Climatic Change* 104 (2011): 481–507, doi10.1007/s10584-009-9786-9.

19. Jonathan Griffith and Margaret Kozick-Kingston, "Arctic Feedbacks: Not All Warming Is Equal," *The Science Teacher* 89, no. 4 (2022): 38–45.

20. Dirk Felzmann, "Students' Conceptions of Glaciers and Ice Ages: Applying the Model of Educational Reconstruction to Improve Learning," *Journal of Geoscience Education* 65, no. 3 (2017): 322–35, doi: 10.5408/16-158.1.

Chapter 3.4

1. Kate Berrisford, "A Simple and Visual Definition of Biodiversity," *The Basics*, December 21, 2021, https://www.nbs.net/articles/a-simple-and-visual-definition-of-biodiversity.

2. Bradley Cardinale et al., "Biodiversity Loss and Its Impact on Humanity," *Nature* 486, no. 7401 (2012): 59–67.

3. Hans-Otto Pörtner et al., "Impacts, Adaptation and Vulnerability Summary for Policymakers," in *Sixth Assessment Report of the Intergovernmental Panel on Climate Change*, eds. Hans-Otto Pörtner et al. (Cambridge, UK: Cambridge University Press, 2022), 9.

4. Pörtner et al., "Impacts, Adaptation and Vulnerability Summary," 28.

5. "Biodiversity—Evidence for Action," Royal Society, https://royalsociety.org/topics-policy/projects/biodiversity/.

6. Cardinale et al., "Biodiversity loss and its impact on humanity."

7. Michel Loreau et al., "Biodiversity and Ecosystem Functioning: Current Knowledge and Future Challenges," *Science* 294, no. 5543 (2001): 804–808.

8. Elsa Cleland, "Biodiversity and Ecosystem Stability," *Nature Education Knowledge* 3, no.10 (2017): 14, doi:org/10.1371/journal.pone.0228692.

9. Suzanne Simard et al., "Net Transfer of Carbon Between Tree Species with Shared Ectomycorrhizal Fungi," *Nature* 38, no. 8 (1997): 579–82; François Teste et al., "Access to Mycorrhizal Networks and Tree Roots: Importance for Seedling Survival and Resource Transfer," *Ecology* 90 (2009): 2808–22, doi:org/10.1038/41557.

10. David Reidmiller, et al., USGCRP, 2018: *Impacts, Risks, and Adaptation in the United States: Fourth National Climate Assessment, Volume II* (U.S. Global Change Research Program, Washington, DC, USA, 2018), 1515. doi: 10.7930/NCA4.2018.

11. Pete Smith et al., "Special Report on Climate Change, Desertification, Land Degradation, Sustainable Land Management, Food Security, and Greenhouse Gas Fluxes in Terrestrial Ecosystems (SR2)" (London: IPCC 650 (2017).

12. David Tilman and David Williams, "Preserving Global Biodiversity Requires Rapid Agricultural Improvements," Royal Society of London, 2021, https://royalsociety.org/topics-policy/projects/biodiversity/preserving- global-biodiversity-agricultural-improvements/.

13. Sandra Díaz et al., *Summary for policymakers of the global assessment report on biodiversity and ecosystem services of the Intergovernmental Science-Policy Platform on Biodiversity and Ecosystem Services* (Bonn, Germany: IPBES secretariat, 2019), doi:org/10.5281/zenodo.3553579.

14. Pörtner et al., "Impacts, Adaptation and Vulnerability," 11.

15. Jherime Kellermann, "The Impacts of Climate Change on Phenology: A Synthesis and Path Forward for Adaptive Management in the Pacific Northwest, Climate Adaptation Science Centers," https://nwcasc.uw.edu/science/project/the-impacts-of-climate-change-on-phenology-a-synthesis-and-path-forward-for-adaptive-management-in-the-pacific-northwest/.

16. "The Grinnell Resurvey Project," Museum of Vertebrate Zoology, UC Berkeley, https://mvz.berkeley.edu/Grinnell/index.html.

17. Loreau et al. "Biodiversity and Ecosystem Functioning."

18. Elena Hamann, Arthur Weis, and Steven Franks, "Two Decades of Evolutionary Changes in *Brassica rapa* in Response to Fluctuations in Precipitation and Severe Drought," *Evolution* 72, no. 12 (2018): 2682–96, doi: 10.1111/evo.13631.

19. Jurriaan M. De Vos, Lucas N. Joppa, John L. Gittleman, Patrick R. Stephens, Stuart L. Pimm, "Estimating the Normal Background Rate of Species Extinction," *Conservation Biology*, August 26, 2014, https://conbio.onlinelibrary.wiley.com/doi/abs/10.1111/cobi.12380.

Chapter 3.5

1. Chi Xu, Timothy Kohler, Timothy Lenton, Jens-Christian Svenning, and Marten Scheffer, "Future of the Human Climate Niche," *Proceedings of the National Academy of Sciences* 117, no. 21 (2020): 11350–355.

2. Andrew Freedman, "Global Warming to Push Billions Outside Climate Range That Has Sustained Society for 6,000 Years, Study Finds," *Washington Post*, May 4, 2020, https://www.washingtonpost.com/weather/2020/05/04/human-climate-niche/.

3. Steven Sherwood and Matthew Huber, "An Adaptability Limit to Climate Change Due to Heat Stress," *Proceedings of the National Academy of Sciences* 107, no. 21 (2010): 9552–55.

4. Freedman, "Global Warming to Push Billions Outside Climate Range."

5. Freedman, "Global Warming to Push Billions Outside Climate Range."

6. Xu et al., "Future of the Human Climate Niche."

7. Eun-Soon Im, Jeremy Pal, and Elfatih Eltahir, "Deadly Heat Waves Projected in the Densely Populated Agricultural Regions of South Asia," *Science Advances* 3, no. 8 (2017), doi: 10.1126/sciadv.1603322.

8. "Abrahm Lustgarten, "The Great Climate Migration," *New York Times*, July 23, 2020, https://www.nytimes.com/interactive/2020/07/23/magazine/climate-migration.html.

9. Alfons Baede et al., "The Climate System: An Overview," *Climate Change 2001: The Scientific Basis* (IPCC, 2001): 38–47.

10. Sarah Kaplan and Brady Dennis, "2021 Brought a Wave of Extreme Weather Disasters. Scientists Say Worse Lies Ahead," *Washington Post*, December 17, 2021, https://www.washingtonpost.com/climate-environment/2021/12/17/climate-change-extreme-weather-future.

11. Stephanie Herring et al., "Explaining Extreme Events of 2016 from a Climate Perspective," *Bulletin of the American Meteorological Society* 99, no. 1 (2018): S1–S140, doi:org/10.1175/BAMS-ExplainingExtremeEvents2018.1.

12. Kaplan and Dennis, "2021 Brought a Wave of Extreme Weather Disasters."

13. James Hansen, Makiko Sato, and Reto Ruedy, "Perception of Climate Change," *PNAS Plus* 109 no. 37 (2012): E2415–E2423, doi:10.1073/pnas.1205276109.

14. Hansen et al., "Perception of Climate Change."

15. Hansen et al., "Perception of Climate Change."

16. Ian Angus, *Facing the Anthropocene: Fossil Capitalism and the Crisis of the Earth System* (New York: NYU Press, 2016), 94.

17. Valerie Masson-Delmotte et al., *IPCC, 2021: Summary for Policymakers, Climate Change 2021: The Physical Science Basis, Contribution of Working Group I to the Sixth Assessment Report of the Intergovernmental Panel on Climate Change* (Cambridge, UK: Cambridge University Press, 2021), 3–32, doi:10.1017/9781009157896.001.

Chapter 4

1. David Bornstein, "A Smorgasbord of Solutions for Global Warming," *New York Times*, April 25, 2018, https://www.nytimes.com/2018/04/25/opinion/a-smorgasbord-of-solutions-for-global-warming.html.

2. National Research Council, *A Framework for K–12 Science Education: Practices, Crosscutting Concepts, and Core Ideas* (Washington, DC: National Academies Press, 2012), 11–12, doi:org/10.17226/13165.

3. Paul Hawken, *Drawdown: The Most Comprehensive Plan Ever Proposed to Reverse Global Warming* (Harlow, England: Penguin Books, 2018), 220.

4. "10 Things: All About Ice," NASA, March 28, 2018, https://sealevel.nasa.gov/news/114/10-things-all-about-ice.

5. Priyadarshi Shukla et al., *Climate Change 2022: Mitigation of Climate Change. Contribution of Working Group III to the Sixth Assessment Report of the Intergovernmental Panel on Climate Change* (Cambridge, UK: Cambridge University Press, 2022), doi: 10.1017/9781009157926.

6. Jeremy Martinich et al., "Reducing Risks Through Emissions Mitigation," in *Impacts, Risks, and Adaptation in the United States: Fourth National Climate Assessment, Volume II*, eds. Dave Reidmiller et al. (Washington, DC: US Global Change Research Program, 2018), 1346–86, doi: 10.7930/NCA4.2018.CH29.

7. Bill McKibben, "In a World on Fire, Stop Burning Things," *New Yorker*, March 18, 2022, https://www.newyorker.com/news/essay/in-a-world-on-fire-stop-burning-things.

8. Hawken, *Drawdown*.

9. Jonathan Foley et al., *The Drawdown Review, Climate Solutions for a New Decade* (Project Drawdown Publication, 2020), doi: 10.13140/RG.2.2.31794.76487.

10. McKibben, "In a World on Fire."

11. Foley et al., *The Drawdown Review.*

12. Michael Irving, "World's Largest Compressed Air Grid 'Batteries' Will Store up to 10gwh," *New Atlas*, April 29, 2021, https://newatlas.com/energy/hydrostor-compressed-air-energy-storage/.

13. Matthew Hutson, "The Renewable-Energy Revolution Will Need Renewable Storage," *New Yorker*, April 18, 2022, https://www.newyorker.com/magazine/2022/04/25/the-renewable-energy-revolution-will-need-renewable-storage.

14. Foley et al., *The Drawdown Review.*

15. Matthew Hutson, "The Renewable-Energy Revolution." 14.

16. Hawken, *Drawdown.*

17. Foley et al., *The Drawdown Review.*

18. Foley et al., *The Drawdown Review.*

19. Coimbra Sirica et al., "New Analysis Reveals That Indigenous Peoples and Local Communities Manage 300,000 Million Metric Tons of Carbon in Their Trees and Soil—33 Times Energy Emissions from 2017," *Rights and Resources*, September 9, 2018, https://rightsandresources.org/blog/new-analysis-reveals-that-indigenous-peoples-and-local-communities-manage-300000-million-metric-tons-of-carbon-in-their-trees-and-soil-33-times-energy-emissions-from-2017/.

20. Erik Hoffner, "Agroforestry: An Ancient 'Indigenous Technology' with Wide Modern Appeal," Mongabay, https://news.mongabay.com/2019/07/agroforestry-an-ancient-indigenous-technology-with-wide-modern-appeal-commentary/, July 15, 2019.

21. McKibben, "In a World on Fire."

22. Thomas Czigler et al., "Laying the Foundation for Zero-Carbon Cement," McKinsey, May 14, 2020, https://www.mckinsey.com/industries/chemicals/our-insights/laying-the-foundation-for-zero-carbon-cement.

23. Keegan Ramsden, "Cement and Concrete: The Environmental Impact," PSCI, November 3, 2020,https://psci.princeton.edu/tips/2020/11/3/cement-and-concrete-the-environmental-impact.

24. I. York and I. Europe, "Concrete Needs to Lose Its Colossal Carbon Footprint," *Nature* 597 (2021): 593–94, *doi: https://doi.org/10.1038/d41586-021-02612-5.*

25. Foley et al., *The Drawdown Review.*

26. "Sources of Greenhouse Gas Emissions," US Environmental Protection Agency, August 5, 2022, https://www.epa.gov/ghgemissions/sources-greenhouse-gas-emissions.

27. Foley et al., *The Drawdown Review.*

28. "Sources of Greenhouse Gas Emissions," US EPA.

29. "Household Air Pollution and Health," World Health Organization, last updated September 22, 2021, https://www.who.int/news-room/fact-sheets/detail/household-air-pollution-and-health.

30. Foley et al., *The Drawdown Review.*

31. Foley et al., *The Drawdown Review.*

32. "Coastal Wetland Restoration," Nature 4 Climate, https://nature4climate.org/science/n4c-pathways/wetlands/coastal-wetland-restoration/.

33. United Nations Department of Economic and Social Affairs, *Growing at a Slower Pace, World Population Is Expected to Reach 9.7 Billion in 2050 and Could Peak at Nearly 11 Billion Around 2100*, June 17, 2019, https://www.un.org/development/desa/en/news/population/world-population-prospects-2019.html.

34. Autonomous University of Barcelona, "USA And EU Are Responsible for the Majority of Ecological Damage Caused by Excess Use of Raw Materials," April 8, 2022, https://phys.org/news/2022-04-usa-eu-responsible-majority-ecological.html.

35. Autonomous University of Barcelona, "USA And EU Are Responsible."

36. National Research Council, *A Framework*.

Chapter 5

1. Dietmar Höttecke and Douglas Allchin, "Reconceptualizing Nature-of-Science Education in the Age of Social Media," *Science Education* 104, no. 4 (2020): 641–66, doi.org/10.1002/sce.21575.

2. Connie Roser-Renouf, Edward Maibach, and Teresa Myers, *American Adolescents' Knowledge, Attitudes and Sources of Information on Climate Change* (Fairfax, VA: George Mason University, 2020), doi: 10.13021/z9by-xp87.

3. Washington Post and the Kaiser Family Foundation, *Washington Post-Kaiser Family Foundation Poll: Climate Change Survey of Adults*, National Opinion Research Center (Ithaca, NY: Roper Center for Public Opinion Research, Cornell University, 2019).

4. John Cook et al., *The Consensus Handbook* (Fairfax, VA: George Mason University, 2018), http://www.climatechangecommunication.org/all/consensus-handbook/, doi:10.13021/G8MM6P.

5. Lizzie Widdicombe, "How Should the Media Talk About Climate Change?," *New Yorker*, October 17, 2020, https://www.newyorker.com/culture/culture-desk/how-should-the-media-talk-about-climate-change.

6. Michael Shermer, "Consilience and Consensus," *Scientific American* 313, no. 6 (2015): 81, doi: 0.1038/scientificamerican1215-81.

7. Washington Post and the Kaiser Family Foundation, *Washington Post-Kaiser Family Foundation Poll: Climate Change Survey of Adults*.

8. Naomi Oreskes, "The Scientific Consensus on Climate Change," *Science* 306, no. 5702 (2004): 1686, doi: 10.1126/science.110361.

9. Geoffrey Supran and Naomi Oreskes, "Rhetoric and Frame Analysis of ExxonMobil's Climate Change Communications," *One Earth* 4, no. 5 (2021): 696–719, doi.org/10.1016/j.oneear.2021.04.014.

10. Kathie Treen, Hywel Williams, and Saffron O'Neill, "Online Misinformation About Climate Change," *Wiley Interdisciplinary Reviews: Climate Change* 11, no. 5 (2020): e665; Liang Wu et al., "Mining Misinformation in Social Media, in *Big Data in Complex and Social Networks*, eds. My T. Thai, Weili Wu, and Hui Xiong (London: Chapman and Hall/CRC, 2016).

11. John Cook et al., *America Misled: How the Fossil Fuel Industry Deliberately Misled Americans About Climate Change* (Fairfax, VA: George Mason University Center for Climate Change Communication, 2019), https://www.climatechangecommunication.org/america-misled/.

12. Treen, Williams, and O'Neill, "Online Misinformation About Climate Change"; Claire Wardle and Hossein Derakhshan, "Thinking About 'Information Disorder': Formats of Misinformation, Disinformation, and Mal-Information," in *Journalism, 'Fake News' & Disinformation: Handbook for Journalism Education and Training*, eds. Cherilyn Ireton and Julie Posetti (UNESCO, 2018), 43–54, https://en.unesco.org/sites/default/files/f._jfnd_handbook_module_2.pdf.

13. Treen, Williams, and O'Neill, "Online Misinformation About Climate Change."

14. Karin Bjornberg et al., "Climate and Environmental Science Denial: A Review of the Scientific Literature Published in 1990–2015," *Journal of Cleaner Production* 167 (2017): 229–41, doi.org/10.1016/j.jclepro.2017.08.066.

15. Riley Dunlap, "Climate Change Skepticism and Denial: An Introduction," *American Behavioral Scientist* 57, no. 6 (2013): 691–98, doi.org/10.1177/00027642134770.

16. Treen, Williams, and O'Neill, "Online Misinformation About Climate Change."

17. John Cook et al., "America Misled."

18. Curt Stager, "Sowing Climate Doubt Among Schoolteachers," *New York Times*, April 27, 2017, https://www.nytimes.com/2017/04/27/opinion/sowing-climate-doubt-among -schoolteachers.html.

19. Craig Idso, Robert Carter, and Fred Singer, *Why Scientists Disagree About Global Warming* (The Heartland Institute, 2015).

20. Anthony Watts and James Taylor, *Climate at a Glance for Teachers and Students* (The Heartland Institute, 2022).

21. Mark Kaufman, "The Carbon Footprint Sham: A 'Successful, Deceptive' PR Campaign," https://mashable.com/feature/carbon-footprint-pr-campaign-sham.

22. Diego Román and K. C. Busch. "Textbooks of Doubt: Using Systemic Functional Analysis to Explore the Framing of Climate Change in Middle-School Science Textbooks," *Environmental Education Research* 22, no. 8 (2016): 1158–80, doi.org/10.1080/13504622 .2015.1091878.

23. "Position Statement: The Teaching of Climate Science," National Science Teachers Association, September 2018, https://www.nsta.org/nstas-official-positions/teaching -climate-science.

24. Cook et al., "America Misled."

25. Pascal Diethelm and Martin McKee, "Denialism: What Is It and How Should Scientists Respond?," *European Journal of Public Health* 19, no. 1 (2009): 2–4, doi: 10.1093 /eurpub/ckn139. PMID: 19158101.

26. Stephan Lewandowsky, Gilles Gignac, and Klaus Oberauer, "The Role of Conspiracist Ideation and Worldviews in Predicting Rejection of Science," *PLoS ONE* 8, no. 10 (2013): e75637, doi.org/10.1371/journal.pone.0075637; Cook et al., "America Misled."

27. Treen, Williams, and O'Neill, "Online Misinformation About Climate Change."

28. Julie Libarkin et al., "A New, Valid Measure of Climate Change Understanding: Associations with Risk Perception," *Climatic Change* 150, no. 3 (2018): 403–16, doi: 10.1007 /s10584-018-2279-y.

29. Adam Corner, Ezra Markowitz, and Nick Pidgeon, "Public Engagement with Climate Change: The Role of Human Values," *WIREs Climate Change* 5 (2014): 411–22, doi.org /10.1002/wcc.269; Robert Gifford, "The Dragons of Inaction: Psychological Barriers That Limit Climate Change Mitigation and Adaptation," *American Psychologist* 66, no. 4 (2011): 290–302, doi: 10.1037/a0023566.

30. Stephan Lewandowsky et al., "The Debunking Handbook 2020," https://sks.to/db2020. doi:10.17910/b7.1182.

31. Anne Armstrong, Marianne Krasny, and Jonathon Schuldt, *Communicating Climate Change: A Guide for Educators* (Ithaca, NY: Cornell University Press; Comstock Publishing Associates, 2018) 43–48, https://www.jstor.org/stable/10.7591/j.ctv941wjn.

32. Kathryn Stevenson et al., "Empowering Children to Change Hearts and Minds on Climate Change Against All Odds," in *Teaching Climate Change in the United States*,

eds. James Henderson and Andrea Drewes (London: Routledge, 2020), 13–14, doi .org/10.4324/9780367179496.

33. W. Vollerberg, J. Iedema, and Q. Raaijmakers, "Intergenerational Transmission and the Formation of Cultural Orientations in Adolescence and Young Adulthood," *Journal of Marriage and Family* 63, no. 4 (2001): 1185–98, http://www.jstor.org/stable/3599823.

34. Lynne Zummo, Brian Donovan, and K. C. Busch, "Complex Influences of Mechanistic Knowledge, Worldview, and Quantitative Reasoning on Climate Change Discourse: Evidence for Ideologically Motivated Reasoning Among Youth," *Journal of Research in Science Teaching* 58, no. 1(2021): 95–127, doi.org/10.1002/tea.21648.

35. Kathryn Stevenson et al., "Over-Coming Skepticism with Education: Interacting Influences of Worldview and Climate Change Knowledge on Perceived Climate Change Risk Among Adolescents," *Climatic Change* 126, no. 3–4 (2014): 293–304.

36. Andrew Guess and Alexander Coppock, "Does Counter-Attitudinal Information Cause Backlash? Results from Three Large Survey Experiments," *British Journal of Political Science* 50, no. 4 (2020): 1497–1515, doi:10.1017/S0007123418000327.

37. Janet Swim et al., "Social Construction of Scientifically Grounded Climate Change Discussions," *Psychology and Climate Change, Human Perceptions, Impacts, and Responses* (2018): 65–93, doi.org/10.1016/B978-0-12-813130-5.00004-7.

38. Asli Sezen-Barrie, Nicole Shea, and Jenna Borman, "Probing into the Sources of Ignorance: Science Teachers' Practices of Constructing Arguments or Rebuttals to Denialism of Climate Change," *Environmental Education Research* 25, no. 6 (2019): 846–66, doi .org/10.1080/13504622.2017.1330949.

39. Treen, Williams, and O'Neill, "Online Misinformation About Climate Change."

40. Swim et al., "Social Construction of Scientifically Grounded Climate Change Discussions."

41. Eric Plutzer et al., "Mixed Messages: How Climate Is Taught in America's Schools" (Oakland, CA: National Center for Science Education, 2016), 17, http://ncse.ngo /files/MixedMessages.Pdf.

Chapter 6

1. Jack Shonkoff and Susan Bales, "Science Does Not Speak for Itself: Translating Child Development Research for the Public and Its Policymakers," *Child Development* 82, no. 1 (2011): 17–32, doi.org/10.1111/j.1467-8624.2010.01538.x.

2. Martha Monroe et al., "Identifying Effective Climate Change Education Strategies: A Systematic Review of the Research," *Environmental Education Research* 25, no. 6 (2019): 791–812, doi.org/10.1080/13504622.2017.1360842.

3. Elizabeth Hufnagel, Gregory Kelly, and Joseph Henderson, "How the Environment Is Positioned in the Next Generation Science Standards: A Critical Discourse Analysis," *Environmental Education Research* 24, no. 5 (2018): 731–53, doi.org/10.1080/13504622 .2017.1334876.

4. Heather Clark, William Sandoval, and Jarod Kawasaki, "Teachers' Uptake of Problematic Assumptions of Climate Change in the NGSS," *Environmental Education Research* 26, no. 8 (2020): 1177–92, doi:10.1080/13504622.2020.1748175.

5. Kristin Gunckel and Sara Tolbert, "The Imperative to Move Toward a Dimension of Care in Engineering Education," *Journal of Research in Science Teaching* 55, no. 7 (2018): 938–61, doi.org/10.1002/tea.21458.

6. Shonkoff and Bales, "Science Does Not Speak for Itself."

7. Stephen Pyne, "The Ecology of Fire," *Nature Education Knowledge* 3, no. 10 (2010): 30.

8. Somini Sengupta, "Wildfire Smoke Is Poisoning California's Kids. Some Pay a Higher Price," *New York Times*, November 26, 2020, https://www.nytimes.com/interactive /2020/11/26/climate/california-smoke-children-health.html.

9. Priya Krishnakumar and Swetha Kannan, "The Worst Fire Season Ever. Again," *Los Angeles Times*, September 12, 2020, https://www.latimes.com/projects/california-fires -damage-climate-change-analysis/.

10. C. Arden Pope et al., "Lung Cancer, Cardiopulmonary Mortality, and Long-Term Exposure to Fine Particulate Air Pollution," *Journal of the American Medical Association* 287, no. 9 (2002): 1132–41, doi.org/10.1001/jama.287.9.1132.

11. Fikile Nxumalo, *Decolonizing Place in Early Childhood Education* (Philadelphia: Routledge, 2019); Robin Kimmerer, *Braiding Sweetgrass: Indigenous Wisdom, Scientific Knowledge and the Teachings of Plants* (Minneapolis: Milkweed, 2013).

12. Jay Johnson et al., "Weaving Indigenous and Sustainability Sciences to Diversify Our Methods," *Sustainability Science* 11, no. 1 (2016): 1–11, doi.org/10.1007/s11625-015 -0349-x.

13. Farhana Sultana, "The Unbearable Heaviness of Climate Coloniality," *Political Geography* 99 (2022): 102638, doi.org/10.1016/j.polgeo.2022.102638.

14. Enrique Salmon, "Kincentric Ecology: Indigenous Perceptions of the Human–Nature Relationship," *Ecological Applications* 10, no. 5, (2000): 1327–32, doi.org/10.2307 /2641288.

15. Leslie Marmon Silko, *Yellow Woman and a Beauty of the Spirit* (New York: Simon and Schuster, 1996): 462–70.

16. Kimmerer, *Braiding Sweetgrass.*

17. Astrid Ulloa, "Indigenous Knowledge Regarding Climate in Colombia," in *Climate and Culture: Multidisciplinary Perspectives on a Warming World,* eds. Giuseppe Feola et al. (Cambridge, UK: Cambridge University Press, 2019), 70.

18. Stephen Garnett et al. "A Spatial Overview of the Global Importance of Indigenous Lands for Conservation," *Nature Sustainability* 1, no. 7 (2018): 369–74, doi: 10.1038 /s41893-018-0100-6.

19. Johnson et al., "Weaving Indigenous and Sustainability Sciences."

20. Johnson et al., "Weaving Indigenous and Sustainability Sciences."

21. Gregory Cajete, *Native Science: Natural Laws of Interdependence,* (Santa Fe: Clear Light Publishers, 2000), 59–83.

22. Kyle Powys Whyte, "On the Role of Traditional Ecological Knowledge as s Collaborative Concept: A Philosophical Study," *Ecological Processes* 2, no. 1 (2013): 1–12, doi.org /10.1186/2192-1709-2-7.

23. DEVEX Editor, "Why Local and Indigenous Communities Are Vital to Sustainable Human Development," *Focus on People and the Planet*, March 15, 2021, https://www .devex.com/news/q-a-why-local-and-indigenous-communities-are-vital-to-sustainable -human-development-99353.

24. Frameworks Institute, *Unleashing the Power of How: An Explanation Declaration*, June 9, 2019, https://www.frameworksinstitute.org/publication/unleashing-the-power-of-how -an-explanation-declaration-2/.

25. Drew Shindell et al., "The Effects of Heat Exposure on Human Mortality Throughout the United States," *GeoHealth* 4, no. 4 (2020): 1–11, doi.org/10.1029/2019GH 000234.

26. Brooke Anderson and Michelle Bell, "Heat Waves in the United States: Mortality Risk During Heat Waves and Effect Modification by Heat Wave Characteristics in

43 US Communities," *Environmental Health Perspectives* 119, no. 2 (2011): 210–18, doi:10.1289/ehp.1002313.

27. Iain Stewart, "Why Should Urban Heat Island Researchers Study History?" *Urban Climate* 30 (2019): 100484, doi: 10.1016/j.uclim.2019.100484.

28. Carly Ziter et al., "Scale-Dependent Interactions Between Tree Canopy Cover and Impervious Surfaces Reduce Daytime Urban Heat During Summer," *Proceedings of the National Academy of Sciences* 116, no. 15 (2019): 7575–80, doi.org/10.1073/pnas.1817561116.

29. US Environmental Protection Agency, *Reducing Urban Heat Islands, Compendium of Strategies: Trees and Vegetation,* 2012, https://www.epa.gov/heat-islands/heat-island-compendium.

30. Brad Plumer and Nadja Popovich, "How Decades of Racist Housing Policy Left Neighborhoods Sweltering," *New York Times*, August 24, 2020, https://www.nytimes.com/interactive/2020/08/24/climate/racism-redlining-cities-global-warming.html.

31. Jeremy Hoffman, Vivek Shandas, and Nicholas Pendleton, "The Effects of Historical Housing Policies on Resident Exposure to Intra-Urban Heat: A Study of 108 US Urban Areas," *Climate* 8, no. 1 (2020): 12, doi.org/10.3390/cli8010012.

32. Plumer and Popovich, "How Decades of Racist Housing Policy Left Neighborhoods Sweltering."

33. Jim Henderson et al., "Expanding the Foundation: Climate Change and Opportunities for Educational Research," *Educational Studies* 53, no. 4 (2017): 412–25, doi:10.1080/00131946.2017.1335640.

Chapter 7

1. Ian Angus, *Facing the Anthropocene: Fossil capitalism and the crisis of the earth system* (New York: NYU Press, 2016).

2. Angus, *Facing the Anthropocene.*

3. Will Steffen et al., *Global Change and the Earth System: A Planet Under Pressure* (Berlin: Springer-Verlag, 2004).

4. Robert McSweeney and Zeke Hausfather, "Mapped: How 'Proxy' Data Reveals the Climate of the Earth's Distant Past," Carbon Brief, March 29, 2021, https://interactive.carbonbrief.org/how-proxy-data-reveals-climate-of-earths-distant-past.

5. James Kirchner, "The *Gaia Hypothesis*: Conjectures and Refutations," *Climatic Change* 58 (2003): 21–45, doi.org/10.1023/A:1023494111532.

6. Jeannine-Marie St. Jacques, Brian Cumming, and John Smol, "A 900-Year Pollen-Inferred Temperature and Effective Moisture Record from Varved Lake Mina, West-Central Minnesota, USA," *Quaternary Science Reviews* 27, nos. 7–8 (2008): 781–96, doi: 10.1016/j.quascirev.2008.01.005; Ben Geyman et al., "Barium in Deep-Sea Bamboo Corals: Phase Associations, Barium Stable Isotopes, and Prospects For Paleoceanography," *Earth and Planetary Science Letters* 525, no. 1 (November 2019), doi.org/10.1016/j.epsl.2019.115751; David Pompeani et al., "The Biogeochemical Consequences of Late Holocene Wildfires in Three Subalpine Lakes from Northern Colorado," *Quaternary Science Reviews* 236 (2020), doi:10.1016/j.quascirev.2020.106293.

7. McSweeney and Hausfather, "Mapped: How 'Proxy' Data Reveals the Climate of the Earth's Distant Past."

8. "What Are Proxy Data?," NOAA National Centers for Environmental Information, April 15, 2016, https://www.ncei.noaa.gov/news/what-are-proxy-data.

9. Matthew Therrell and Makayla Trotter, "Waniyetu Wówapi: Native American Records of Weather and Climate," *Bulletin of the American Meteorological Society* 92, no. 5 (2011): 583–92, doi.org/10.1175/2011BAMS3146.1.

10. "How Can Tree Rings Teach Us About Climate?," National Centers for Environmental Information, March 11, 2016, https://www.ncei.noaa.gov/news/how-can-tree-rings-teach-us-about-climate.

11. Valerie Trouet, *Tree Story: The History of the World Written in Rings* (Baltimore: Johns Hopkins University Press, 2020), 12–13.

12. "Ice Core," NOAA National Centers for Environmental Information, June18, 2020, https://www.ncdc.noaa.gov/news/picture-climate-what-can-we-learn-ice.

13. Robert Mulvaney, "Ask the Experts: How Are Past Temperatures Determined from an Ice Core?," *Scientific American*, June 1, 2005.

14. Paul Pearson, "Oxygen Isotopes in Foraminifera: Overview and Historical Review," *Paleontological Society Papers* 18 (2012): 1–38, doi.org/10.1017/S1089332600002539.

15. USGS Climate Research and Development Program, Paleoclimate Research, "Innovative Paleoclimate Methods," October 20, 2022, https://www.usgs.gov/programs/climate-research-and-development-program/news/innovative-paleoclimate-methods.

16. McSweeney and Hausfather, "Mapped: How 'Proxy' Data Reveals the Climate of the Earth's Distant Past."

17. National Research Council, *Surface Temperature Reconstructions for the Last 2,000 Years* (Washington, DC: National Academies Press, 2006), doi.org/10.17226/11676.

18. Michael Mann, "The Value of Multiple Proxies," *Science* 297, no. 5586 (2002): 1481–82, doi: 10.1126/science.1074318.

Chapter 8

1. Paul Edwards, *A Vast Machine: Computer Models, Climate Data, and the Politics of Global Warming* (Cambridge, MA: MIT Press, 2010), 23–26.

2. Banu Dur and Uyan Inanc, "Data Visualization and Infographics in Visual Communication Design Education at the Age of Information," *Journal of Arts and Humanities* 3, no. 5 (2014): 39–50.

3. Luciana Gatti et al., "Amazonia as a Carbon Source Linked to Deforestation and Climate Change," *Nature* 595 (2021): 388–93, doi.org/10.1038/s41586-021-03629-6.

4. Beth Covitt et al., "Understanding and Responding to Challenges Students Face When Engaging in Carbon Cycle Pool-and-Flux Reasoning," *Journal of Environmental Education* 52, no. 2 (2021): 98–117, doi: 10.1080/00958964.2020.1847882.

5. Lynne Zummo and Sara Dozier, "Using Epistemic Instructional Activities to Support Secondary Science Teachers' Social Construction of Knowledge of Anthropogenic Climate Change During a Professional Learning Experience," *Journal of Geoscience Education* 70, no. 4 (2021): 530–45, doi.org/10.1080/10899995.2021.1986785.

6. Concord Consortium, "Thinking and Doing with Data: Designing 2030," 2019, 34, https://designing2030.concord.org/2019-meeting.html.

7. Hilary Geoghegan, Alexander Arnall, and Giuseppe Feola, "Climate and Culture: Taking Stock and Moving Forward," in *Climate and Culture: Multidisciplinary Perspectives on a Warming World*, eds. Giuseppe Feola, Hilary Geoghegan, and Alex Arnall (Cambridge, UK: Cambridge University Press, 2019), 1–18.

8. Birgit Schneider, "Climate Model Simulation Visualization from a Visual Studies Perspective," *Wiley Interdisciplinary Reviews: Climate Change* 3, no. 2 (2012): 185–93, doi: 10.1002/wcc.162.

9. Stephen Norton and Frederick Suppe, "Why Atmospheric Modeling Is Good Science," in *Changing the Atmosphere: Expert Knowledge and Environmental Governance*, eds. Clark Miller and Paul Edwards (Cambridge, MA: MIT Press, 2001): 88–133, doi.org/10.7551/mitpress/1789.001.0001.

10. Edwards, *A Vast Machine*.

11. Matthias Heymann, Gabriele Gramelsberger, and Martin Mahony, "Introduction," in *Cultures of Prediction in Atmospheric and Climate Science: Epistemic and Cultural Shifts in Computer-based Modelling and Simulation*, eds. Matthias Heymann et al. London: (Routledge, 2017), 27.

12. Gabriele Gramelsberger and Johann Feichter, "Modelling the Climate System: An Overview," in *Climate Change and Policy: The Calculability of Climate Change and the Challenge of Uncertainty*, eds. Gabriele Gramelsberger and Johann Feichter, (Berlin: Springer Science & Business Media, 2011), 9–90.

13. Heymann et al., *Cultures of Prediction in Atmospheric and Climate Science*, 25.

14. Norton and Suppe, "Why Atmospheric Modeling Is Good Science," 136.

15. Zeke Hausfather, "Analysis: How Well Have Climate Models Projected Global Warming?," Carbon Brief, May 10, 2017, https://www.carbonbrief.org/analysis-how-well-have-climate-models-projected-global-warming/.

16. USGCRP, *Impacts, Risks, and Adaptation in the United States: Fourth National Climate Assessment, Volume II* (Washington, DC: US Global Change Research Program, 2018): Appendix 5, 209, doi: 10.7930/NCA4.2018.

17. Valérie Masson-Delmotte et al., "Climate Change 2021: The Physical Science Basis," *Contribution of Working Group I to the Sixth Assessment Report of the Intergovernmental Panel on Climate Change: Summary for Policymakers,* 2021, 22, doi:10.1017/9781009157896.001.

18. Olivia Levrini et al., "Recognition and Operationalization of Future-Scaffolding Skills: Results from an Empirical Study of a Teaching–Learning Module on Climate Change and Futures Thinking," *Science Education* 105, no. 2 (2021): 281–308, https://doi.org/10.1002/sce.21612.

Chapter 9

1. Devarati Bhattacharya, Kimberly Steward, and Cory Forbes, "Empirical Research on K-16 Climate Education: A Systematic Review of the Literature," *Journal of Geoscience Education* 69, no. 3 (2021): 223–47, doi: 10.1080/10899995.2020.1838848.

2. Cindy Passmore, Christina Schwarz, and Jocelyn Mankowski, "Developing and Using Models," in *Helping Students Make Sense of the World Using Next Generation Science and Engineering Practices*, eds. Christina Schwarz, Cindy Passmore, and Brian Reiser (Arlington, VA: NSTA Press, 2017), 109–34.

3. Kelsie Fowler, Mark Windschitl, and Claus Auning, "A Layered Approach to Scientific Modeling, Creating Scaffolds That Allow All Students to Show the Most of What They Know," *Science Teacher* 88, no. 1 (2020): 24–36.

4. Martha Monroe et al., "Identifying Effective Climate Change Education Strategies: A Systematic Review of the Research," *Environmental Education Research* 25, no. 6 (2019): 791–812, doi.org/10.1080/13504622.2017.1360842.

5. Mark Windschitl, Jessica Thompson, and Melissa L. Braaten, *Ambitious Science Teaching* (Cambridge, MA: Harvard Education Press, 2018).

6. Laura Zangori et al., "Student Development of Model-Based Reasoning About Carbon Cycling and Climate Change in a Socio-Scientific Issues Unit," *Journal of Research in*

Science Teaching 54, no. 10 (2017): 1249–73; Eliza Bobek and Barbara Tversky, "Creating Visual Explanations Improves Learning," *Cognitive Research: Principles and Implications* 1, no.1(2016): 27, doi: 10.1186/s41235-016-0031-6.

7. Heather Clark, William Sandoval, and Jarod Kawasaki, "Teachers' Uptake of Problematic Assumptions of Climate Change in the NGSS," *Environmental Education Research* 26, no. 8 (2020): 1171–92, doi:10.1080/13504622.2020.1748175.

8. Matthew Ballew et al., "Systems Thinking as a Pathway to Global Warming Beliefs and Attitudes Through an Ecological Worldview," *PNAS* 116, no. 17 (2019): 8214–19, doi:org/10.1073/pnas.1819310116.

Chapter 10

1. Sarah Jaquette Ray, *A Field Guide to Climate Anxiety: How to Keep Your Cool on a Warming Planet* (Oakland: University of California Press, 2020), 2.

2. Karen O'Brien, Elin Selboe, and Bronwyn Hayward, "Exploring Youth Activism on Climate Change: Dutiful, Disruptive, and Dangerous Dissent," *Ecology and Society* 23, no. 3 (2018): 42, doi.org/10.5751/ES-10287-230342.

3. Paul Hawken, *Regeneration* (New York: Penguin, 2021), 10.

4. National Academies of Sciences, Engineering, and Medicine, *How People Learn II: Learners, Contexts, and Cultures* (Washington, DC: National Academies Press, 2018), 1–10, doi: org/10.17226/24783.

5. Ray, *A Field Guide to Climate Anxiety,* 124.

6. Nicole Seymour, *Bad Environmentalism: Irony and Irreverence in the Ecological Age,* (Minneapolis: University of Minnesota Press, 2018), 63.

7. Ray, *A Field Guide to Climate Anxiety,* 120.

8. Bob Doppelt, *Transformational Resilience: How Building Human Resilience to Climate Disruption Can Safeguard Society and Increase Wellbeing* (New York: Routledge, 2016), 7.

9. Kristin Haltinner and Dilshani Sarathchandra, "Climate Change Skepticism as a Psychological Coping Strategy," *Sociology Compass* 12, no. 6 (2018): 5, doi.org/10.1111 /soc4.12586.; Charlie Kurth and Panu Pihkala, "Eco-Anxiety: What It Is and Why It Matters," *Frontiers of Psychology*, 13:981814 (2022): 1–13, doi: 10.3389/fpsyg.2022 .981814.

10. Kurth and Pihkala, "Eco-Anxiety," 4.

11. "Climate Change Education : How to Address Eco-Anxiety with Students?," Office for Climate Education, January 24, 2022, https://www.oce.global/en/news/climate-change -education-how-address-eco-anxiety-students#footnote-5.

12. Maria Ojala et al., "Anxiety, Worry, and Grief in a Time of Environmental and Climate Crisis: A Narrative Review," *Annual Review of Environment and Resources* 46 (2021): 35–58, doi.org/10.1146/annurev-environ-012220- 022716.

13. Panu Pihkala, "Eco-Anxiety and Environmental Education," *Sustainability* 12, no. 23 (2020): 10149, doi.org/10.3390/su122310149.

14. Avit Bhowmik et al., "Powers of 10: Seeking 'Sweet Spots' for Rapid Climate and Sustainability Actions Between Individual and Global Scales," *Environmental Research Letters* 15, no. 9 (2020):1, doi.org/10.1088/1748-9326/ab9ed0.

15. Christina Kwauk and Rebecca Winthrop, *Unleashing the Creativity of Teachers and Students to Combat Climate Change: An Opportunity for Global Leadership* (Washington, DC: Brookings Institution), 8, March 26, 2021, https://www.brookings.edu/research /unleashing-the-creativity-of-teachers-and-students-to-combat-climate-change-an -opportunity-for-global-leadership/.

16. Danielle Lawson et al., "Intergenerational learning: Are children key in spurring climate action?" *Global Environmental Change* 53 (2018): 207, doi.org/10.1016/j.gloenvcha .2018.10.002.

17. Jiaqi Wang et al., "How Do Parents and Children Promote Each Other? The Impact of Intergenerational Learning on Willingness to Save Energy," *Energy Research & Social Science* 87 (2022): 12–13, doi.org/10.1016/j.erss.2021.102465.

18. Kwauk and Winthrop, *Unleashing the Creativity of Teachers and Students to Combat Climate Change,* 9.

19. Mizuko Ito et al., *Connected Learning: An Agenda for Research and Design* (Irvine, CA: Digital Media and Learning Research Hub, 2013).

20. Ray, *A Field Guide to Climate Anxiety,*112.

21. Jen Kretser and Erin Griffin, "Taking Back Our Future: Empowering Youth Through Climate Summits," in *Teaching Climate Change in the United States,* eds. Joseph Henderson and Andrea Drewes (London: Routledge, 2020), 147; Nicole Rom and Kristen Iverson Poppleton, "Engagement for Climate Action" in *Teaching Climate Change in the United States,* eds. Joseph Henderson and Andrea Drewes (London: Routledge, 2020), 154.

22. Rom and Poppleton, "Engagement for Climate Action," 156.

23. Mary Annaïse Heglar, "Climate Change Isn't the First Existential Threat: People of Color Know All About Building Movements, Courage, and Survival," *ZORA*, February 19, 2019, https://zora.medium.com/sorry-yall-but-climate-change-ain-t-the-first -existential-threat-b3c999267aa0.

Acknowledgments

Writing a book like this is a journey of discovery and exhilaration interspersed with episodes of paralyzing self-doubt. Generous and caring people made it possible for me to press forward through the harder hours and to imagine there would be something useful, perhaps inspiring, at the end of the process.

I am deeply indebted to five visionary teachers, masters of their craft, who allowed me to observe learners discussing their uncertain futures and document what their students created to represent their expanding knowledge. I was unprepared for students' candid remarks about climate change, their daily desires to seek deeper understandings of the more-than-human world, and emerging traces of emotional resilience in the face of unknowns just over the horizon. My boundless gratitude goes out to Jessica Torvik Lee, Colleen LaMotte, Dr. Carolyn Colley, Molly Ravits, and Erin Smith.

I could not have sustained this writing project without the support of my wife, Dr. Pamela Joseph. You endured my endless musings about wind turbines and Antarctic ice shelves—ideas I processed out loud over our morning coffees and neighborhood walks. You were patient as my office became a quagmire of piled source materials. It helped me too that you were also writing a book and that we could share the ups and downs of serious scholarly work. I took everything you said to heart.

About the Author

Mark Windschitl is a former secondary science teacher and currently a professor in the area of teaching, learning, and curriculum at the University of Washington. He is the lead author of *Ambitious Science Teaching* (Harvard Education Press) and publishes research on teacher and student learning, classroom discourse, and preservice teacher education. He also teaches scholarly writing at the university.

Index